DATE DUE

W9-DDD-736

Color, Sex, & Poetry

EVERYWOMAN: Studies in History,
Literature and Culture

Susan Gubar and Joan Hoff-Wilson
General Editors

BLACKS IN THE DIASPORA

Darlene Clark Hine and John McCluskey, Jr.
General Editors

Color, Sex, & Poetry

Three Women Writers
of the Harlem Renaissance

Gloria T. Hull

INDIANA UNIVERSITY PRESS
BLOOMINGTON & INDIANAPOLIS

The following archives, organizations, and publishers have given permission to reprint materials to which they hold the rights (specific credits appear in the Notes section): Collection of American Literature, The Beinecke Rare Book and Manuscript Library, Yale University, New Haven, Connecticut; Fisk University manuscript holdings, Nashville, Tennessee; Moorland-Spingarn Research Center, Howard University, Washington, D.C.; Morris Library, University of Delaware, Newark, Delaware; The Schomburg Center for Research in Black Culture, New York Public Library; Woodruff Library, Atlanta University Center; National Urban League, New York; Ohio Historical Society; The Atlantic Monthly Company; Broadside Press; Harper & Row; Alfred A. Knopf, Inc.; and University Press of America.

Library of Congress Cataloging-in-Publication Data

Hull, Gloria T.
Color, sex, and poetry.

(Everywoman : studies in history, literature, and
culture) (Blacks in the diaspora)
Bibliography: p.
Includes index.
1. American poetry—Afro-American authors—History
and criticism.   2. American poetry—Women authors—
History and criticism.   3. American poetry—20th
century—History and criticism.   4. Dunbar-Nelson,
Alice Moore, 1875–1935—Criticism and interpretation.
5. Grimké, Angelina Weld, 1880–1958—Criticism and
interpretation.   6. Johnson, Georgia Douglas Camp,
1886–1966—Criticism and interpretation.   7. Harlem
Renaissance.   8. Women and literature—United States.
9. Afro-Americans in literature.   10. Afro-American
women poets—New York (City)—Biography.   I. Title.
II. Series: Everywoman.   III. Series: Blacks in
diaspora.
PS153.N5H84   1987   811'.52'099287   86-45580
ISBN 0-253-34974-5
ISBN 0-253-20430-5 (pbk.)

1   2   3   4   5   91   90   89   88   87

Contents

Three Poems   vii
Preface   ix

CHAPTER I: INTRODUCTION

Color, Sex, and Poetry in the Harlem Renaissance   *1*

CHAPTER II

Alice Dunbar-Nelson (1875–1935)   *33*

CHAPTER III

Angelina Weld Grimké (1880–1956)   *107*

CHAPTER IV

Georgia Douglas Johnson (1880–1966)   *155*

CHAPTER V: AFTERWORD

Color, Sex, and Poetry: The Renaissance Legacy   *212*

Notes   217
Index   235

Three Poems

Georgia in My Dreams

> *The dark bottom of the slumbering ocean*
> *is a mirror*
> *Sea mirror, densely shining*
> *Come—and see*
> *Georgia Douglas Johnson*
> *sorceress treading through my sleeping*
> *treading lightly*
> *calling*
> *dreaming me*

She walked me through her narrow hallway
dusty with papers
as easy in the piles of clutter
as a witch's cat

She wanted me to know that
though they burned them for her funeral
she woman wrote every poem, play, novel, story
that we were stepping over

Wanted me to know—before I saw it—
that her Half-way House still held her
that the red-pink roses she had planted
should not die

If Two
(for Angelina)

If I could paint this in words
I'd be like Angelina
These were the scenes she loved
This gorgeous sunset parading itself
    across the evening sky
Lighting up orange flares and cobalt streamers
Thin-needled pine stalks
    gently fingering the blue

Lining layers of subtle color
  even prettier than a rainbow
Saffron, bright amber, pure amethyst, beryl hues

Angelina, you favored these delicate shades
Seeking clear chromatics for the dissonant half-tones
  of your strangely muted life

The tints are vibrant still
  behind this darkening curtain
The gracile pines—their mood now changed to indigo—
  are menacing the night

Miss Alice

She loves me, she loves me not
She loves me, she loves me not

Stuck up 'risto lady
with your snub-turned nose and your fancy clothes
I wouldn't speak to you either
if I passed you on the street
My hair's too wild,
my skin is dark
So why did you bother me?
And why did I bother you?—
Clanging in your boxes and your unquiet bed

Those press releases were not enough
You wanted the whole damn story, the record set straight
Your daring rescued from the backyards and the barbeques
You knew your stellar spot was center stage

But I still don't really like you, queenly lady
(Lady, how do you feel about me?)
Yet if I said we were not sisters
Rain curses, Goddess strike me
for telling one awful lie

Gloria Hull
1985/86

PREFACE

This book began in 1975 with the first two articles I ever wrote and published—a brief, coauthored digest of the Harlem Renaissance, and a survey of Afro-American women poets from Phillis Wheatley to Margaret Walker. At the time, I had no definite plans for this volume which has materialized, but was simply pursuing an increasingly ardent interest in black women writers, poetry, and the Harlem Renaissance. Though I was initially researching seven female poets of the period, the focus gradually narrowed to five, then finally to three. Assisted by a Faculty Research Grant from the University of Delaware, I spent the summer of 1976 working at the Moorland-Spingarn Research Center, Howard University, Washington, D.C. The wealth of material available there on Angelina Weld Grimké culminated in a long bio-critical essay. The following summer, I participated in the Afro-American Literature institute conducted at Yale University by Robert Steptoe, Henry Louis Gates, and Sherley Ann Williams. There, I began testing my hypothesis that the Harlem Renaissance did need "rewriting." Then, during my 1977–78 sabbatical leave, I became thoroughly acquainted with Alice Dunbar-Nelson through editing her manuscript diary and reading a great deal of her other archival documents, which were conveniently located at her niece's home in Wilmington, Delaware.

My work—which was now assuming shape—received a second boost in 1979, when I was awarded a National Endowment for the Humanities Summer Stipend for further development of the project. And when the Rockefeller Foundation granted me a full 1979–80 fellowship, I was able to do the requisite, remaining travel and research—to New York City, Fisk University, Atlanta, Georgia and, again, Washington, D.C., which became my base. At the end of the year, I had written a hefty chapter on Georgia Douglas Johnson and was plotting out the remainder of the writing. Seeing other books through publication, teaching, and diverse professional commitments required so much immediate attention that it was not until a summer 1985 break between two Fulbright years in Jamaica that I finally finished this *Color, Sex, and Poetry: Three Women Writers of the Harlem Renaissance*. By this time, Indiana University Press had contracted to publish the work.

Any fruit that takes ten years to mature must surely owe its existence to much good fortune and many good people. Though I cannot specify each and every useful idea, cheering word, or act of kindness, I acknowledge and am grateful for them all. I have already mentioned the institutions and agencies that facilitated my progress by giving me time and money—both critical necessities. Then there are the libraries and librarians, all of whom were professional and courteous. But there were some whose generosity exceeded the requirements of duty—for example, Esme Bhan and Janet Sims-Wood at Howard University, Diane Lachatanere at the Schomburg Center, and Gloria Mims of the Atlanta University Library. My home university reference librarian, Laura Shepard, deserves notice, too, for the numerous pieces of information that she checked and double-checked. Pauline A. Young allowed me to use Dunbar-Nelson's papers and richly shared her memories and information. Typist Betty Sherman has labored with me through every chapter, every draft, meeting my impossible deadlines and watchfully straightening footnotes and pages.

I remember sitting around dinner tables all along the United States' Northeast corridor with Patricia Bell Scott and Barbara Smith, while their wonderful questions prompted me to tell the stories that helped to keep my enthusiasm for this project alive. Kevin Kerrane, an English department colleague at Delaware, and Ellen Morgan paid special attention to what I had written about Grimké. Zack Bowen, the department chair, read the manuscript and, like Barbara, commented in detail on the introduction. I also thank Michele Gibbs for her warm words about that chapter. Martha Terry Zingo was my official and unofficial researcher, and in ways too numerous to mention unfailingly supported me and my writing.

Other sisters and friends to whom I owe more than this roll call of gratitude can indicate are: Geraldine McIntosh, E. Ethelbert Miller, Thelma A. Higgins, Konda Mason, E. Jean Lanyon, and Maggie Andersen. The nurturing environment of the 1977–80 Black Feminist Retreat Group with which I was affiliated (and which included such members as Carroll Oliver, Audre Lorde, Demita Frazier, Cheryl Clarke, Lorraine Bethel, and Beverly Smith) reminds me to be grateful for the feminist, black feminist, black/women's studies movements that have provided the climate and models for this kind of scholarship. For their spiritual well-wishes, I want to note Faith Queman, Amy Klainer ("Just do it, Gloria") and especially Jan Nelson, whose continuous presence was an indispensable boon. And no acknowledgment would be complete without praise sounds for the love and energy of my immediate family: Mrs. Jimmie Thompson, Anthony Delroy Wellington, and Adrian Prentice Hull. For all of the aid, and all of the people-spirits both named here and unnamed who contributed to this work, I give thanks.

From the very beginning, I saw myself as writing a book for those who would care about these three women not only because of their unique individualities, but also because of what they represent: black women/ writers struggling against unfavorable odds to create their personal and artistic selves. Amid the current black female literary renaissance, we are moved to reclaim foremothers for the lessons and the blessing that they give us. This process of recovery is slowly but surely constructing a truer American literary history and, it is hoped, hastening the day when writers like Dunbar-Nelson, Grimké, and Georgia Douglas Johnson will require no extraordinary efforts to be known and appreciated for who they really are.

Color, Sex, & Poetry

CHAPTER I • INTRODUCTION

Color, Sex, and Poetry
in the
Harlem Renaissance

The year is 1927:

Alice Dunbar-Nelson is writing lively, informative columns in the Washington, D.C., *Eagle* about musical and literary prizes being offered to black artists, the black-and-tan cabarets of Harlem, James Weldon Johnson's *God's Trombones*, the Pan-African Congress, and the musical shows "Rang Tang" and "Africana." Her poem "April Is on the Way" wins honorable mention at the annual *Opportunity* awards dinner and is published that same year in *Ebony and Topaz*.[1]

Angelina Weld Grimké receives a friendly note from Langston Hughes on May 8, 1927, and is enjoying the distinction of having more of her poems included in Countee Cullen's landmark 1927 collection, *Caroling Dusk: An Anthology of Verse by Negro Poets*, than any other woman writer.[2]

Georgia Douglas Johnson, already renowned as a poet, receives first place in the 1927 *Opportunity* competition for her folk drama *Plumes*. Five months later, she is featured by society writer Geraldyn Dismond in the October 29, 1927, "Through the Lorgnette" column of the Pittsburgh *Courier*.

Georgia Douglas Johnson's Saturday Nighters salon at her Washington, D.C., home is especially brilliant this year. Grimké was, in Gwendolyn Bennett's words, a "particularly pleasing" component of a "charming medley" of participants on June 4, 1927, while Dunbar-Nelson was the

---

The National Urban League's *Opportunity* magazine was an important source of "New Negro" information and an indispensable outlet for Harlem Renaissance writers (together with the NAACP's *Crisis*). In this July 1926 cover, poet-artist Gwendolyn Bennett reinterprets popular jazz and African motifs from a female point of view. (Photo courtesy of the National Urban League, New York.)

guest of honor at a July 23, 1927, evening, where there was "much poetry and discussion and salad and wine and tea."[3]

In this wide range of ways at the height of the Harlem Renaissance, these three women writers—Alice Dunbar-Nelson, Angelina Weld Grimké, and Georgia Douglas Johnson—are contributing to the brightness of the period. Their varied backgrounds and experiences both accord with and diverge from the flow of the movement. Yet, because of sheer timing, they were swept fortuitously into the New Negro cultural awakening of the 1920s.

Viewed from one angle, the Harlem Renaissance was what Nathan Huggins has called it, "a channeling of energy from political and social criticism into poetry, fiction, music, and art."[4] A historical cause that helped to generate it was the founding of such organizations as the National Association for the Advancement of Colored People, the National Urban League, and the Association for the Study of Negro Life and History, which fostered a growing mood of racial confidence, assertiveness, and protest. W. E. B. DuBois's Talented Tenth became the New Negro shedding old, demeaning stereotypes and assuming a bold new face. The Great Migration of blacks from South to North brought more money and freedom, along with an air of excitement, opportunity, and drama. World War I had introduced black soldiers to a wider world of tolerance, thus intensifying their abhorrence of American racial prejudice. In general, United States blacks added their voices to the international outcry of black self-assertion. As seen most clearly in Garveyism, this attitude involved race solidarity and pride and a conscious connection with the African homeland. All of these moods and ideas emerged as newly articulated themes in the art and literature of the period.

Although the designation *Harlem* Renaissance discounts other geographical activity, the development of that black metropolis as a race capital located within the cultural capital of the country made it the acknowledged locus of the movement. In particular, the proximity to the publishing world was crucial. It facilitated opportunities for mainstream outlets that augmented those provided by race magazines such as *Opportunity, Crisis,* and, to a lesser extent, the *Messenger.* In the same way, white patronage from downtown was worth more than the prizes awarded in the *Opportunity* and *Crisis* annual contests. White participation in the Renaissance is a reminder that the 1920s were also the time of the Jazz Age and the Lost Generation, and of experimentation with black themes by white writers like Eugene O'Neill, DuBose Heyward, and Julia Peterkin. Freudian-influenced whites were fascinated with the potential naturalness and exoticism of blacks and with these manifestations in all forms ranging from Harlem street life to the singing and dancing of black musicals such as *Shuffle Along* (1921) and *Running Wild* (1923). Fresh developments in music were paralleled by the rise of fine artists like Aaron Douglas, Sargent Johnson, Augusta Savage, and Richmond Barthé, who likewise mined the racial dimensions of their talent.

In literature, names from an earlier era continued to be called—Fenton Johnson, Alice Dunbar-Nelson, W. E. B. Dubois, James Weldon Johnson, and others. Many new writers surfaced—notably, Claude McKay, Jean Toomer, Countee Cullen, Jessie Fauset, Langston Hughes, Nella Larsen, Eric Walrond, Rudolph Fisher, Gwendolyn Bennett, Arna Bontemps, Willis Richardson, Helene Johnson, and Zora Neale Hurston. Utilizing the major genres of poetry, short stories, novels, and plays, these writers produced a remarkable and diverse body of work. Timeless subject matter in traditional modes competed with more daring topics, approaches, and techniques. This juxtaposition of generations and concepts of art led to a critical debate between what are most often designated as the genteel and the bohemian schools. Alice Dunbar-Nelson pictured it as conflict between "those to whom literature is a beautiful dignified mistress" and those to whom it is "a strident, dishevelled gutter-snipe."[5] True it was that jazz, free verse, primitivism, and sensationalism attracted more attention than conventional verse and mannered depictions of Afro-American life. History and folklore (both rural and urban), satire, issues of identity and power all found expression in this Harlem Renaissance work, which, on the whole, came more assuredly from an ethnic center.

As one commentator put it, any investigation of the Harlem Renaissance must recognize its "emotive and symbolic character."[6] Ever since the period, those writing about it have done so with their various analytic methodologies glazed by their own subjective biases, needs, and imaginations. Historians have de-emphasized the magic of the era by reconstructing its social and political causation. Many participants and onlookers have cast highly flavored memoirs. Textual scrutiny has revealed the thematic and linguistic strategies of the writers. During the 1970s, a black-is-beautiful generation saw itself adumbrated by the earlier age, while some harsher critics viewed it as another baleful lesson in racial co-optation. The social historians' picture of a glittering interracial assemblage of the avant-garde is balanced by crime and poverty statistics for the black working class. And this list could be extended even further. Yet, however idiosyncratic or scholarly, these many approaches have not adequately dealt with women during the period. The absence of critical studies on black women artists is real, as well as "emotive and symbolic." It is beginning to be addressed through current widespread interest in Zora Neale Hurston and through work by mostly black female critics on other lesser-known figures.

The focus here is on three individual women writers. But what can be said about the overall place of women in the Harlem Renaissance? What were they doing, these Negro women so beautifully described by Elise Johnson McDougald in 1925? " . . . a colorful pageant of individuals, each differently endowed. Like the red and yellow of the tiger-lily, the skin of one is brilliant against the star-lit darkness of a racial sister. From grace to strength, they vary in infinite degree. . . . "[7] The general female populace— to whom the Renaissance was an unknown or unheeded phenomenon— was maintaining the basic foundation of the world, as usual. McDougald places these "ordinary" women into four categories. The smallest segment is the leisured wives and daughters of business and professional men who are "free to preside over the family" and enjoy the "luxuries of well-appointed homes, modest motors, tennis, golf and country clubs, trips to Europe and California." The second category comprises active, progressive women who are themselves in business and the professions. They are secretaries, administrators, doctors, lawyers, dentists, social workers, probation officers, nurses, librarians, pharmacists, and, above all, school teachers, whose sympathy and judgment in the classroom make them a mighty force for spiritual and mental balance among black youth. The third group, the many women in the trades and industry, are ignored by labor unions and only recognized in cookery, where they are not allowed to advance to managerial positions. The "spirit of stress and struggles" that characterizes groups two and three is augmented by their additional roles as wives, lovers, and mothers (many without husbands). The fourth group fares worst of all. For these domestic and casual workers, "health and morale suffer" because of the material conditions of their lives.

Representations of these women can be found in the bourgeoise characters of Jessie Fauset's and Nella Larsen's novels and in the exquisite but doomed women of Jean Toomer's *Cane*. Langston Hughes imaged the survival strength of a Madam Alberta K. Johnson:

> My name is Johnson—
> Madam Alberta K.

> The Madam stands for business
> I'm smart that way.
> . . . .
> I do cooking,
> Day's work, too!
> Alberta K. Johnson—
> *Madam* to you.[8]

while a relatively unknown poet, Blanche Taylor Dickinson, told the mini-saga of a girl dazzled by store window displays, who bought a dress, waved her "soft black hair," and applied cosmetics to make herself "neat and fair." Then

> She slipped the dress on carefully,
> Her vain dream fell away. . . .
> The mirror showed a brownskin girl
> She hadn't seen all day![9]

Other women's lives touched more closely the phenomena of the movement, and some of them contributed in major ways to the activity of the period. Most significantly, Jessie Fauset was one of the impresarios of the Renaissance (along with such people as Alain Locke and Charles S. Johnson) because of her key position as literary editor of *The Crisis* and her intellectual evenings, which functioned as stages for cultural happenings. Indispensable behind-the-scenes support for Renaissance artists and activities was provided by two other notable women, Regina Anderson and Ethel Ray Nance. Nance was Charles Johnson's secretary at *Opportunity* magazine and, as such, functioned as his scout, assistant, clearinghouse, and hostess. One of her apartment mates was Anderson, who was a librarian at the Harlem public library on 135th Street (which helped to promote black creativity). Nance describes her as "our life saver," "very special," and a "delicate little person" who "loved to have people around her." She continues:

> But, being in the library at 135th Street, she [Regina] came in contact with
> all these people . . . some writers were very fortunate being associated with
> her closely. And, worked very hard. She would bring home seven or eight
> books at night as these new books came out. She made a digest—enough to
> give some kind of short review for the next day.[10]

Their apartment at fashionable 580 St. Nicholas Avenue, "Dream Haven," was a shelter for new arrivals like Hurston, an informal gathering place for writers and artists like Cullen, Walrond, and Hughes, and, like Fauset's home, a forum for meetings, people, and ideas. In fact, Regina Anderson and Gwendolyn Bennett gave Charles Johnson the suggestion for his celebrated 1924 Civic Club dinner, where black writers of all generations were brought into contact with sympathetic white writers and publishers.[11]

In Washington, D.C., Georgia Douglas Johnson extended the list of black women who were hostesses to the Renaissance:

> In the living room of her S Street house behind the flourishing rose bushes, a freewheeling jumble of the gifted, famous, and odd came together on Saturday nights. There were the poets Waring Cuney, Mae Miller, Sterling Brown, Angelina Grimké, and Albert Rice. There were the artists Richard Bruce Nugent and Mae Howard Jackson. Writers like Jean Toomer and Alice Dunbar-Nelson (former wife of Paul Laurence Dunbar), and philosopher-critic Locke came regularly to enjoy the train of famous and to-be-famous visitors. Langston Hughes used to bring Vachel Lindsay; Edna St. Vincent Millay and Waldo Frank came because of Toomer; James Weldon Johnson and W. E. B. DuBois enjoyed their senior sage role there; occasionally, Countee Cullen and, more often, the suave Eric Walrond accompanied Locke. Rebecca West came once to encourage Georgia Johnson's poetry. H. G. Wells went away from one of the Saturday nights saddened by so much talent straining to burst out of the ghetto of American arts and letters.[12]

Johnson's role as cultural sponsor was all the more important because she played it outside of Harlem, New York, thus becoming a nexus for the intercity connections that helped to make the movement a truly national one.

Even in as unlikely a place as Lynchburg, Virginia, another female poet, Anne Spencer, was helping to "unpretentiously initiate a cultural and intellectual awakening."[13] James Weldon Johnson had discovered Spencer shortly before the 1920s and first published her poems in his *Book of American Negro Poetry* (1922). She had also established a local chapter of the NAACP in her southern city. Brought thus into the political and artistic ferment of the age, Spencer's home at 1313 Pierce Street became a popular stopover point for black leaders and artists traveling between the North and South, as well as a Renaissance focus for the state. Drawn to her doors were the likes of Roland Hayes, Marian Anderson, W. E. B. DuBois, Walter White, Mary McLeod Bethune, and Georgia Douglas Johnson.

Of course, from a feminist perspective, it is ironic that one of the notable ways women contributed to the period was through hostelrying-hostessing-salon keeping, refinements of their traditional domestic roles extended into the artistic and cultural arena. Most notably, A'Lelia Walker used her late mother's fortune to give large parties where famous guests of all classes and callings from home and abroad rubbed shoulders with one another. She and Carl Van Vechten were the fete-givers supreme of this party-mad era. And Geraldyn Dismond reported them in the *Inter-State Tattler*.

In other areas, too, women made their presence felt. There were the chorines whose unkempt (Afro-Americans say "rusty") knees Dunbar-Nelson execrated in one of her columns. There were also Garveyite daughters, actresses like Nora Holt and Rose McLendon, and singers such as Bessie Smith, Ethel Waters, and Billie Holiday. Most importantly, black women augmented the rich outpouring of literature. Major talents like Jessie Fauset, Georgia Douglas Johnson, Gwendolyn Bennett, and Zora Neale Hurston made their mark across a range of genres. Some, like Nella Larsen, Anne Spencer, and Helene Johnson, excelled in one specific form. Still others, especially poets such as Clarissa Scott Delaney and Lucy Ariel Williams, flashed briefly and less brightly.

Yet, despite what appears to be full participation of women in the Harlem Renaissance, one can discern broad social factors and patterns of exclusion. One of the most basic is how male attitudes toward women impinged upon them, how men's so-called personal biases were translated into something larger that had deleterious effects. This became especially invidious when such men were in influential and critical positions. They then made blatant the antifemale prejudice inherent in the whole of society. An excellent, though upsetting, case in point is Alain Leroy Locke, who was such an indispensable personage that Langston Hughes said he helped to "mid-wife" the Renaissance into being.[14] A Harvard-trained Ph.D., Rhodes scholar, and Howard University philosophy professor, Locke gave definitive shape to "the New Negro" in his 1925 anthology of that name. More importantly, his smooth, learned manner inspired patrons to make of him a conduit for their largesse to black artists. Thus, Locke dispensed not only money but also advice, support, and vital aid to many needful young writers. His handling of his role was controversial, but no one denied its centrality.

The problem with Locke, however, is that he behaved misogynistically and actively favored men. From the standpoint of the 1980s his unequal treatment of women makes his position all the more controversial. A "certified misogynist," he customarily "dismissed female students on the first class day with the promise of an automatic grade of C."[15] Owen Dodson explains: "He [Locke] didn't believe in women's lib for instance. If women enrolled in his classes as seniors, he'd say, 'You come here at your own risk.'"[16] This contempt for women and disparagement of their intellect inevitably carried over into his judgments and actions, with precious few exceptions. One of these was Zora Neale Hurston, whom, for some reason, Locke liked and recommended. Yet, there was still something in his attitude that caused her to label him "a malicious, spiteful little snot," who "lends out his patronage. . . . And God help you if you get on without letting him represent you."[17]

Locke's behavior becomes even more problematic because of his obvious partiality toward young males, to whom he was sexually attracted. Locke, in fact, functioned within a homosexual coterie of friendship and patronage that suggests that literary events were, in more than a few instances, tied to "bedroom politics" and "sexual croneyism"—as they no doubt may have been in the heterosexual world also. The point here, though, is that women were definitely excluded from Locke's beneficence and this particular sphere of favoritism. One story is illustrative. Cullen, whose homosexuality was openly tittered about, once described to Hughes a weekend he had spent with Locke: "Hughes crackled with curiosity, wanting to know about Howard, the city, and Locke. 'Is Mr. Locke married?' he wondered." Locke had begun a correspondence with Hughes after reading his early poems in the *Crisis*. Finally Hughes decided to "take Locke up on his repeated offers of a special relationship," perhaps with Cullen's urging. Eventually, in the summer of 1924, Locke came to see Hughes in Paris, "promising to bring him details of a possible Howard scholarship, offering to introduce him to famous Parisians." There, they had a "glorious time" and also met again in Venice. It was Locke who introduced Hughes to the wealthy, eccentric patron Mrs. Charlotte Osgood Mason (affectionately known as "Godmother") and "secured what amounted to a blank check" for him.[18]

The operation of a circle is further, and interestingly, revealed in this passage about Richard Bruce Nugent, a handsome, "self-conscious decadent who had shortened his name to Richard Bruce to allay maternal embarrassment about his homosexuality":

> Georgia Douglas Johnson believed in Nugent's promise and mothered his neuroses when he returned to Washington in 1924. Alain Locke pursued him, offering Godmother's largesse if the young man would discipline his talents. But it was meeting Hughes at Georgia Johnson's one winter evening in 1925, and walking each other home "back and forth all night," that was the turning point in Nugent's life. He followed Hughes to New York, met Van Vechten, and fashioned his personality . . . after Van Vechten's libertine [character] Peter Whiffle. . . . [19]

Carl Van Vechten, photographer, writer, columnist, and critic, was notorious for his lifestyle and his novel *Nigger Heaven*. He frequented the "transvestite floor shows, sex circuses, and marijuana parlors along 140th Street,"[20] and his lavish parties were said to resemble a "speakeasy deluxe peopled by literary figures, stage and screen celebrities, prizefighters, dancers, elegant homosexuals, and Lorelei Lee gold diggers."[21]

> Yet this was the figure whose assistance to the growth of the Harlem Renaissance . . . was probably greater than that of any other white American. It was Van Vechten who talked Frank Crowninshield, the editor of *Vanity Fair*, into publishing some of the first poems of Countee Cullen and Langston Hughes, and who encouraged Alfred Knopf to bring out Hughes' first collection [*The Weary Blues*, 1925]. Among other editors and publishers of his acquaintance, he tirelessly promoted the work and the careers of the young Harlem writers.

This personality-patronage issue broadens into general revelations about the customary male circles of power and friendship, which during the period crossed racial lines. In his autobiography *The Big Sea*, Hughes recalls that Alfred A. Knopf, Jr., James Weldon Johnson, and Carl Van Vechten annually celebrated their common birthday together. In 1928, Charles Chesnutt, Afro-American fiction writer of an earlier generation, asked Johnson to assist him in bringing out a new edition of his novel *The House Behind the Cedars*. Johnson graciously responded: "I shall make some preliminary inquiries among publishers that I know well, and when you come to New York it will be a great pleasure to me to introduce you to these publishers."[22] Johnson also wrote the following to Edwin R. Embree, president of the Rosenwald Fund on August 22, 1931: "I got in touch with Langston Hughes and he tells me that he has written you about a scholarship. I need not say that I hope he will get it."[23]

Hughes was particularly fortunate. In Depression-stricken 1933, he returned from Russia to the United States as the guest of Noel Sullivan, "a rugged, shy bachelor whose family was one of San Francisco's oldest and richest." He was met at the dock by a "liveried chauffeur" and given a Carmel cottage in which to write.[24] Even Claude McKay, whose personality was difficult, had incredible "luck." During 1924, he was penning second-rate poetry and receiving money from Walter White and radical philanthropist Louise Bryant, and fifty-dollar monthly grants arranged by James Weldon Johnson and Walter White from the Garland Fund—all to write an execrable novel, "Color Scheme," which even Knopf rejected and left to die "of its own considerable defects."[25]

After its failure, he reworked similar material into an equally flawed second novel and wrote a few short stories. In France, disillusioned and broke in 1926, he asked Schomburg for money, then subsequently obtained greater assistance from Bryant. She persuaded her husband, diplomat William Bullit, to edit McKay's stories, and Bullit also got for him a $500 advance from Alfred Harcourt of Harcourt, Brace. Meanwhile, Bryant herself "was in New York with McKay's stories, charging through publishers' offices like an evangelist, preaching McKay's genius and showering desks with manuscript. . . . " She retained for him a prestigious agent who negotiated a contract with Harper's to expand one of the stories into a novel. "With an advance and expense money from Bryant to pump him up," McKay was able to finish *Home to Harlem* in 1927.

Manna such as this was never showered upon the women writers of the period. Locke secured Mrs. Mason's backing for Hurston, Van Vechten helped Gwendolyn Bennett, Walter White volunteered to have his secretary type Larsen's *Quicksand,* and women received a good word or a small favor here and there. Yet the Renaissance, despite its veneer of equal opportunity, was a time when not only Harlem and the Negro, but men as usual were "in vogue." In a world that values and caters more to males, they enjoyed the lion's share of all the available goods and, in the field of literature, were more apt to be seriously encouraged as professional writers. This was not solely a matter of merit. For example, in 1926, McKay's reputation rested on *Harlem Shadows,* a volume of poetry published in 1922. He had been writing badly since (and was continuing to do so). Nevertheless, Bryant, White, Johnson, and others generously aided him. His novel that resulted, *Home to Harlem,* benefited not only from all this moral and material support (with which he should have produced something creditable) but from its exploitation of popular Harlem low-life themes.

The issue here is not whether friends—male or female, homosexual or heterosexual—should help one another. However, when the persons are men with power and position who almost exclusively benefit their male friends, then women suffer. In addition, all of this happens while the fiction of pure individual worth is maintained. It is telling that when James Weldon Johnson was assisting Chesnutt, Dunbar-Nelson was complaining about the "curious selfishness" she found in his crowd,[26] and in 1931, when Johnson was unofficially endorsing Hughes to the Rosenwald Fund, she and Georgia Douglas Johnson were desperately applying for jobs and grants. At no point during their lives did anyone ever provide them with leisure to write. The need for this creative space preoccupied Johnson. A

1928 newspaper article revealed that her "great fear" was that she would not be able to accomplish her artistic goals, for, "although she works incessantly, her time is too much taken up with making a living to give very much of it to literary work."[27]

True, quieter, less-visible female support networks existed, and women were sometimes able to serve their sisters. Nevertheless, because of women's less-advantaged status, these networks could often only amount to consolation circles for the disfranchised. Even when female spheres of patronage and aid were possible, they did not always realize their potential because of women's interests, positions, or socialization. An interesting case in point from the period is provided by hair-straightening heiress A'Lelia Walker. She spent freely on "the circle of handsome women attending her," "the effete men . . . who organized her socials" (she was "especially fond of homosexuals"), and "her retinue of domestics." Her lavish parties made her "Harlem's principal salon-keeper, doing for the Renaissance what Mabel Dodge had done before the war for the artists and intellectuals of Greenwich Village": "But to the intellectuals and artists of Harlem she opened her houses and almost never her purse."[28]

Class (not in the sense of money) and caste differences operating on both sides prevented someone like Dunbar-Nelson from gaining some sort of place within Walker's circle of handsome women, which included French princess Violette Murat, who had come to the United States with Harold Jackman, Cullen's lifelong intimate, and was "perhaps too fond of women for some Harlemites."[29] It would have been difficult, but not impossible, for them to move past their superficial differences. Though not an intellectual, A'Lelia was not unintelligent; and Dunbar-Nelson, for her part, loved eating, drinking, and playing bridge as much as A'Lelia, although she generally cloaked her bohemian self with proper manners and social squeamishness. Had A'Lelia Walker been made to see that aiding other women (albeit artistic and intellectual New Negro ones, whom she probably mistrusted as a type) was a good project, many could have benefited. She was feminist enough to specify in her will that the Walker Manufacturing Company be perpetually headed by a female.[30]

Clearly, where the personality-patronage issue is concerned, individuals are most strongly drawn to their type. This observation raises the question of Harlem Renaissance fraternization and its relation to female role expectations. True to the upbeat flavor of the era (and to masculine behavioral norms), a great deal of this professionally vital male socializing occurred after hours in bars and over bottles. For example, after Walter White had enlisted writer Sinclair Lewis to help McKay, Lewis kept his promise by "spending two nights drinking and talking about writing with McKay at Harry's Bar, and taking a careful look at the unfinished novel."[31] At this time, even women's smoking was appalling. Ethel Ray Nance recounts being shocked when she first saw Jessie Fauset sitting at a table in the Civic Club with DuBois and smoking: "but she was very graceful about it. . . . And as I sat there, I thought, when I write home to my father, I guess I just won't mention this part of it."[32] Despite the fact that women did "go out," most of them—unlike the notorious actress Nora Holt—were not liberated enough to drink and/or talk about writing all night in a bar. Respectable, conscious black women were especially careful to counter negative stereotypes of themselves as low and sluttish. Female socialization can also be seen in women's relative reluctance to promote themselves confidently and boldly. Doing so helped to make Hurston a scandalous topic.

In the same way that women could not blithely "hang out" in bars or hop freighters to France and North Africa, they all could not, at the drop of the Renaissance, come flocking to New York City. They were much more likely to be tied to place via husbands, children, familial responsibilities, parental prohibitions, lack of fresh opportunities or the spirit of adventure, and so on. Although Jessie Fauset, Gwendolyn Bennett, and Helene Johnson were in Harlem during its heyday, Georgia Douglas Johnson and Angelina Grimké lived in Washington, D.C., while Alice Dunbar-Nelson orbited between Philadelphia and Wilmington, Delaware. Certainly, they were adversely affected by geographical immobility and being located away from the New York social and literary scene.

It is also instructive that, in this revolutionary movement that officially proclaimed its youthfulness, older men seem to have fared better than older women. Dunbar-Nelson, Grimké, Johnson, Anne Spencer, and Jessie Fauset were, like James Weldon Johnson and Claude McKay, born before 1890, and not after the turn of the century as were younger figures such as Hughes, Cullen, and Bennett. This means that quite a number of the women writers who were discovered or who received first-time prominence during the period did not fit the brash, youthful model. This was evident in the view and treatment of them that tended to make them passé rather than venerable. Recognizing this fact, women as unlike each other as Georgia Johnson and Zora Neale Hurston used false birthdates that represented them as being younger than they really were. In Hurston's case very recent scholarship has revealed that she was actually an additional decade older than her already corrected birthdate of 1901 indicates.[33] The new date of 1891 edges her into this older generation of women born in the late nineteenth century. Between 1927 and 1930, when Johnson ap-

plied to the Harmon Foundation, she cited her birthdate as 1888, an un-
truth that added two more years to the six by which she customarily
shortened her life. She rightly suspected that, in this instance, it was better
to be thirty-nine rather than forty-one or forty-seven. Obviously, Time
"brushing cold fingers through [one's] hair" (in Johnson's poetic words)
was a liability for women in more areas than romance.[34]

Other specifically literary factors further illuminate the status of women
writers in the Harlem Renaissance. A principal one is the issue of poetry as
a genre. During the period, it was, in a real sense, the preeminent form—
based on its universality, accessibility for would-be writers, suitability for
magazine publication, and classical heritage as the highest expression of
cultured, lyric sensibility. The big three writers of the era—McKay, Cullen,
and Hughes—made their reputations as poets. And most of the notable
women writers of the period were poets, with only Larsen and Hurston not
essaying verse. In addition to Johnson, Dunbar-Nelson, and Grimké, six
others produced significant work—Anne Spencer, Jessie Fauset, Effie Lee
Newsome, Gwendolyn Bennett, Helene Johnson, and the lesser-known
Gladys Mae Casely Hayford.

Anne Spencer is an arresting poet because of the originality of her material and approach. Working in forms that are an eccentric mixture of free
verse and rhymed, iambic-based lines, she treated subjects as varied as her
titles: "Before the Feast of Shushan," "At the Carnival," "The Wife-
Woman," "Dunbar," "Letter to My Sister," "Lines to a Nasturtium,"
"Neighbors," and "Creed." She is most modern in her predilection for
casting herself into roles, her sense of woman-self and female identity, and
her style, which is characterized by terseness, apt or unusual diction, and
vivid images and metaphors. Known best as a novelist, Fauset is usually
represented in anthologies by her love poems. Some of them are distinguished by the French titles she gave them and by her sometimes humorous and ironic cast of mind. Effie Lee Newsome primarily wrote children's verse based on nature lore.

Gwendolyn Bennett and Helene Johnson are the stellar poets of the
younger generation. Bennett's poetry can be quite impressive. She was, by
occupation, an artist, and consequently in her work she envisions scenes,
paints still lifes, and expresses herself especially well in color. Of all the
women poets, Helene Johnson's work most reflects the qualities commonly designated as characteristic of the Renaissance. She took "the 'racial' bull by the horns" (as James Weldon Johnson put it),[35] and also
wrote poems in the new colloquial-folk-slang style popular during that
time. Although the bulk of her poems are traditional romance and nature

lyrics, her "Sonnet to a Negro in Harlem" is pro-black and militant. In her frequently reprinted "Poem," she waxes ecstatic over the "Little brown boy / Slim, dark, big-eyed," who croons love songs to his banjo down at the Lafayette Theater.

Gladys Mae Hayford's distinctions are being born in Africa and having two of her poems—"Nativity" (in which the Christ Child is black) and "The Serving Girl"—published in the *Atlantic Monthly*. A Fanti, she committed herself to imbuing "our own people with the idea of their own beauty, superiority and individuality." Because Africa for her was a very real place, her poems have a concrete specificity not usually found in some other Harlem Renaissance works on that theme. She talks about blue lappah, frangipani blossoms, and the brass ankle bells that guard "Brown Baby Cobina." Her regularly accented couplets also employ various lyric personae and speak naturally about love and sex (particularly "Rainy Season Love Song"). "The Serving Girl" catches her themes and style:

> The calabash wherein she served my food,
> Was smooth and polished as sandalwood:
> Fish, as white as the foam of the sea,
> Peppered, and golden fried for me.
> She brought palm wine that carelessly slips
> From the sleeping palm tree's honeyed lips.
> But who can guess, or even surmise
> The countless things she served with her eyes?

Lyric poetry has long been considered the proper genre for women, defining them as surely in literature as the home has defined them in society. Yet, despite poetry's historical, across-the-board respectability, when women write it, it somehow becomes a lesser form than when it is handled by men. Furthermore, during the 1920s as in other periods, there was always professional pressure to create a novel. In 1924, when Walter White was succoring McKay, what White wanted him to do was generate "book-length fiction that would be snapped up by the public rather than critically acclaimed but barely read poetry."[36] It is not surprising then that many of the female poets tried their hand at imaginative prose although, during the Renaissance proper, only Fauset, Larsen, Bennett, and Hurston published fiction. Women both kept themselves and were kept in their lyric sphere.

The three women who are the focus of this study—Dunbar-Nelson, Grimké, and Georgia Douglas Johnson—have been granted the niche they occupy in literary history because of their poetry. Their names are rarely called unless that is the topic. This narrow treatment reduces their status as writers, and seeing them solely as poets is one of the first misconceptions that a close scrutiny rectifies. Beginning with her very first publication, Dunbar-Nelson wrote short stories and continued to do so until the end of her life, even though most of them were published before the 1920s. Essays, journalism, a diary, and an occasional play received more of her attention than did verse. Grimké was both a poet and a dramatist, who could also write a creditable piece of short fiction. Johnson, too, worked in these three forms, adding to them some now-lost unpublished essays and longer fiction. If poetry does remain a convenient and useful entrée to these women's literary output, that avenue must be widened to accommodate their other interests. Investigating them through their total writings, in conjunction with their color and race, and their gender, yields a much more accurate picture of them (and often, by extension, of their cohorts) as earlier twentieth-century black women writers. Their lives and their works are of dual importance. Not nearly enough has been known about them; thus, biographical information—interesting in itself—is also necessary for giving them personal and literary substantiation and for the practice of a holistic scholarship.

Even though some particularities keep these three women writers individually and collectively unique, they constitute a coherent and representative trio to study. They are similar, yet different enough to give requisite breadth and variety (thus making understanding and generalization even more valid and persuasive). As mentioned earlier, they were not based in New York City, and they belonged to the same older generation, having been born in 1875 and 1880. Consequently, they already had achievements to their credit when they were "picked up," as it were, in the 1920s. Given the dynamics of the black cultural elite, it is also not surprising that they associated with one another personally and professionally. For instance: Dunbar-Nelson wrote a Harmon Foundation recommendation for Johnson and reviewed her books; Johnson gave Grimké warm and friendly care. There is no record of direct interaction between Dunbar-Nelson and Grimké (although they surely knew each other), but Johnson was demonstrably close to the two of them.

All three writers had considerable contemporary reputations. The only female poet to publish not just one, but three, volumes of her work during the period, Johnson was hailed as the foremost woman poet of the age. Her plays also won Renaissance prizes, and her role as nexus gave her extensive recognition. Grimké was known for her family name and the notoriety of her 1916–20 problem drama *Rachel;* and she became a well-represented poet of the period. The Dunbar name was even more illustrious for Dunbar-Nelson. It, coupled with her earlier accomplishments and her multifarious involvements, especially in journalism and speaking, gave her high visibility. From today's vantage point, these writers still emerge as important, and for reasons that enlarge those recognized by their contemporaries. Johnson can be even better appreciated for her pseudonymous, multi-genred prolificacy. Grimké is burnished by the depth of her unpublished work, especially her lesbian poetry. The surfacing of Dunbar-Nelson's diary and discoveries about her other unpublished writing enhance her standing. For all of them, there can now be a vastly better comprehension of their lives as writers and remarkable women.

The vagaries of literary fortune further hold them together as a unit. Enough of their documents survived to make them major figures for study. Though Johnson's voluminous papers were summarily dumped on the day of her funeral, she had published enough to provide a substantial corpus, especially when it is supplemented by her long correspondence and contacts with luminaries from the period. Because of Dunbar-Nelson's connection with famous black poet Paul Laurence Dunbar and the consciousness of her historian-librarian niece about the worth of both Dunbar and her aunt, Dunbar-Nelson's papers have been treasured. Grimké's position as scion of the famous black Grimké family (which included lawyer-diplomat Archibald, cleric Francis, and diarist Charlotte Forten) led to her materials being preserved along with theirs. In a world where the remains of black women have not been universally valued and are relatively difficult to find, having a sizable body of original, archival material on a related group of three early writers is indeed a rare boon. (Anne Spencer, who kept her own rich collection until her death in 1975, would have accorded well with this trio. However, she had granted exclusive access to another researcher, J. Lee Greene.)[37]

A final point of general comparison among Dunbar-Nelson, Grimké, and Georgia Douglas Johnson is that no biography or literary criticism of any length or definitive significance has been written about them. They desperately need—and deserve—long overdue scholarly attention. Another related, unfortunate similarity is that too much of what they wrote is not easily and generally available because it either is out-of-print or was never published. Assessing them accurately requires one to consider both their published and unpublished writings, taking care to distinguish, especially when it is crucial, between them. It is hoped that, in the not-too-distant future, new editions and anthologies will present them in a freshly altered and fuller light.

Color defined the Harlem Renaissance. Philosophically and practically, it was a racial movement whose overriding preoccupation can be seen in all of its aspects and manifestations—the name of the era (where Harlem is synonymous with black), its debates and manifestos (Locke's "The New Negro" and Hughes's "The Negro Artist and the Racial Mountain"), book titles (Georgia Johnson's *Bronze,* Cullen's *Color, The Ballad of the Brown Girl,* and *Copper Sun*), artistic illustrations (the African motifs of Aaron Douglas and Gwendolyn Bennett), and so on. Indeed, during the 1920s, Alice Dunbar-Nelson, Angelina Grimké, and Georgia Douglas Johnson were participating in a literary movement that was, by self-definition, race oriented. How they were affected by this general reality emerged from their own specific realities as black women. Racial attitudes of the larger society, Harlem Renaissance dictates, and personal experience all combined to determine the handling of color in their writings.

Reflecting their nearness to the miscegenation of slavery, these three women were visibly mixed blooded. Grimké was a light brown quadroon, whose mother was white and father mulatto; Johnson herself said that she was born "a little yellow girl"; and Dunbar-Nelson could pass for white when she chose to. The Harlem Renaissance was preoccupied with the array of Afro-American skin tones, ranging across (in Claude McKay's catalogue) "chocolate, chestnut, coffee, ebony, cream, [and] yellow."[38] This rainbow began to be celebrated in art, even if the entire spectrum was still not as widely accepted in real life, where the same old light-minded hierarchy operated. Of course, the matter of color has always had a heavier impact on black women. Like McKay, men rhapsodized about their teasing browns, chocolate-to-the-bones, and lemon yellows, but many still preferred to marry the paler shades. Deep historical links between fair color and beauty, and fair color and class affiliation, are not easily broken. Even during this "natural" period that glorified blackness and exploited primitivism, the stage show chorines were creams and high browns (which was apparently what the promoters and public accepted), and Wallace Thurman, tortured himself by his own black skin, could relevantly present the agony of a self-hating dark heroine in his 1929 novel, *The Blacker the Berry.*

Though not of the "tragic mulatto" variety, these three women writers' situations came from ambivalences different from but no less complicated than those of Thurman's Emma Lou. The roots of their color complexes and preoccupations can be traced to their personal history; the roots of their racial consciousness to the combination of personal history and American racism. Grimké's attitudes seem to have been simpler and clearer than either Dunbar-Nelson's or Johnson's. Growing up with liberal and

politically committed white and black people who—though themselves
privileged—actively strove for racial betterment, she understood well in-
tra- and interracial prejudice. These sympathies she translated directly into
her literary work.

Lynching and the sorrow of having children are the dual themes of the
drama and fiction that she produced before the Renaissance heyday, so
much so that even a radical partisan wonders about her absolute fixation
upon these subjects. For the 1925 *Opportunity* contest, she sent Charles
Johnson a never-published story that expanded her militant focus into other
race themes of the period. "Jettisoned" is about a black woman domestic
named Miss Lucy, who decides not to pose as "old Black mammy" in order
to visit her passing daughter in Long Island, New York. Her option is to
remain with her sweet, young surrogate daughter, Mary Lou. In addition to
this incidental treatment of the popular passing motif, the story also features
average black folk characters who are, in Johnson's enthusiastic judgment,
"real, unpretensious, and lovable."[39] Both these facts situated the piece
firmly in the literary mode of the age. In "Jettisoned," Grimké used dialect to
aid in picturing Miss Lucy, a racial-literary strategy that she had attempted
years earlier in some Dunbar-derivative poetry.

Miscegenation was a major factor in Georgia Douglas Johnson's life and
art. Undoubtedly because of her own identity, she "nourished a whole
generation of Eurasians and other 'Mixed breeds,' " in the words of Cedric
Dover.[40] Her involvement is further indicated by such works as two lost
novels entitled *One and One Makes Three* and *White Men's Children*, and a
poem called "Aliens," a neo-treatment of the tragic mulatto that she pas-
sionately dedicated "To You—Everywhere!"[41] Treated comically, miscegenation also underlay her prize-winning play *Blue Blood* (1926). During
the Renaissance years, her creativity focused heavily on racial themes,
especially in her realistic one-act plays. *Plumes*, a "folk tragedy," fulfilled
the contemporary requirements for "real Negro literature"—"a Negro author, a Negro subject, and a Negro audience."[42] *A Sunday Morning in the
South* survives from among her dramatic protests against lynching, while a
primitive African melodrama called *Popoplikahu*, which was being rehearsed in 1926, has been lost. Johnson also wrote what she called plays of
"average Negro life" and historical dramas such as *William and Ellen Craft*.
Later, she continued her racial slant in war and brotherhood poems and
songs, and in other interracial projects. Her political activity was not, however, as relentlessly race-oriented as Dunbar-Nelson's.

Perhaps she was referring only to her poetry, but Johnson told Arna
Bontemps in 1941 that she really did not enjoy "writing racially": "When-

ever I can, I forget my special call to sorrow and live as happily as I may."[43] This remark is strikingly similar to Anne Spencer's statement introducing herself in *Caroling Dusk:* "I write about some of the things I love. But have no civilized articulation for the things I hate."[44] Like Spencer, other women writers eschewed "hateful" topics of prejudice and injustice. Choosing to do so placed them out of the fashionable mainstream (to the detriment of their contemporary and posthumous reputations). Johnson succumbed to external pressure and wrote a volume of obligatory race poetry, *Bronze: A Book of Verse,* in 1922. Using a self-conscious and indirect style, she speaks here with the voice of a black woman-mother for her persecuted but rising race. However, this is her weakest book. Johnson later confessed that she attempted *Bronze* because someone had said, after she published *The Heart of a Woman* (1918), that she had "no feeling for the race."[45] In times of black political consciousness, writers are pressured to toe the racial line. Unfortunately, these post-Victorian black women authors could not always effectively reconcile their color, sex, and poetry, poetry here encompassing also their poetics (concepts of literature) and their imaginative writing in general.

Dunbar-Nelson was the most uncomfortable of all with mixing race and belletristic literature. Throughout her career, she maintained a sharp demarcation between black concerns and her literary work. Though race was the keynote and unification for practically everything else that she did, it rarely sounded in her poems and stories. In her two pre-Renaissance volumes of Creole stories, the fiction, as one critic put it, "has no characteristics peculiar to her race."[46] Even in poetry that she wrote during the Renaissance, the thematic separation is basically maintained, although she did make some slight attempt to modernize her subjects and style. At the same time, her articles and newspaper columns had the militantly black ring of the period. She advocates "Negro Literature for Negro Pupils," exposes the racism on Mississippi levees during the floods, discusses black theater, and praises black sororities and fraternities for fostering race pride.

Interestingly, two of her unpublished Creole stories written during the first of the century tackle the more daring, racial topic of black Creole males who problematically decide to pass as white. When she proposed enlarging one of them, "The Stones of the Village," into a novel, Bliss Perry of the *Atlantic Monthly* discouraged her in 1900 by saying that the present American public disliked "color-line" fiction.[47] Maybe Perry spoke as a white reader who was tiring, say, of Charles Chesnutt, who had explicitly treated the color line in his 1899 collection, *The Wife of His Youth,* and more realistically dealt with racial concerns (passing and an interracial romance in the Reconstruction South) in his just-published novel, *The House Behind the Cedars* (1900). When the subject achieved fresh popularity in the 1920s, Dunbar-Nelson did not resurrect her old manuscripts. It would have been informative to see their reception.

Dunbar-Nelson's split authorial personality suggests the duality (not to say confusion) of her own attitudes regarding blackness. She was secretly ashamed of some aspect of her birth and parentage, and ambivalent about dark-skinned, lower-class blacks. As a "brass ankles," that is, a "white nigger," she resented intraracial animosity directed at those of her caste. Yet, she worked with zeal for black people as a race in political parties and the black women's club movement. Allegiance to Afro-American heritage can also be discerned in other aspects and activities of her life—for example, the foods she loved and her immersion in a black oratorical tradition. Yet, even in the receptive atmosphere of the Harlem Renaissance, she did not creatively use such material.

Large amounts of ambivalence, white blood, and caste privilege did not obliterate the basic race-color reality of these three women's existence. They were all touched by it and all responded in their lives and writing. However, only Johnson contributed significantly to the race literature of the Harlem Renaissance period. Grimké had passed her creative peak, and Dunbar-Nelson hardly ever treated race themes in the imaginative genres that counted. Clearly if one narrowly judges the worth of writers associated with the era by what they produced on race during those specific years, then these and other women writers will be devalued.

The lives of Afro-American women have always been determined as much by their gender as by their race. Not surprisingly, Dunbar-Nelson, Grimké, and Johnson were all three schoolteachers trained in female fields (English and music). Their domestic configurations are varied, but still show women's limited options in a patriarchal society. Johnson's situation (the most traditional) was that of wife to a husband who discouraged her writing, and mother of two sons whose care emotionally and financially burdened her. Dunbar-Nelson acted out romances with her first two husbands before settling down in a rather egalitarian marriage with a man whose sexist attitudes were not stifling. Despite her marriages, however, her home base was almost always a gynocentric arrangement involving her mother and sister. A motherless child, Grimké was the daughter of a stern father; she chose not to marry and ended her life alone.

Johnson seemed to have rested easiest in her sexual roles. Dunbar-Nelson suspected her of having an affair in the early 1920s, and her friend the playwright-poet Owen Dodson commented that, even at eighty, she did not hide her "wrinkled bosom." Dunbar-Nelson experienced difficulty finding satisfying outlets for her passionate nature, especially since she was sexually attracted to both men and women. Grimké was a thwarted lesbian who forswore lasting intimacy at an early age. What she and her father diagnosed as laziness in her character may really have been an understandable psychological listlessness.

At the outset of this study, no data suggested that these three writers were anything other than conventionally heterosexual women. What emerged regarding their sexuality prompts further speculation about the hidden nature of women's sexual lives in general and, more specifically, about lesbian invisibility. It also highlights some of the difficulties of doing lesbian-feminist scholarship, where the subjects feel constrained even in their private utterances from expressing themselves clearly and fully. For the sensitive researcher, there is often a gap between what one knows and what can be "proved," especially to those readers who demand a kind of evidence about the individual and the meaning of her work that could not be produced for heterosexual subjects. Yet, it is obvious that both Grimké and Dunbar-Nelson had sexual psyches that cut across the usual grain and were manifested in their lives and writing.

In part because of their female status, Johnson and Dunbar-Nelson waged a running battle with the wolf of financial hardship. For example, during the Renaissance, Johnson was "in the grip of genteel poverty,"[48] and in 1942 at the age of sixty-two, found herself hoping for a few hours work in a clerical pool. With this and indeed all of their problems, they were sustained by their intuitive strength and spirituality (a resource that Grimké lacked). In particular, Johnson, who acted more like the "crazy lady" she was as she grew older, radiated a living energy that made people speak of her "soothing balm" and "basking in deep spirituality" at her home, which she had christened "Half-Way House." Unlike Dunbar-Nelson's predominantly female support groups, Johnson's circle included women friends and a homosexual coterie that she "mothered."

These three women writers are as feminine as they were aracial in their poetry. As her contemporary critics noted, Georgia Johnson sang "the heart of a woman" in her gemlike lyrics, although they failed to hear the irony, discontent, and quiet sedition that undercut some of their apparent sentimentality. Women characters also hold center stage in her 1920s plays, while her later short short story "Free" is a remarkable vignette of female bonding. Dunbar-Nelson's poetry—which she viewed as secondary and wrote sporadically—also mined feminine and traditional lyric topics such as nature and love, with one poem, "I Sit and Sew," being feminist in spirit. Generally speaking, how she handled gender in her work betrays the same kind of ambivalence that marked her treatment of race. For Dunbar-Nelson, there was always a dichotomy—fostered perhaps by female role and self-image conflicts—between the "inside" and the "outside." Externally, she was liberated in her carriage, doing radical women's work and making her way in the male journalistic profession. Yet, she succumbed to playing the good little helpless woman, and assumed poses of modest authorship—although less so as she matured. Almost all of the women in her work are depicted as traditional, with none of the interests and mettle that she herself possessed.

Dunbar-Nelson's general problem may simply have been a deep inability to use her own real experience as raw material for realistic art—even during the Renaissance, which encouraged such. One wonders if a modern, feminist acceptance of the "personal" as legitimate literary subject matter would have made her any more capable of doing so. All three of these women were released into the freedom of the self only through the lyric "I" persona. It should be said, however, that Johnson's work was not negatively affected by the fact that she did not draw from a more real autobiographical base. But creating in this way—had she been able to—could only have enhanced Dunbar-Nelson's output. Her colorful life would have produced writing in the same way that, say, the adventures of Hughes and McKay (safe and accepted because they were males) were translated into their poetry and fiction.

Like Johnson, Grimké is more feminine and personal in her poetry, and more racial in her drama and fiction. To the usual universal lyric topics, she adds the theme of lesbian love, predominantly in her unpublished poems. Not being able to write openly from her sexual self, as well as not being able to print whatever she did manage to write, blighted her creativity and reputation as a poet. If she and Dunbar-Nelson could have penned their lesbian poetry unfettered by internal or external constraints, their corpus would have benefited. The peculiarly female image of cloistering appears in Grimké's work, suggesting her own narrow, sheltered life and recalling similar images in Dunbar-Nelson's stories. Her two major characters (Rachel and Mara) are women, whose depiction is idealized and faintly autobiographical.

Contrasting widely as female personalities, Grimké, Dunbar-Nelson, and Georgia Douglas Johnson shared definite similarities as lyric, women poets. Evaluated solely by the poems that were published in Harlem Renaissance magazines and anthologies, they appear as traditional, feminine verse-makers who treated themes of love, death, sorrow, nature, selfhood, and identity, with a smattering of indirectly handled racial material (Johnson's "Old Black Men" and "Suppliant"; Grimké's "Tenebris"; and Dunbar-Nelson's "April Is on the Way"). Furthermore, male anthologists like James Weldon Johnson used some of their most sex-stereotyped work. Thus, Georgia Johnson is always represented by "I Want to Die While You Love Me" and never by "Ivy," which ironically addresses the usual "clinging vine" definition of women. That women, poetry, and women poets were not accorded maximum status did not improve the situation.

To varying degrees, women were important in all three writers' authorial lives and literary imaginations. They are positively evoked, from the outmoded feminine ideals that Dunbar-Nelson strangely enshrined, to Johnson's realistic black female folk characters, to Grimké's sensitive young delicate women. Expanding the view of this trio as women writers to fields beyond their poetry shows them in a truer light. It is difficult to say whether they saw themselves as part of a female literary tradition. During her heyday, Johnson was compared with Sara Teasdale and Edna St. Vincent Millay. Locke, at least, saw them as belonging to the same school of "modern feminist realism."[49] Dunbar-Nelson and Johnson, especially, knew themselves to be part of a contemporary group that included women as well as men. And the women sometimes aided each other. In Johnson's own words, Jessie Fauset "very generously helped her to gather together material for her first book,"[50] while Dunbar-Nelson wrote her an unavailing Harmon Foundation recommendation. Grimké's ceasing to write was almost certainly caused in part by her relative isolation. Like Nella Larsen (also after 1930), she secluded herself and was never artistically heard from again.

Yet, it required considerable courage for these early twentieth-century women to put themselves forth as writers. This they bravely did, despite their deferent gestures, their securing males to "offer their books" to publishers, and so forth. Johnson dedicated *An Autumn Love Cycle* to white woman writer and critic Zona Gale in gratitude for her encouragement. But all of her books are prefaced by men—poet-anthologist William Stanley Braithwaite, W. E. B. DuBois, and Alain Locke, respectively. However, any contrary evidence notwithstanding, on some basic and indispensable level, these three black women were serious about themselves as writers.

Certain features of their poetics further help to explain them and their positions as female literary artists of the Harlem Renaissance. Dunbar-Nelson held an exalted, high-art concept of literature that complemented her generally classical and orthodox taste. In fact, this ivory-tower conception contributed as much as her personal ambivalence to her not using her real self and experience in her art. Judging from their work, it appears that Grimké and Johnson operated from a broader, but still basically orthodox, position. Certainly, the three of them subscribed to romantic philosophies and notions of poetry. Grimké most fully articulated these ideas in a 1925 statement that she wrote. She declares that her poems arise from within herself as the reflection of moods that find symbolic analogues in nature, and even employs the image of the harp favored in romantic critical theory: "And what is word? May it not be a sort of singing in the harp strings of the mind? Then on the principle of sympathetic vibration is there not in nature a harp singing also to be found. . . . "[51] Romantic concepts help account for their use of poetry as a vehicle for brief expression of intense emotion, a concentration on the ideal, and a lavish use of nature and natural images.

Generally speaking, they shied away from experimentation with more modern styles and modes of verse. Of course, in the 1920s, Carl Sandburg, William Carlos Williams, the imagists, Harriet Monroe, and others were introducing *vers libre* and similar flexible poetic forms. The black writers were adding to this their ethnically derived innovations of rhythm, dialect, jazz, and blues. In one poem, "At April," Grimké uses a kind of syncopation to admonish "brown girl trees" to "toss your gay lovely heads."[52] Dunbar-Nelson tried to capture the new, more colloquial and direct tone in a few of her poems of the period. But Johnson adhered to rhymed and metered stanzas throughout, never even developing a facility for free verse.

The gender-class-literary dimensions of how they wrote gain illuminating perspective when placed alongside the song lyrics of the period's black blueswomen. Critic Barbara Christian suggests:

> It might be said that the genuine poetry of the black woman appeared not in literature but in the lyrics of blues singers like Bessie Smith. . . . Perhaps because the blues was seen as "race music" and catered to a black audience, black women were better able to articulate themselves as individuals and as part of a racial group in that art form.[53]

Cheryl Wall puts the matter even more forcefully when she says: "Free of the burdens of an alien tradition, a Bessie Smith could establish the standard of her art; in the process she would compose a more honest poetry than any of her literary sisters'."[54] One aspect of Bessie Smith's "honesty" was a raunchy, woman-proud sexuality that echoed the explicitness of this licentious era. Reared as proper, middle-class, almost Victorian black women who were trained to be proofs of black female morals and mod-

esty, Dunbar-Nelson, Grimké, and Johnson could only treat sex roman-
tically and obliquely in their work—although, as Dunbar-Nelson vividly
proves, they could be quite "naughty" in private life. The younger Helene
Johnson was able to say to her "brown boy," "I loves you all over"; but
this is a far cry from Bessie Smith's "I'm gonna drink good moonshine and
run these browns down."[55] Their restrained treatment of sex also helped to
place them outside the sensational mainstream.

The lack of formal innovation exhibited by these three poets (were
women conditioned to be less daring?) combined with their conventional,
age-old themes (were these deemed more suitable for the lyric feminine
sensibility?) made their work relatively unexciting in a renaissance awakening that required some flash and newness. Because of temperament and
socialization, they did not loudly raise their voices in protest, pride, or
primitivism. The quality of their achievement could not obliterate this
difference. Nor could the fact that, for the first time in Afro-American
literary history, women were entering the scribal tradition in more than
token fashion, and largely as poets. Before, there had been the anomalous
Phillis Wheatley, Harriet Wilson, Francis Ellen Watkins Harper, some ex-
slave narrators (Harriet Brent Jacobs, Ellen Craft, and Elizabeth Keckley),
and documentary writers such as Charlotte Forten, Ida B. Wells, and Mary
Church Terrell. Perhaps the women writers of the Harlem Renaissance
were truly having more of a nascence than a re-nascence.

Dunbar-Nelson, Grimké, and Johnson knew that winning their way as
authors necessitated demonstrating talent in genres other than poetry that
were considered more major and difficult, and that also carried greater
rewards. To be perfectly accurate, Dunbar-Nelson considered the short
story her most representative genre and also wrote plays. Grimké expended almost as much effort on drama as poetry and wrote a few short
stories, even planning at one point to take a short-story writing course.
Johnson focused on drama for a major portion of her career and wrote a
little fiction. Her success in the three forms is more even, for Grimké's gifts
really were lyrical while a latter-day assessment shows that Dunbar-
Nelson's excellence came in noncanonical forms. Grimké was the only one
who did not write a novel. Dunbar-Nelson worked on four throughout her
life, and Johnson on one or two. A problem they had in common was not
conceiving ideas and plots that were inherently of novel proportions. They
found themselves making up word counts and "rounding up" necessary
pages. Having been destroyed, Johnson's "White Men's Children" (which
she described as "a novel dealing with the interplay of bloods") cannot be
evaluated. Publishers considered but apparently did not accept it. In 1942,

a Rosenwald Foundation executive volunteered that he had "taken a great deal of pleasure" in reading the work,[56] thus leaving behind the only documented opinion about it. Dunbar-Nelson's loosely written novels—which do not fall predominantly in the Renaissance period—did not sustain reader interest as tight fictional constructs. In the early 1900s, one of them, "Confessions of a Lazy Woman," was accepted for publication, but the contract was canceled when the firm underwent changes. "This Lofty Oak," the final one she wrote at the end of her life, merits attention as fictionalized biography, with her, a woman writer, setting down for posterity the fascinating life history of another self-made woman who was her intimate friend.

None of them—except Dunbar-Nelson—wrote modern realistic fiction that utilized the increasingly important urban setting. However, the experience of the two women novelists who did, Fauset and Larsen, is instructive. The first is disparaged for her proper, bourgeoise characters, milieu, tone, and point of view. In actuality, other novels by male writers—for example, those by Wallace Thurman and McKay's *Home to Harlem*—are as badly flawed in their way as Fauset's were in hers. However, because her faults were seen as sex-related ones that put her out-of-step with the avant-garde of her era, she is disproportionately minimized. David Lewis states further that "respectable critical reaction to the fiction of DuBois, Fauset, and Larsen was no match, in the short term, for the commercial success of *Home to Harlem,* [or] the controversy of *The Blacker the Berry.*"[57] Larsen, who wrote good psychological fiction from a black female perspective, was generally appreciated but not truly understood. Interestingly, some of Dunbar-Nelson's best unpublished stories rely on psychological probing of her characters.

Final pieces of individual data further explain these three women's work. Again, Grimké is easiest of all to summarize. She could not really write or publish her lesbian poems and never collected a volume of her work, although she projected one sometime around 1920. Because of mainly personal factors, she was not prolific—not even in her métier, poetry. She leaves the impression of a talented writer whose potential was never realized. Her strengths were her fine sensibility, descriptive power, and quiet drama.

Inadequate volume was certainly not one of Georgia Douglas Johnson's problems. In 1944, she catalogued the unpublished work she had on hand: "three new books of poetry, thirty plays both one and three act, thirty short stories, a novel, a book of philosophy, a book of exquisite sayings, . . . twenty songs."[58] There was, in addition, a biography of her late husband entitled "The Black Cabinet" and her reminiscences of her Renaissance Saturday Nighters, which she called "Literary Salon." When publication proved vain, she consoled herself by recalling that Balzac had left behind forty unpublished novels at his death. Unfortunately, with one or two exceptions, only what she published during her lifetime survived her. Based on this, she emerges as the most well-rounded, well-realized in the traditional literary genres. Erlene Stetson summarizes her major poetry like this:

> Over-all, all three volumes as musical lyrics form a sonata. The movement is from the intensely subjective world of the woman in the spring of life who is yet naive enough to shout her pain, to the summer of life, the red and fire of *Bronze* when motherhood, marriage and race exacts its toll on the female psyche and finally, to the autumnal season of realism and objectivity "when love's triumphant day is done" (*Autumn*, p. 47).[59]

This sonata displays her poetic literateness and aptly chosen images and conceits.

She used her admirable dramaturgical skills in one-act plays that focused on racial issues, mostly through female characters. One really wishes that other of her short stories had survived to see if she customarily reached the achievement level of "Free." Being definitive about her is short-circuited by the work of hers lost to pseudonymous publication. Also, her poignant, late lyrical admission that "one lives too long" could be applied to her as a writer. Though she strove to remain current (like Dunbar-Nelson, going so far as to attempt a filmscript), her themes of miscegenation, passing, and brotherhood—even more so than her poetic style—were anachronistic in the years before her death in 1966.

Of these three women writers, it is Dunbar-Nelson whose literary position calls for the most radical revision. Long noted as a romantic poet and writer of local-color sketches, she reemerges as a unique chronicler of black female experience in her diary, a first-rate essayist and journalist, and a fictionist whose total output (including unpublished stories) reveals a breadth and interest beyond her recognized Creole pieces. Unfortunately, the work that she excelled in is noncanonical, ephemeral, and unavailable. She is the only one who approached the status of professional writer. Thus, publication, which was important to all three women for self-realization, was more critical to her for economic livelihood. Trying to earn money by her pen (something she once bitterly remarked that fate had decreed should not happen) was an ambition that her marriage to litterateur Paul Laurence Dunbar helped to set. That it was more necessary did not make it happen. How she was affected by the marketplace is partially indicated by the fact that she found outlets for her slighter, color-less stories quicker than for her meatier ones. Like Georgia Douglas Johnson she also wrote pulp romance. Hers was embarrassingly poor; Johnson's may have been published under pen names in magazines like *Tan Confessions*.

Dunbar-Nelson did not resort to self-subsidized publication, even though at the time, and especially for black writers, it was not so heavily stigmatized as a "vanity" enterprise (just as contemporary self-publication by women writers has taken on different meaning). By the time of the Harlem Renaissance, however, mainstream channels were opening (albeit selectively and unimpartially). Therefore, in 1925, Charles Johnson dissuaded Grimké from paying to have "Jettisoned" printed, saying, "A story such as this should sell itself."[60] In 1919, she had shared the initial cost of publishing *Rachel* with the Cornhill Company. Georgia Johnson's unprecedented three books of poetry owed their existence to her own money (for example, her 1918 *Heart of a Woman* was also published by Cornhill). Pleading for herself with reference to the Harmon awards in 1928, she said, "[I] cannot pay for another volume being published."[61]

Dunbar-Nelson's rejections were sometimes caused by the weakness of her work. As reviewers accurately noted, she is good at description but not with plot, while her matter is diverting but her style commonplace. Her ease with language and journalistic habits often betrayed her into hasty, prolix writing, which she did not strenuously revise. In poetry, she relied heavily on thematic and stylistic contrast. The twin subject of war and peace is one of her major motifs—in all genres. Her living through three wars (both hot and cold), being black and political (at a time when whether Afro-Americans should fight for the United States was a controversial racial debate), and working as executive secretary for the Friends American Inter-Racial Peace Committee help to explain this choice. Perhaps because it is the only forum where she starred herself, Dunbar-Nelson's diary presents her strongest and most distinctive voice.

This, then, introduces the three women writers of the Harlem Renaissance who constitute this study: Alice Dunbar-Nelson, Angelina Weld Grimké, and Georgia Douglas Johnson. The unearthing of hitherto unknown biographical and critical material about them corrects the prevailing myopic view of them as women and as writers. Generally speaking, their reputations are enhanced. But even those sceptics or resolute traditionalists who choose not to revise their opinions will now know more precisely how these figures came to be who they were. However, it would require a willful blindness to continue to see Dunbar-Nelson only as Paul Laurence Dunbar's elegant, poetic appendage, or Grimké as a shy lyricist who simply did not publish enough, or Georgia Douglas Johnson as the contented "poet-housewife."

Concomitantly, focusing on them has brought with it a changed perspective on other Harlem Renaissance writers, male and female. Though not a part of this study, Anne Spencer, for instance, is also explained by what has been learned about the core three. The four of them form a coherent contrast to the younger women poets and the female novelists of the period. Grimké, Johnson, and Dunbar-Nelson were certainly elder stateswomen and literary foremothers for the succeeding generation to reckon with. Blanche Taylor Dickinson suggested this when she named Johnson as one of her favorite poets.[62] In that genre, Johnson holds her place as "foremost," since the designation implies productivity and reputation, as well as achievement. However, in many ways, Grimké and Spencer are better and more original. It is interesting to see affinities between Gwendolyn Bennett and Grimké, while Helene Johnson and Gladys Hayford become all the more singular when placed alongside the rest of their sisters. Only secondarily poets, Fauset and Dunbar-Nelson push a consideration of these women into other forms. When this happens, the two of them and Johnson can receive more of the credit that they are due, and Grimké and Bennett can, too, be appreciated for their multi-genred achievement. These women poets wrought well in drama and fiction, and in nonliterary forms.

Directly comparing Johnson, Dunbar-Nelson, and Grimké with male poets and writers of the period would force them into a competition whose rules were formulated without them in mind. In colloquial parlance, it was not their "ball game." They themselves could not help playing it, but conscious critics do not have to tally a traditional score. It is far more instructive to imagine how Hughes's and Johnson's careers would have differed if they could have exchanged sexes, or whether Cullen's love and nature lyrics and poems of attenuated protest would have received the same favorable treatment had he been a woman writer. Certainly, it becomes harder to casually place these three in some inferior echelon below such of their contemporaries as Frank Horne or Arna Bontemps.

This matter of comparison symbolizes how much has been learned about the sexual-literary politics of the New Negro era. In myriad ways, both subtle and blatant, women were penalized for their gender. These ranged from "blaming the victim" for the inevitable results of her female socialization to outright sexist exclusion. Though Locke may still be respected for his erudition and insightful criticism, his iconic status as cultural entrepreneur has been tarnished. For reasons beyond those previously thought, Charles S. Johnson emerges as a much more important and admirable mentor. Posterity also has a better sense of the gender-related "breaks" that boosted the careers and permanent reputations of "major" writers like Hughes and McKay. Whatever these women were not able to accomplish was exacerbated by the age and has been further multiplied by their perennial critical treatment. Even David L. Lewis, who wrote a brilliant and indispensable social history of the period, *When Harlem Was in Vogue* (1982), largely ignores the women poets. And though he later supplemented his statement with more positive information, Lewis slurs Georgia Johnson's literary salon as one of the places in Philadelphia or Washington, D.C., "where belles-lettres meant Saturday night adventures in tidy parlors, among mostly tidy-minded literati."[63] Although she was a woman, neither Johnson's house nor her mind was tidy. And some of the same people who glittered on the Harlem scene attended her affairs.

To speak more positively, looking at these three writers enables one to see the "Harlem Renaissance" (if that designation is maintained) as a large and diverse movement in Afro-American literary history that went beyond what a small "in-crowd" was helping one another to do in New York City. Encompassing it requires a broadening of temporal, geographical, and critical boundaries. More literarily still, it becomes clear that women writers are tyrannized by periodization, the hierarchy of canonical forms, critical rankings of major and minor, and generalizations about literary periods. Indeed, generalizations about the characteristics of an era are often arrived at without weighting women's work. In this case, Dunbar-Nelson, Grimké, and Johnson sometimes pick up—and even extend—the dominant temper of the age, as when Johnson explores the black female folk psyche in *Plumes* or Grimké combines imagist and Renaissance racial techniques in her poem "The Black Finger." At other times, the pure fact of their being and what they write constitute an implicit challenge to the more visible modes. Dunbar-Nelson's diary, which she kept in 1921 and then from 1926 to 1931, is an excellent example. Generally, studying these women writers and the way they have been handled fosters a wariness about superficial, incomplete knowledge, oversimplifications, and the "bandwagoning" approach to criticism and teaching.

Without women writers, the Harlem Renaissance would have been a bleaker place. Though not blindingly vivid, the color they added completed the total spectrum. Not only did women play their usual and some additional special roles, but the work that they produced clearly—if sometimes "slantwise"—embodied the female half of human experience and swelled the ranks of the New Negro artists. Poetry, in particular, would have suffered had they not been writing. Johnson's plays and Dunbar-Nelson's essays and columns would also have left lacunae. When their lifetime of work is included, Dunbar-Nelson, Grimké, and Georgia Johnson become even more important. Their writings are significant as notable literary responses of earlier twentieth-century Afro-American women writers to the determining facts of race and gender as filtered through their personal and artistic consciousness. The resulting beauty and complexity is valuable for both historical and literary reasons.

One final word *in propria persona*. Even though it is neat and convenient to continue doing so, we need to stop hyper-emphasizing the Harlem Renaissance, often by repeating the same handful of works and critical clichés. Or, if we decide to use it as an originating point of focus, we must remember that there was significant literature both before and after, and that, in all three periods, black women writers live.

CHAPTER II

Alice Dunbar-Nelson
(1875–1935)

Ensconced with her family in West Medford, Massachusetts, Alice wrote Paul Laurence Dunbar, her husband in Washington, D.C., a March 7, 1899, letter recounting some remarkable personal history that she had recently learned from her mother:

> Another thing I didn't know. She [Mama], nor any of our family didn't know of the emancipation proclamation for two years! The owners fled with their slaves [from Opelousas, Louisiana] to a wild district in Texas and there held out against the law. Finally the old Judge was threatened with arrest, so he called the slaves together one morning and read the proclamation, and then like a man told them how long he had withheld the news. It must have been a dramatic scene the way mama puts it, the inflexible Yankee soldiers on each side of the white-haired old man, his sobbing daughters and wife, the open-mouthed, indignant and unforgiving slaves, for most of them were of mixed Indian blood. She says he broke down and sobbing like a child threw out his hands and begged them too if they would return to Louisiana with them he would try to pay them back wages.[1]

This plantation melodrama continued with some of the ex-slaves remaining in Texas, while others—including Alice's mother, Patricia—made the three-month journey back to Opelousas in "big covered wagons, swimming the Sabine and Red Rivers," "where the Judge tried to make amends by giving them cabins and starting them in life."

Alice Ruth Moore as she appeared about the time of her 1898 marriage to Paul Laurence Dunbar.

A more mature Alice Dunbar-Nelson. (Photo courtesy of the Ohio Historical Society.)

At this point, either Mother Patricia tired of talking, or Alice tired of writing. Alice probably told this tale to Paul as an attempt to match the famed southern narratives of his mother (which often served as the basis for his writing) with some "roots" lore of her own. She never referred to or used the story in any public context, for—unlike Dunbar, who was Negroid in color and features—she would not choose to emphasize slave ancestry among her personal data. Dunbar-Nelson would much rather have been taken as a descendant of Louisiana's (preferably free) *gens de couleur*, those mixed-blood, "colored" people who considered themselves superior to pure Negroes, especially those who had been slaves. Throughout her life, ambiguities regarding race and color are apparent in her behavior, comments, and writings. Of course, these ambiguities never reached "tragic mulatto" proportions, but as with Georgia Douglas Johnson and her "mixed-breed" preoccupation, and the clearly race-crossed Angelina Grimké, they were crucial on both personal and artistic levels.

Precisely what Mother Patricia did upon returning to Louisiana is not known. However, she eventually made her way to the New Orleans metropolis, became a seamstress, and gave birth to two daughters—Alice's older sister, Mary Leila, and later Alice Ruth herself on July 19, 1875. Details about the father, Joseph Moore, are scarce. The family always referred to him as a "seaman" or "merchant marine," a description substantiated by a May 6, 1929, letter to Dunbar-Nelson from one "(Capt.) Harry Dean" of Chicago, Illinois. He writes:

> I am sure you cannot remember me. Your husband, Paul Dunbar, and I were chums in Chicago in 1893. Subsequently, while sailing out of New Orleans, when in company with your father, I first met you there. Subsequently, while peddling ostrich plumes, in Wilmington, Delaware, your husband, Dr. [*sic*] Nelson, was good enough to buy from me some gorgeous plumes for you.

Alice was born with reddish-blonde curls that darkened to red to auburn, and was fair enough to "pass" for white. Given her mother's black and American Indian blood, she seems to have received considerably more Caucasian influence from her father. The specifics are shrouded in history, but there was something irregular, something shameful about her birth that Alice alluded to years later in a private letter to Paul. Remonstrating with him about "deriding" her and inflicting "bitterness and hurts," she wells up: "Dearest,—dearest—I hate to write this—How often, oh how pitifully often, when scarce meaning it, perhaps, you have thrust my parentage in my face. There!''[2] What there was to thrust in her face could have been white ancestry, illegitimacy, or perhaps a combination of the two. At any rate, with this background, she assumed a prominent place in the racially mixed Creole society of postbellum New Orleans.

Dunbar-Nelson's twenty-one years in New Orleans laid the foundation for many of her later interests and activities. After a public school education and graduation from the two-year teachers' program of Straight College (now Dillard University) in 1892, she began teaching, a vocation she followed for the next thirty-six years of her life. For her, as for countless other educated black women, it was one of the very few—some would say the only—safe, secure, relatively fulfilling career options. During this time, she studied art and music (she played the piano and cello), thus beginning an informed taste for the fine arts that continued to erupt in rhapsodies for grand opera, classical composers, and Old Masters in her public and private utterances. In a 1921 diary entry, she writes about "salivating . . . [her] starved soul in the loveliness" of the Chicago Art Museum, which she described as "a dream of beauty." Altogether, she preferred "sweet convention," "good drawing," "low tones and harmony" to modernistic "scarecrow art"[3]—a leaning toward the orthodox that is also reflected in other aspects of her life such as her poetry.

The youthful Miss Moore was also president of the "Whittier Club" and acted in dramas that it presented. This activity provided an outlet for her theatrical personality and an early base for the plays and movie scripts that she subsequently wrote. Even at this stage, she had ventured into journalism, combining it with women's concerns (two lifelong preoccupations, which persisted in being frequently yoked). At nineteen, she wrote the "Woman's Column" for the *Journal of the Lodge,* seemingly the newspaper for an artistic-fraternal organization. Its August 18, 1894, issue features her on the front page.[4] Below a photograph captioned "A Brilliant Southern Writer" and adjacent to her column, there is an article headed "Know Each Other" which provides information about Dunbar-Nelson not found elsewhere.

Among other things, it proclaims that

> Miss Moore is noted for her modest and unassuming ways, cultured and refined manners and brilliant attainments. She has the honor of being the only colored female stenographer and type-writer in this city ["employed

as bookkeeper and type-writer for the Paragon Printing Company, the largest colored establishment in the country"]. She is one of our prominent and efficient school teachers; a brilliant and versatile writer, and is a contributor to several journals in the North and South. . . . and her excellent articles in behalf of race and sex have elicted [*sic*] commendatory expressions from all sections. Miss Moore is a member of St. Luke's P.E. [Protestant Episcopal] Church; a leading member of one of our prominent literary societies and withal, a popular member of our social circles, and has a host of friends and admirers.

What particularly stands out here is that, at this early date, Dunbar-Nelson is picking up printing skills that she will eventually use in coediting a paper during the early 1920s with her third husband; she is writing "in behalf of race and sex," the twin themes of her life; and she is attracting notice for both her personal charm and professional attainments. Though she had already achieved much, much more was expected of her.

That she was carving her niche as writer is also very evident. Unlike Georgia Douglas Johnson, who wrote nothing of significance until she was thirty years old, Dunbar-Nelson clearly became an author while still in her teens. Indeed, her first published book, *Violets and Other Tales,* appeared in 1895, when she was only twenty years old.[5] The volume culminates this period of Dunbar-Nelson's life and indicates her future directions as a writer.

After a title page bordered in the pretty five-petaled flower that names it, *Violets* begins with a dedication, "To my friend of November 5, 1892." This friend, who was dead at least by 1913, was one of Dunbar-Nelson's teachers.[6] Perhaps this teacher was inspirational, but Dunbar-Nelson never says so. She only commemorated that date for the rest of her life—for example, writing in her 1928 diary, "Awake in my berth repeating the old phrase, 'To my friend of November 5, 1892.' "[7] And on November 5, 1930, she starts her entry with the exact phrase, then proceeds: "And in 1892, November 5 came the day after election day—and there at my place every day on the table for 38 years is the little silver Harrison spoon to commemorate a beautiful friendship."[8] Whatever its nature, the impression was certainly lasting. That Dunbar-Nelson kept the day so faithfully also attests to her prodigious memory and her penchant for sentiment.

The young author introduces the book with two paragraphs that are remarkable for their modesty, diffidence, and ladylike tone of casual authorship. She describes her "maiden effort" as "a little thing with absolutely nothing to commend it, that seeks to do nothing more than amuse."

Her hopes for the work are equally slight: "If perchance this collection of idle thoughts may serve to while away an hour or two, or lift for a brief space the load of care from someone's mind, their purpose has been served—the author is satisfied." Whether she heard enough testimonials of entertainment and cheer to please her cannot be ascertained. However, in later years, Dunbar-Nelson disparaged her juvenile publication. Writing to bibliophile Arthur Schomburg, she confessed:

> I am heartily ashamed of "Violets" and would not have given Mr. Bolivar a copy had he not importuned me for it as a "curiosity." . . . Perhaps Mr. Bolivar showed you a decenter volume, "The Goodness of St. Rocque." . . . I am not so ashamed of that, though it is bad enough. Please don't want "Violets" in your collection; such sheer slop as that would spoil the whole.[9]

Actually, even allowing for a bit of posing, Dunbar-Nelson need not have been so harsh in her retrospective judgment. An unbiased reader is much more likely to concur with Sylvanie F. Williams's prefatory statement: "There is much in this book that is good; much that is crude; some that is poor: but all give that assurance of something great and noble when the bud of promise . . . will have matured into that fuller growth of blossoming flower. . . . "

Violets is a potpourri of short stories, sketches, essays, reviews, and poetry encompassing a variety of tones and techniques. The individual pieces are usually brief, slight, impressionistic—but some of them possess charm and interest. "Anarchy Alley" is an almost onomatopoeic description of the densely teeming four squares of New Orleans' Exchange Alley, "a Latinized portion of America, a bit of Europe, perhaps, the restless, chafing, anarchistic Europe of to-day, in the midst of the quieter democratic institution of our republic" (p. 50). Dunbar-Nelson reviews Gustave Flaubert's *Salammbô,* praising it for sensuous beauty but decrying its tendency to degrade the mind. In another essay, she writes provocatively about a newly discovered Buddhist history that sheds light on Jesus Christ's unknown years. One selection, "The Bee Man," is a fairy tale about a beekeeper whose innate nature causes him to become a beekeeper again even after he is given a second life by a good fairy. Another uses narrative stream-of-consciousness. And three of the best stories in the volume— "Titee," "A Carnival Jangle," and "Little Miss Sophie"—are repeated in her later book, *The Goodness of St. Rocque* (1899).

Fourteen of the twenty-nine selections are poems. Their titles are informative: "Three Thoughts," "A Plaint," "Impressions," "In Memoriam,"

"At Bay St. Louis," "New Year's Day," "Chalmette," "Amid the Roses," and so on. These are mostly conceits, elegiac poems, occasional poems, love and courtship lyrics. "Paul to Virginia (Fin De Siecle)" begins:

> I really must confess, my dear,
>   I cannot help but love you,
> For of all girls I ever knew,
>   There's none I place above you;
> But then you know it's rather hard,
>   To dangle aimless at your skirt,
> And watch your every movement so,
>   *For I am jealous, and you're a flirt.* (P. 83)

Each of the three succeeding stanzas concludes with the last-line refrain. Stylistically, her major weakness in these mostly conventionally rhymed and metered forms is prolixity. There is also very little that is original in her young poetic voice.

The title story, "Violets" (a title that she also used to designate her later, best-known poem), is, to a certain extent, typical of the volume. It is a pathetic little tale of an innocent young girl who dies of heartbreak. Part I has her tying "a bunch of violets with a tress of her pretty brown hair" and sending it as an Easter token to her lover together with a long, tender letter that recounts their romance. Part II comprises the following Easter, when she lies dead in her casket, fingers "locked softly over a bunch of violets; violets and tube-roses in her soft, brown hair." In Part III, a man in a distant city asks his "regal-looking" wife (a definite foil to the sweet heroine) if she ever sent him some flowers and, after her disdainful reply, throws them into the fire: "And the Easter bells chimed a solemn requiem as the flames slowly licked up the faded violets. Was it merely fancy on the wife's part, or did the husband really sigh,—a long, quivering breath of remembrance?" (p. 17). Thus, the tale ends.

Philosophically, it is reminiscent of another work in the collection, "The Maiden's Dream," which begins:

> The maid had been reading love-poetry, where the world lay bathed in moon-light, fragrant with dew-wet roses and jasmine, harmonious with the clear tinkle of mandolin and guitar. . . . And there stole into her consciousness, words, thoughts, not of her own, yet she read them not, nor heard them spoken. . . . (P. 85)

Thereupon follows a paean to "Love, most potent, most tyrannical, and most gentle of the passions," a paean that ranges over history, heavens, nature, famous and infamous scenes of real, mythic, and literary lovers. After being thrilled by the amorous words crowding her mind, the dreamer awakes, whispering to the lover at her side to "Take all of me—I am thine own, heart, soul / Brain, body, all." What is presented here is a refined, literary version of a young woman whose head is full of romance. Whether autobiographical or merely a use of expected convention, it is not surprising to find Dunbar-Nelson employing such a consciousness as the locus for a number of her pieces. This persona is obviously also intelligent, with a wit and humor that surface in the wry description of a football game ("Ten Minutes' Musing") and a recounting of being chloroformed in the dentist's chair ("In Unconsciousness").

Of greater interest is a thematic ambivalence about woman's concept of self and proper role in the world. This is objectified as conflict between the sanctioned way of wife/mother/family and the more uncertain path of the "brave new woman who scorns to sigh."[10] Three stories are particularly relevant. The first, "A Story of Vengeance," is a dramatic monologue spoken by "a lonely woman," "an old maid," to her friend, who is happy with "kind husband, lovely children." To explain why she never married, she recounts her affair with Bernard. For him, she

> gave up all my most ambitious plans and cherished schemes, because he disliked women whose names were constantly in the mouth of the public. . . . became quiet, sedate, dignified, renounced too some of my best and dearest friends. . . . lived, breathed, thought, acted only for him. . . . (P. 101)

When he returned to an old flame, she took up her long-forgotten plans, succeeded triumphantly, and engineered a revenge that ruined his life. Instead of relenting when he returned and begged forgiveness, she sneered and disclosed her actions—but then suffered a deluge of love and remorse that now torment her "outcast, forsaken, loveless" existence.

The second story, "At Eventide," presents the conflict between private sphere and public career even more forcefully. The heroine is "tempted" by "Ambition" to seek fame as a singer—despite her lover's wish that "My wife must be mine and mine alone. I want not a woman whom the world claims, and shouts her name abroad. My wife and my home must be inviolate" (p. 162). After they separate, she eventually discovers that "Fame was but an empty bubble while love was supreme and the only happiness, after all." When she seeks him again, he rejects her as a "soiled lily," a "gaudy sun-flower," leaving her "to writhe and groan in despair."

Finally, in "The Woman," a secretary muses on the question, "Why should well-salaried women marry?" and concludes:

> . . . your independent working woman of to-day comes as near being ideal in her equable self poise as can be imagined. So why should she hasten to give this liberty up in exchange for a serfdom, sweet sometimes, it is true, but which too often becomes galling and unendurable. (P. 25)

She is the most liberated of the lot but closes her thoughts by saying that whatever else a working woman might do, she will still cuddle as gracefully as her unemancipated sister because "it comes natural, you see." Clearly, in these stories, the author buttresses the traditional and romantic view of women.

Dunbar-Nelson is writing in a trasitional era—when Victorian ideas maintained force, but when social and legal changes were widening women's lives and increasing their participation in paid labor. Work outside the home was still felt to detract from true femininity and was seen as temporary/secondary. As a young, informed, progressive black woman, Dunbar-Nelson reflects the contemporary debate, but also her own personal-historical experiences of work and women's roles. Her stance in *Violets* anticipates her vexing pattern of being more orthodox in her literary writings than in the ethics that guided her own behavior. Whatever else was operative, there is a definite conflict between abstract feminine ideals (which she tended to enshrine in her fine art) and her active, ambitious personality and economic needs.

In *Violets*, a well-read, conspicuously talented young writer is trying on voices, trying out authorial strategies. Overall, the advanced juvenilia of the volume is a dress rehearsal for Dunbar-Nelson's more mature performances. This first period of her life set some major patterns—racial ambiguity, Creole materials and themes, vocational pursuits, cultural involvements, journalistic work, women's concerns and issues, racial activism, and multi-genred writing. These will continue to define her in the years to come.

ii

Following the almost archetypal Afro-American migratory pattern, Dunbar-Nelson left New Orleans in 1896 for the wider opportunities of the North. The move was both an individual and a family one. Leila's husband, James Young, set up a prosperous catering business outside Boston in Medford, Massachusetts, bringing Mother Patricia and Alice, as well as his wife, with him. Massachusetts, still the cradle of liberty and liberal ideals, was a congenial location. With the family in West Medford, Alice enjoyed her own "little room," where she "sat many a night and dreamed things while . . . [watching] the Mystic [River] flow silvery away in the distance." She also took advantage of the area's rich history by doing such things as "browsing around Longfellow's haunts and Lowell's home" and attending the dedication of the Robert Gould Shaw monument in Boston.[11]

In 1897, she began teaching school in Brooklyn, New York, and living with Viola Earle Matthews there at 33 Poplar Street. Her other major occupation was conducting evening and Sunday classes at the White Rose Mission, which she helped Mrs. Matthews to establish. (It later became the White Rose Home for Girls in Harlem.) Until she resigned in the spring of 1898, the work kept her very busy. Coming home one night, she cried: "Exhausted? I feel like a dishrag. 62 untamed odoriferous kids all day, 23 fiends in the manual training class to-night. Fiends, just fiends pure and simple."[12] Relations with her colleagues at her first assignment, Public School 83, also contributed to the strain. As she tells it,

> I leave the school Thursday, the third [February 3, 1898], and go to #66, a school where there are neither colored teachers or pupils. I can always get along with white people. There was always an intense feeling in #83 against me on the part of the Downing clicque [sic]—social fuss, you know. As long as I had the principal, who is white and the former head of department Miss Goodwin, also white on my side, I was all right. These last two were staunch supporters of mine. I made my friends exclusively with the white teachers, ate with them, went to and fro with them. Well, Miss Lyons made me practically *hors de combat.* My two best friends got transfers immediately—so I had to follow their example. I look forward with great pleasure to my new school.[13]

Even though she was charmed with her new situation in Brownsville, east New York City, where the children were all Polish Jews and the all white teachers "jolly," Dunbar-Nelson worked just as hard—especially after she received an unprecedented promotion to teach the young, difficult students.

Her account of her first meeting with the manual training class is both amusing and instructive. She described the boys as "the toughest, most God-forsaken hoodlums you ever saw, average age 14, but I'd met their counterparts in New Orleans. They were inclined to jeer and act horribly."[14] Her patience lasted for fifty-seven minutes, when she was forced to grab a fifteen-year-old by the collar, drag him to the center of the floor, lecture him in four to five word sentences punctuated with shakes, then reseat him, wincing: "One boy whistled. The others looked on in respectful silence. The class was dismissed in perfect order." After class, one boy her height (about six feet tall) asked if she went to a gym. "Yes," she replied, "and I'm willing to undertake to knock you down if you want." He declined, and left beaming with respect and admiration. Dunbar-Nelson said it was a pity to have to be brutal, but . . .

Dunbar-Nelson displayed this robustness of physique and spirit until she died. When she was fifty-four years old, she took her dog Duke and a "stout stick" at midnight to lock up the open garage.[15] These pictures vary from the outward image of feminine gentility projected by her elegant dress and decorous carriage. Even in matters such as this, Dunbar-Nelson's "inside" and "outside" did not always match—a phenomenon that, in a sense, "cloaked" her and that renders posthumous interpretation of her character doubly intriguing.

At this stage of her life, Dunbar-Nelson had also become active in the growing black women's club movement. An 1899 article, "Women in Clubdom," summarizes her contributions:

> She has been both inspector and secretary of the W.R.C. of the department of Louisiana and Mississippi. After her removal to Boston she became a member of the Massachusetts corps. Three years ago she was secretary of the National Association of Colored Women. She is a member of the Woman's Era club of Boston, and has worked in the White Rose mission in New York.[16]

In the body of the article, Dunbar-Nelson talks about the good work being done by Afro-American women in Boston, Colorado, New Orleans, Philadelphia, Tuskegee and other places through mothers' meetings, journals, hospitals, aid for soldiers, and the like. She describes in some detail the outreach of the White Rose Mission, which is located in a populous black settlement and "has for its special interest the reclaiming of little children from the street": "It conducts a free kindergarten [which she organized and ran], a manual training class, mothers' meetings, a Sunday evening Bible class, and other lines of work, which have been found valuable and successful."

However exciting the North, her teaching, and club work may have been, this second period of Dunbar-Nelson's life is most notable for the event that assured her claim to fame: her marriage to Paul Laurence Dunbar, the poet from Ohio whose dialect verse catapulted him into prominence as America's first famous black *litterateur.* Though their union was brief, its influence on her was permanent. Forever after, she played the role of great man's widow, a role that was her insurance against obscurity and was a concrete means of livelihood. Ironically (but not unexpectedly), when she died—after twenty-nine years of widowhood, a second known husband, and many illustrious accomplishments of her own—the Philadelphia *Afro-American* ran a banner story with this headline: "Alice Ruth Moore's 2 Husbands / First, A Volatile Genius; Second, a Calm Newsman / Washingtonians Recall Romance of the Dunbars / Mrs. [Mary Church] Terrell Recalls When Wife of Poet Borrowed / an Ice Cream Freezer."[17]

The Moore-Dunbar marriage rivaled in celebrity the later Harlem Renaissance uniting of poet Countee Cullen and W. E. B. DuBois's daughter Yolande—though it lacked that extravagance. Furthermore, Paul and Alice saw themselves as a darker-skinned version of their famous models, Robert Browning and Elizabeth Barrett. Shortly after their March 6, 1898, wedding, Alice penned a comment to Paul that makes this reference and defines the romantic-literary nature of their relationship: "Paul, my precious bijou, I see that the Barrett-Browning idea has fastened itself upon you. Thus far we have done as our models, there is but one thing left—for you to write a Pippa Passes and I an Aurora Leigh. Then we can rest content. (Oh conceit!)"[18] The two of them went through a storybook romance and courtship, a quiet elopement-style wedding, a short and tumultuous marriage, and an almost public breaking up. During the course of their limelighted days together, each affected the other's life at both the private and public levels, with Alice in particular entering the world of professional authorship as the relatively unknown female half of a male-versus-female/famous-versus-unknown writing pair.

Quickly told, their story runs thus. In 1895, Paul saw one of her poems and her picture in a Boston magazine and began corresponding with her. Their letters progressed from formal to cordial to friendly to intimate over the next two years. When they finally met in New York City on the eve of his February 6, 1897, departure for a reading tour of England, they became engaged. Her work in Brooklyn and his in the Library of Congress, Washington, D.C., kept them separated and—if their letters are to be believed—hating each moment apart. Eventually, passion overrode practical considerations (Alice trying to finish the school year, married women teachers not being allowed). They made their initially secret marriage public, and Alice joined him in Washington, where they became a glittering part of the city's black society.

Though they relented in the face of Alice's determination, her family had strongly opposed the marriage. Virginia Cunningham, an early Dunbar critic, frankly spells out the reasons:

> The Moores did not approve of Paul's having scraped an acquaintance with Alice through letters; they were ashamed of his having a washwoman for a mother and of his lack of college training. Whether they said so or not, they were also ashamed of his black skin, so much darker than Alice's. . . . Then, too, the family felt the usual mistrust of poets as money earners, and it is possible that they disapproved of Paul's connection with a minstrel show like "Clorindy."[19]

These issues did not help the solidity of the marriage's foundation and probably contributed to its later demise. Yet, at the outset, nothing seemed to mar its beauty. Newspapers touted them as a well-matched couple and—consistent with sexist norms—more than one article concluded with references to Alice's loveliness (taking no note of Paul's lithe, dark handsomeness). Two instances are illustrative.

> Mrs. Dunbar is a woman of much grace and attraction of manner, with a true and happy disposition. She is a perfect helpmeet, rendering him the assistance that a woman of superior intellect, discrimination, and culture may extend to a literary husband.[20]

> Mrs. Dunbar is a young and beautiful woman. She is a native of New Orleans, and has all the soft, pretty ways of manner and speech of the southern woman in general. She is tall and slender, somewhat stately, with great, melting black eyes, and wavy black hair, combed down over her ears in the princess style. Mrs. Dunbar was a teacher in the public schools of Brooklyn before her marriage and is as refined and cultivated as she is attractive.[21]

The private side of the Dunbar's relationship as revealed in their letters is much more interesting than the public record. Its dynamics illuminate Alice—almost harshly so—and also allow for the tracing of undercurrents that eventually swept the two apart.

In the first place, Alice tended to sweetly "nag" Paul about being a "good boy," being true, resisting temptation, evil, and the dangers of drink, not making her jealous, taking care of himself, choosing suitable associates, being mindful of what he wrote, watching what he did, and so on. She could also be manipulative, inquisitive, and dictatorial. Before they were wed, she directed him not to go near the Tenderloin, the New York district frequented by black musicians and show people, but to stay at a "first-class *white* hostelry," where he would "be away from the—well niggers." She said it was time for him to shed those ties and take "some decently dignified stand in the world":

> You see I think more of your name and reputation than you do. I want you to be dignified, reserved, difficult of access. You cheapen yourself too

often by being too friendly with inferior folks, and your wife doesn't want it. You will be better appreciated if you are more reserved. See?[22]

Being too tired to choose words, she told him to forgive her brusqueness. The next month, she ordered him to cut off his "adolescent" moustache. And she frequently sent him lists of questions to answer about his business and activities—for example: "How in earth did your expenses get to be $55? And what was the mighty discussion you had with Bro' Washin'ton? And did he agree to pay you $100 . . . ?"[23]

She juxtaposed this tone with one that was more loving, demure, and deferent. On one occasion, she was led to apologize for her ardor: "Pardon me, dear, if I rhapsodize, but I love you, my husband that is to be."[24] She could resort to baby-talk: "I wish I could see you. I'm blue and tired and I 'wants to be petted.' "[25] In matters of domestic economy, she spelled out for herself a very conventional role:

> I will help you to save, not spend. I wish I could add some to the income, but the only things I can do are write, teach, and be a stenographer, and keep books and give lessons in some things. I can do fancy work too, but it's slow and doesn't pay, and folks don't take lessons in things much, and you wouldn't want me to be at some other man's elbow taking dictation, would you? and school-boards don't allow married women to teach, and editors won't accept my scribbling, so I guess I'll have to stay at home and watch over the family exchequer, eh?[26]

Dunbar-Nelson certainly revealed some unattractive traits in her interaction with Paul. They seem to have sprung from her strong personality and her desire to be the good-guiding wife, while maintaining an acceptable degree of dependent femininity (two inherently conflicting roles).

Given the age, it is not surprising that the question of premarital sex was a large one. Clearly, they wanted it, but resisted—until they finally succumbed. In fact, Alice's fear that she may have been pregnant probably helped to precipitate their clandestine marriage. In February or March 1898, she writes: "Paul—Paul—Eleven days may be an awful short time in which to draw conclusions—but, but, but, I have so many queer things happening [to] me, the sudden stopping of—well *something* being the worst." As early as January, she had proposed they marry secretly; in February, she had pleaded, "Have pity on my weakness for the dear God's sake, and make me yours *legally.*"[27] After he did, he accused her of "forcing" the issue and she remonstrated that she thought she was doing what was best for them. In a March 23 letter, she is so apparently anguished and angry about his reproaches that she says let the marriage be annulled. Suffering through a miserable mood almost two years later, she asks Paul a set of revealing, rhetorical questions: "Do you love me? I am so blue. Aren't you sorry I made you marry me? Tricked you into it, didn't I?"[28]

The rigid proscriptions against sex before marriage, with their heavier weight on women, helped push them into a near-classic, near-sordid scenario. It helps to remember that in 1898 Alice was only twenty-three years old and apparently experientially naïve about certain things. However, their sexual passion continued strong. It is refreshing to find Alice writing—albeit in code and to her husband—regarding matters about which most women remained silent. In a March 23, 1901, letter that she termed "naughty" and "wicked" and asked him to tear up, Alice confides:

> I should have had a visit from my country cousin—you know whom I mean on the 19th and she hasn't shown up. . . . You know Sir Peter called on Miss Venus so seldom within the past some weeks that it makes it all the more likely that it isn't measles. "Seldom visits make long friends." . . . How is Sir P.? To-morrow will be two weeks since he and Miss V. had a visit together and she has been making some solicitous inquiries as to his health.

During the next month's separation, she threatened to "play solitaire" with Miss Venus if he did not hurry home.[29]

Finally, it bears mentioning that the young couple never had a child, although they had fantasized about a baby from the beginning. Alice took treatments to prepare herself. On April 15, 1901, she told Paul that she had been going almost daily to her physician "to be tortured": "After that it will all be over and Dr. Parsons says her work will be done and yours begin. If nothing does, she and I are clear. It will all be your fault." Such pressure as this must not have been pleasant. At any rate, whose infertility was to blame is a moot question—since neither of them ever produced children either together or with other partners.

Pinpointing precisely what caused the critical breakdown in their relationship is an impossible task. Certainly, the matters that distressed Alice's family at the outset were operative, as were the history and tensions revealed in the foregoing discussion. Three months after they began living together, they had a serious enough quarrel that Alice left Washington to stay for a time in West Medford. She insisted that she loved and missed Paul terribly but could not take his moodiness and temper. She also blamed herself a bit for the non-homeyness of their domicile. It is well to recall that Alice liked living with her mother, sister, and family, and that Paul's unusually close friendship with his widowed mother, who shared the Washington residence, made the two of them quite comfortable together. Overall, much of the couple's fighting strikes one as a histrionic clashing of wills. Alice showed insight into this when she wrote to Paul in September 1898: "I am about convinced of one thing, that all this nonsense about self-introspection, self-centeredness, broodiness and this eternal posing is simply morbid, fanciful nonsense, in us both, arising from inordinate conceit."[30] She advised: "Let us lay aside the mask of theatricalism, the 'Sentimental Tommy' of our natures and stand face to face in the daylight."[31]

More concrete problems arose from their frequent separations because of Paul's engagements, his alcoholism (mistakenly induced by a doctor who prescribed liquor to alleviate his tuberculosis symptoms), and his dependency on heroin tablets. Details are vague, but it appears that while on a binge one night in 1902, he beat Alice and then spread lies and a "vile story" about her.[32] She said she could have overlooked the brutality, "but the slander I could not stand": "I never saw him again after that night. I was genuinely afraid of him. Disgusted, too, for this was only a culmination of the misery of four bitter years." Family and friends tried to reconcile them for many months. Paul himself begged forgiveness in contrite letters and moving poems. Enough heartrending pressure to soften a mountain of marble was put on Alice—but she remained absolutely obdurate (which reveals a great deal about her stubborn nature). She refused to reply, refused to see him for a moment, refused to visit him on his sick- or deathbed (although she made confidential inquiries of his physician about his condition).

Therefore, when Paul died in Dayton, Ohio, on February 9, 1906, he and Alice were estranged. Yet the world gave respect to her as his wife, sending her numerous condolences, requests for information and souvenirs, and commercial propositions. Her career as his widow was officially launched.

The other, very important side of Dunbar-Nelson's relationship with Dunbar was their dynamic as a professional writing couple. This aspect ran more smoothly than the strictly personal one, although there probably was spillover between the two currents. In fact, there may have been some professional competition and jealousy—perhaps more so on Alice's part since she was the less celebrated (though no less ambitious) of the two. Yet it is also possible that Paul might have harbored reservations about a wife who was a potential rival. Still, it seems that the two of them genuinely supported and encouraged each other's writing. For the time they were together, their authorial lives intertwined.

After their engagement, Alice urged Paul to exert himself as a literary man and said no, he was not, as he opined, mediocre. She continued:

"Whatever ambition I may have had for myself I have lost in you. To stand by your side, urging, helping, strengthening, encouraging you is now my prayer. To be an inspiration to you, a comforter and a real helpmeet, this is what I want."[33] What Dunbar-Nelson says here could have been lifted straight from one of her *Violets* stories. Was this statement more of her feminine role-playing? Had she thus strongly internalized the societally sanctioned role of "helpmeet"? Did she honestly believe that this was what she wanted and what would make her happy with her literary husband-to-be? Given her temperament and their turbulent interaction, she was never able to fulfill this questionable vow wholly and successfully. However, she rendered Paul concrete aid as secretary and business manager.

An October 7, 1899, article in *Literary Life* reports that: "Mrs. Dunbar is her husband's stenographer and typewritist, taking down in shorthand from his dictation, and afterward making a typewritten transcription from her notes and his pen-written manuscript."[34] A 1902 publication mentions that "she writes short stories and acts as secretary and general helpmeet to her husband."[35] Beyond this, "Alice, who possessed the shrewd business sense he [Paul] lacked, acted as his manager, choosing not only his speaking engagements but even poems which would most appeal to his audiences."[36] Virginia Cunningham recounts a telling anecdote. With Paul away, Alice opened a Western Union invitation for him to speak while the messenger waited for an answer:

> "Will come," Alice replied, knowing that Paul would be free. "Fee fifty—" She stopped. On a sudden impulse she doubled Paul's usual charge. "Fee one hundred dollars," she wrote firmly. If the club wanted Paul enough to telegraph instead of write, they would want him enough to pay one hundred dollars [which they did].[37]

That she tried to involve herself in all aspects of his work is further attested to by her January 29, 1898, request that he let her into his confidence regarding the plots and details of his novel and new book of poems.

Despite this apparent submersion of her ego, Alice's development as a writer was furthered during her time with Paul. On January 15, 1898, she talked about publishing "a book of plantation nursery rhymes and folk tales" and asked, "Can I 'collaborate' with you?" The self-esteem that this request reveals is likewise shown in the way she shared her writing progress with him: "Wrote a 3000 word ghost-story last night—called 'St. John's Eve' which I am going to send in to the Black Cat competition and also two poems [underlined seven times]. . . . *They are very fine.* I have

[just] bundled them off. . . . Am I not almost too literary, too—intellectual, in fact."[38] Interestingly, here she is both bragging about and disparaging herself. On occasion, Alice also communicated her discouragement:

> You ask me why don't I write those little sketches out? Oh dear, it makes a weariness come over me to think of it. I've written and written and been repulsed and rebuffed until I feel that it isn't any more use. Eight years ago I sent out my first MS and eight months ago I swore off. Of course, I have no right to expect better, but it makes me very bitter sometimes and—oh well, let's talk of the weather.[39]

It also seems that she and Paul discussed story ideas. In August 1898, she asked him, "If you don't want the story, would you mind my building up a tale of that contrived [?] whist game of ours?" There is no irrefragable evidence to support it, but one gets the feeling that they may have had a hand in each other's work. Alice builds a picture of idyllic joint creativity when she asks Paul to "bring the typewriter and the Sat. Eve. Post work [to West Medford] and we can do our stories all over undisturbed."[40]

Fortunately for Alice, Dunbar's agent and publisher became hers. Her second volume of short stories, *The Goodness of St. Rocque* (1899), which was "seen through the press" by him, was published by Dodd, Mead and Co. as a companion volume to his *Poems of Cabin and Field*.[41] Contemporary notices of her work almost always mentioned that she was his wife and otherwise yoked her with him. Many commentators did not know that she was already a published author. They called *St. Rocque* her first book and made statements such as, "It is rather interesting to learn that Mrs. Paul Lawrence Dunbar will join her gifted husband in the field of letters."[42] An April 21, 1900, article in the Philadelphia *Post* entitled "Paul Dunbar's Gifted Wife" begins: "Literary marriages are by no means the rule, and that the foremost writer of his race should be rivaled in the telling of short stories by his wife makes the appearance of Mrs. Paul Laurence Dunbar in the field of literature a matter worthy of note." One writer for the New York *Evening Sun* took a much more cynical view of the situation. Lumping Alice with Mrs. Edwin Markham, Mrs. Robert Louis Stevenson, and others, he declared:

> Wives of great men are many of them reminding us nowadays of the peculiar and practical advantages of their position. . . . Mrs. Paul Lawrence Dunbar appears in print to the extent of several stanzas—not through any machinations of the Muse or inspiration from Pegasus plainly—but because she is Mrs. Paul Lawrence Dunbar. . . . Was there ever such a short cut to fame as this?[43]

True, Alice, an aspiring writer, benefited from stepping into the spotlight with Paul. And unfortunately, this commentator was evaluating her solely on her poetry, rather than her prose. Yet to conclude that she has no talent is tantamount to critical slander. Furthermore, whatever "breaks" she received from her marital position could be seen as compensation for the usual handicaps accompanying gender (and race). Judging Dunbar-Nelson fairly requires looking at her work more closely, and on its own terms.

When approached in this manner, her major achievement of this period, *The Goodness of St. Rocque and Other Stories,*[44] shows Dunbar-Nelson to be working within the limitations of her talent, epoch, and genre but nevertheless producing readable short fiction that reveals a good deal about her as an early black female writer.

The stories here are longer, more developed, and better overall than those in *Violets*. They are set firmly in New Orleans and fully utilize the Creole history and distinctive culture of the city. Of course, this fact invited comparison with George Washington Cable, "the novelist of the Creoles," much of whose "charm of description," one critic thought, had been caught by Dunbar-Nelson.[45] The volume was generally reviewed as a collection of "delightful Creole stories, all bright and full of the true Creole air of easy-going . . . brief and pleasing, instinct with the passion and romance of the people who will ever be associated with such names as Bayou Teche and Lake Pontchartrain."[46] With this material, Dunbar-Nelson is drawing on her own intimate knowledge. She is also exploiting the local-color literary tradition popular at the time, a school of writing associated with women, notably Kate Chopin (also of Louisiana) and, further away from home, Sarah Orne Jewett.

Strictly speaking, only two of the pieces are merely sketches—one of a place ("By the Bayou St. John") and the other a dialect rendition of a person ("The Praline Woman"). Throughout, Dunbar-Nelson achieves a local flavor through the part-English, part-French, accented speech of her characters. "A Carnival Jangle" recreates the tragic din of Mardi Gras. "M'sieu Fortier's Violin" reflects Dunbar-Nelson's enthusiasm for the French Opera through a little, old, lovable Creole male. A similar protagonist is used in "Mr. Baptiste," who dies in the middle of a dock strike that involved black scab labor (a motif she was to return to later in her 1914 story "Hope Deferred").[47] The heroine of "La Juanita" is a "petite, half-Spanish, half-French beauty" who defies her strict Grandpère for a despised American sea captain (whom the family ultimately accepts after he saves a fleet of vessels from the town). "Titee" also ends happily—although Dunbar-Nelson had to revise the *Violets* conclusion, in which the good-hearted young Titee dies. This somewhat helps to alleviate the preponderance of sad endings.

The title story, "The Goodness of St. Rocque," is interesting for a number of reasons. First of all, it depicts a love triangle—two young women in competition for a man. In the romantic tradition of color-contrasted heroines popular with Byron, Sir Walter Scott, and others, Manuela is tall, slender, graceful and dark, while Claralie is blue-eyed, blonde, and petite. To vanquish her rival, Manuela resorts to a voodoo madam whose stratagems also enlist the aid of the Catholic St. Rocque (thus showing the alliance of these two religious traditions, one outlawed, the other sanctioned). Dunbar-Nelson's mother believed in the "black arts" and passed along to her daughter a sense of the spiritual and mystical aspects of existence. Other references to superstition are made in the story. Before the errant Theophile is safely secured, he sends Manuela a box of bonbons,

> but being a Creole, and therefore superstitiously careful, and having been reared by a wise and experienced maman to mistrust the gifts of a recreant lover, Manuela quietly thrusts bonbons, box, and card into the kitchen fire, and the Friday following placed the second candle of her nouvena in St. Rocque. (P. 11)

Finally, the story is replete with Old World Creole traditions, with their emphasis on the maintenance of family, formality, and a closed society.

In 1919, Angelina Grimké published a story of black female madness and infanticide entitled "The Closing Door." This "closing door" is a perfect symbol for the experiences of many of the women in *The Goodness of St. Rocque*. Indeed, one of the stories, "Sister Josepha" concludes with a young woman consigning herself to the convent in this manner: she "paused at the entrance, and gazed with swift longing eyes in the direction of narrow, squalid Chartres Street, then, with a gulping sob, followed the rest, and vanished behind the heavy door" (p. 172). Camille, a little "brown" orphan, had grown up at the Convent du Sacré Coeur with "the rest of the waifs; scraps of French and American civilization." When she was fifteen and "almost fully ripened into a glorious tropical beauty," a lady and gentleman wished to adopt her: "The woman suited her; but the man! . . . Untutored in worldly knowledge, she could not divine the meaning of the pronounced leers and admiration of her physical charms which gleamed in the man's face, but she knew it made her feel creepy, and stoutly refused to go" (p. 159).

Rebuked by the Mother Superior, Camille decides to take the veil; but the life of a nun does not suit her. She grows tired of "holy joy," "churchly pleasures," and compares her life with others: "For her were the gray things, the neutral tinted skies, the ugly garb, the coarse meats; for them the rainbow, the ethereal airiness of earthly joys, the bonbons and glacés of the world" (p. 164). At a fête service one day, she falls in love with a pair of tender, handsome eyes: "Perchance, had Sister Josepha been in the world, the eyes would have been an incident. But in this home of self-repression and retrospection, it was a life-story" (p. 168). She plans to run away, but stops when she realizes "the deception of the life she would lead, and the cruel self-torture of wonder at her own identity." Thus, she vanishes sorrowfully behind the convent door. Dunbar-Nelson's exploration of this "heavy door" of illegitimacy, racism, sexism, female vulnerability, and forced convent life is quite remarkable.

Annette in "The Fisherman of Pass Christian" closes herself behind a door. Because of disappointment in love, she gives up her plans to be an opera singer. For the same reason, Odalie (in the story of that name) takes up the cloistered life. "Tony's Wife" has the door slammed in her face when she is put out in the cold after her cruel "husband's" death. And poor "Little Miss Sophie"—after years of heartbreak and drudgery that are briefly and pathetically lightened at the end—suffers the ultimate closed door of death.

Metaphorically—and often literally—all these women are shut in. Partly, Dunbar-Nelson is continuing certain eroding conventions of the romantic heroine. Partly, she is simply portraying the real limitations and lack of options borne by women. Beyond this, the closing door is semiotic shorthand for an almost existential female dread. Still, it is distressing to see so many protagonists in these stories sink and succumb. This helps to highlight how thoroughly Dunbar-Nelson separated herself and her actual experience from her writings and did not see what happened to her, her own possibilities, as grist for her creative mill.

Unfortunately, though she describes two women characters as having "small brown hands" ("When the Bayou Overflows" and "Sister Josepha"), her stories are also separated from her black experience. As one critic phrased it, *St. Rocque* "has no characteristics peculiar to her race."[48] Despite Dunbar-Nelson's New Orleans heritage of mixed blood and light skin, it is necessary to remember that her position in America was always that of a colored/Negro/black person.

Reviews of the book were generally favorable. They note that Dunbar-Nelson's "sympathetic and refined manner gives a literary value" to the "slight incidents and simple characters" that she has found "in quiet corners"; that "within her rather narrow limitations," she "shows understanding of character, and an eye for interesting occurrences."[49] Inevitably, she was compared with Paul L. Dunbar. One reviewer commented that her work had "an individuality and charm of its own, while sharing some of the qualities found in the work of her husband."[50] (What the reviewer thought these were would have been interesting to know.) Another praised her "fair amount of invention," "pretty" writing, and "avoidance of the racial dialect which the name of the Dunbars is likely to suggest."[51] The most racially condescending review came from Dallas, Texas. It expressed "surprise" at "the ability of this colored writer" and at the "ease and culture" of her tales.[52]

From the viewpoint of style, contemporary critics were on target when they noted that she was good at description, but weak with plot, and that her style was commonplace, while the matter was diverting.[53] In an attempt to achieve intimacy and immediacy, Dunbar-Nelson addressed her audience with "you know" and "you see." But today's readers dislike being grabbed from behind the fictional veil of illusion. Furthermore, to them, even her most developed stories seem sketchlike, without the density of idea, texture, and resonance expected from the postmodern short story.

However, Dunbar-Nelson was writing after the establishment and Americanization of the short story, but mostly before the early twentieth-century, Chekhov-influenced innovations in the form. She had the then-prevailing concept of the short story—which was to set the scene, introduce the principal characters, manipulate them through some external action to a climax and denouement, and to tell all this from the point of view of an outside, omniscient author. Today, her plots often seem predictable, her situations hackneyed or melodramatic, her narrative style unsophisticated—but a modern reader has this reaction to most late nineteeth-century fiction aimed at a popular audience. Also, at this time, very few black writers had attempted the short story. The predominantly white reading public had been conditioned to expect black fictional characters to be either tragic mulattoes or happy plantation slaves. Because she concocted stories that bore no relation to most black life, she skirted the problems that these stereotypes presented. Thus, it is well to remember that she is not writing out of an established black short-story tradition—especially not a black female tradition—but is in her own way helping to create one.

The Goodness of St. Rocque does fulfill some of the promise augured by Dunbar-Nelson's earlier book. Also, it is not weakened by the inclusion of derivative poetry. When asked by an editor for a poem in 1900, she confessed to being short on poetic inspiration and added, jocularly: "Mr. Dunbar tells me that I average one poem in six months, and that there will be none due for several weeks to come."[54] During this period, she definitely concentrated on short fiction. As late as 1928, a newspaper article reported that she "considers her short stories her most representative work."[55] Significantly, at no time during her life did she seem to regard herself primarily as a poet.

In addition to those in *The Goodness of St. Rocque,* Dunbar-Nelson wrote many other short stories—some published, some not. More still were left incomplete and are scattered as holographs and drafts in various forms and stages through her manuscript remains. One group of the finished pieces is slighter and more irritating than *St. Rocque;* another group is more ambitious, interesting, even intriguing.

The less satisfying stories tend to be impossible anecdotes of thwarted or feuding lovers that abruptly end happily. The heroines are fluffy, idle, haughty, silly, while the men are handsome and idle. Two of them written in her vein of the Creole love story, "The Bicycle Race" and "At Mandeville," are signed with the pseudonym of "Monroe Wright." Perhaps Dunbar-Nelson thought a new name would bring fresh consideration to this hackneyed material. "George Brenton: Artist" is really about Margaret Drake, a "little old maid" slightly past thirty who lives for friends and an absconding lover and "never talked of herself." Another somewhat different story is "Mrs. Newly-Wed and Her Servants." Written in December 1898, while Alice resided with Paul at 1934 Fourth Street, N.W., Washington, D.C., it is a quasi-autobiographical sketch. "Little Mrs. Newly-Wed" woefully recites her servant problems. She had had ten "girls" in as many months, all of them from "the camp," "that disreputable part of the town just below the Sixth street hill where a lot of colored folks have congregated." One notes the clear class and perhaps social contrast between Mrs. Newly-Wed and the servant women. The general impression left by these airy, unreal stories is of a black woman writing with her back turned to herself in some fanciful space of aracial and authorial privilege.

The interesting group of Dunbar-Nelson's stories treats realistic material in more daring ways. One category of "tenement stories" (her designation) reflects her settlement work and her teaching on New York City's East Side. In a January 23, 1898, letter to Paul, she reported a visit to the home of one of her students, where she found a German woman married to "a shiftless, dirty Negro" who drank, beat her, and neglected her and the children. They were about to be evicted from two smelly, squalid rooms, had no coal, no food, a nursing baby, a toddler with chickenpox, etc. She and a coworker brought some aid. Dunbar-Nelson said that such scenes were familiar to her, but she was still not hardened to them. Then, too, as early as *Violets*, she had attempted a "neighborhood" tale called, appropriately, "In Our Neighborhood."

"The Revenge of James Brown" (finally published as a young people's story by the Methodist Episcopal Church in 1929) is set in Steenth Street near Third Avenue, with characters such as Banjo Liz, Scrappy Franks, and McEneny. It tells of young Jimmy Brown's rejection of the "Pure in Heart" mission and consequent adolescent coming-of-age.[56] "Miss Tillman's Protege" (an unpublished work) focuses on a philanthropic but selfish and condescending woman who tries to adopt little Hattie Gurton because of preconceived notions about Hattie's horrible home life, which is really loving and comfortable. These stories are another type of local-color fiction produced by Dunbar-Nelson. She details the alleys and fire escapes of Steenth Street, as well as "the substratum for which the mission was designed": "Thin, hungry-looking women in strange gowns; stout, over-worked women with fretful babies; flashy young women in cheap picture hats, and fidgety children in soiled pinafores." And the characters speak an appropriate dialect, rendered as well as Dunbar-Nelson can manage: "An' phwat do they be sittin' up a mission fur? Sure, it's not me, but them wot wurrks out wot needs it." Dunbar-Nelson's continued attention to class and class conflict makes one wonder whether she used class as a psychological metaphor to replace race in her writings. Since she was not always able, for a variety of internal and external reasons, to express buried racial feeling, portraying opposing classes may have been her way—perhaps unconsciously—of hinting at group differences and hierarchical oppression.

Another category of story incorporates black Creole life but moves beyond the safe, predominantly love themes of *St. Rocque* to overt treatment of race and passing. Published in *The Southern Workman*, "The Pearl in the Oyster" chronicles the rise and fall of Auguste Picou, a Creole fair enough to live as white, but whose grandfather was black. He comes to grief because, racially, he tries to have it both ways. He rejects the Negro side gallery and his brown-skinned childhood friend in favor of white uptown life, then seeks to reenter the now-closed Creole fold in order to play corrupt ward politics. His ironically shallow solution is to take his wife and child and "go away somewhere where we are not known, and we will start life again, but whether we decide to be white or black, we will stick to it."

An unpublished typescript, "The Stones of the Village," is even more tragic. Having been rejected as a "White Nigger" by "all the boys, white and black and yellow," Victor Grabert becomes a famous lawyer whose past has been obscured by death and chance. But the specter of race haunts him, driving him to Negrophobia, then eventually to madness and a fatal heart attack. In these two stories, Dunbar-Nelson treats the popular Afro-American literary themes of the "color line"—passing—and the tragic mulatto from her own particular vantage. She also reveals the anti-black sentiment of the Creole people. Auguste's mother declares vehemently, "'My son wid what day call Negre!' Non, non!" Victor's Grandmère snatches him from a crowd of children, hissing, "What you mean playin' in de strit wid dose niggers?" How much of this sentiment Dunbar-Nelson internalized, and on what side of the fence she felt herself to be sitting, are matters for speculation.

Dunbar-Nelson's manuscript story "Ellen Fenton" is singular in her canon. A strikingly modern work, it is reminiscent of Doris Lessing's "To Room 19" in its exploration of a domestic woman's painful growth into a consciousness of self. At age forty, Ellen Fenton is "looked up to by every one in the town," "pointed out as the model woman," "constantly held up as the worthy and progressive twentieth century woman with a large field, who was unspoiled by semi-public life, and unnarrowed by a large family." Yet, vague feelings of unhappiness prompt her to begin "getting acquainted with myself, as it were." She "discontentedly awakens" to a "new found self," which she locks away in the secret joy of her heart because others cannot comprehend the changes in her ideas and behavior.

> She had always been a woman, who in addition to the multiple cares of her household and public philanthropy, to use the cant phrase, "lived her own life." She was discovering now that the term was a misnomer. The average woman, she found, who "lives her own life," in reality, lives others', and has no life of her own.

To her surprise, she discovers one day that her husband Herbert has been undergoing a similar metamorphosis. Therefore, Ellen achieves supreme happiness "for in finding herself, she had also found Herbert, and he had found himself and her."

"Ellen Fenton" reflects Dunbar-Nelson's lifelong fascination with psychology (as do other of her works). However, if she had done more of this sensitive probing of female consciousness, contemporary readers would be even more inclined to see her as a germinally feminist writer. What she does not do in this story is sustain a clear link between Ellen's condition and her feminine gender roles. And the reader's positing the link is undercut by Herbert's parallel crisis, which makes of everything a more generalized conflict between the self and a spiritually repressive society. As Ellen sorrowfully muses at the end: "But how many lives were wasted, how many went out into the Great Unknown, all unconscious of themselves or their fellow-men."

Sometime around 1902, Dunbar-Nelson projected another volume of short stories called "Women and Men" (a title that further reminds one of Lessing's *A Man and Two Women*), which was to include "Ellen Fenton," "Victor Grabert," "George Brenton," and nine others (about half of which either were not written or did not survive among her papers).[57] This book did not materialize. However, a 1902 statement in the Chicago *Recorder* that "some of the leading magazines of the country regularly print Mrs. Dunbar's short stories"[58] is substantiated by the correspondence between herself and her agent, Paul R. Reynolds. On February 15, 1902, she received a check for $34.96, after commission and postage, for "A Foreordained Affair," one of her airy love stories. On April 9, 1902, she inquires about his placing "a collection of short stories, most of which have been published in various newspapers, etc., on New York tenement life. I believe you sold some of them."[59] "A Frenchtown Interlude," another slight domestic romance, complete with rivals and reconciliation, was sold to a St. Louis magazine called *The Mirror* for fifty dollars.[60] She netted thirty dollars for an unknown "The Romance of a Kitchen" on January 31, 1903. And her story "The Ball Dress" appeared in *Leslie's Weekly*, December 12, 1901.

The correspondence also makes plain many unsuccessful attempts at publication. On December 14, 1900, Walter Page of Doubleday, Page and Company rejects a collection of her short stories, saying short stories are "the most difficult thing in the market." Her letters to Reynolds show that she kept him supplied with a steady stream of material, much of which came back to her. Though Dunbar-Nelson tried her hand at longer fiction, this too proved unprofitable. To Bliss Perry of *The Atlantic Monthly*, she proposed expanding "The Stones of the Village" into a novel. In an August 22, 1900 reply, he cautioned her against "padding" and offered his opinion that at present the American public had a "dislike" for treatment of "the color-line."

Dunbar-Nelson also essayed two novels, both of which were deemed too short to satisfy publication requirements. Reynolds critiques the first of these, "The Confessions of a Lazy Woman," in a July 27, 1900, letter. He points out that people do not, as a rule, like stories that are told in diary form (as this one was), and that it suffers from lack of action, plot, and climax:

> The idea of a lazy woman who laughs at her neighbors and the rest of the world for their anxiety to accomplish their work, clean their houses, ac-

cumulate money or what not, is an amusing conception, and your heroine makes a number of observations which are very acute and very humorous often. But I think after the reader is once familiar with the conception there is a certain monotony about it.

Dunbar-Nelson continued to work on the novel, all the while expressing to Paul, her husband, her "disgust" and damning it as "inane, senseless drivel" that she must be writing for "amusement."[61] Despite its weaknesses, A. S. Barnes & Company accepted "Confessions of a Lazy Woman" for publication in the fall of 1902. However, they broke the contract in 1903 because of "certain changes in the firm," which their February 18 letter did not spell out.

Her second novelette was called "A Modern Undine." The seventy-nine-page version extant among Dunbar-Nelson's papers tells the fairly interesting story of Marion, a decorous, self-centered, introverted, prickly-sensitive, twenty-four-year-old Southern woman. After her marriage, she retreats further into paranoia and obsessive mothering of her crippled son. Just when she and her husband are beginning to air the refuse between them, he has to leave town. From a professional opinion written to Dunbar-Nelson in 1903,[62] it appears that Marion and Howard are reunited, for the critic objected to her finding her husband "far too easily." He thought, further, that the whole story needed more "development—more incident—more character drawing of the sort that makes the characters reveal themselves in speech & action." (Talking about her characters is indeed one of her narrative faults.) On the positive side, Dunbar-Nelson's descriptive method is her way of attending to her protagonist's psychological makeup, which is, in fact, the work's strongest attraction:

> There it was again, the old irritating personal note which she struck in every conversation; which she had sounded the night they had talked by the phosphorescent waters. The most impersonal appearing woman, she was unable to get beyond her own ego, unable to see any allusions save through the medium of her own self-consciousness.

After this period, Dunbar-Nelson's attention to fiction waned. However, at least two typescripts indicate that she continued writing short stories until the end of her life. "Summer Session," which carries her 1934 Philadelphia address, is a meshing of the love and detective fiction traditions. The undated "His Great Career" is a snappily written, surprise-ending story whose climax is quite effective.

Dunbar-Nelson wrote her stories in the same way that she "produced literature" (her phrase) of all types: with facile quickness. A short story required about one week, and when she was writing longer pieces, she did so on the so-many-words-per-day plan. Whether this characteristic haste affected the quality of her output is difficult to say conclusively. This question raises the corollary issue of how seriously Dunbar-Nelson took—was able to take—herself as a writer. Some evidence reenforces the casual, dilettantish, unconfident impression conveyed by her first book, *Violets*. For instance, in an August 27, 1901, letter to Mr. Reynolds, her agent, she writes: "I hope soon to do some new short Creole stories, and if you really wish to be bothered with almost hopeless stuff, I shall send them to you."[63] Another letter smacks of an unprofessionalism about details that is reminiscent of Georgia Douglas Johnson in her scatterbrained middle age:

> I have trimmed the story again. . . . This ought to bring it down to three thousand. I may have been mistaken in the count; sometimes one is likely to say the same figure twice, which would make quite a difference. I did not know whether it was necessary to re-copy it, so took the lazier plan.

Yet, this offhandedness is belied by the time, energy, and emotion that she put into her work. She even expressed "disappointment" to Paul on March 25, 1901, at the price Reynolds got for her stories, but consoled herself by reflecting, "but I suppose I must wait for reputation before I can command prices." These antithetical facts suggest that Dunbar-Nelson was torn by that pull of "contrary instincts," which Virginia Woolf identified as the birthright of literary women.

Overall, this second period of Dunbar-Nelson's life was brief, but full. An observer is left with the impression that she acted out romances in her life and art—to the diminution of both. Clearly, her personal traits indicated that, being in her late twenties, she had not yet become a fully mature, post-Saturn cycle person. As a writer, her major achievements occurred in short fiction, a form that never again occupied her so totally. Perhaps the most lasting effect of these years was her association with Paul Laurence Dunbar, an association that was often galling but served as part of the arsenal that helped her through the world as a black woman/writer.

iii

The third phase of Dunbar-Nelson's life is cleanly demarcated by her rupture with Paul L. Dunbar and 1902 move to Wilmington, Delaware, which becomes for her a solid base. Thus begins a period of personal readjustment and of educational and political involvement where creative writing is relegated to second place. The turn of the century brought many startling advances in science and society. Dunbar-Nelson seems to reflect these changes in her progress from late Victorian heroinism to an even more active participation in the modern age.

During mid-1902, Dunbar-Nelson was breaking up the Washington, D.C., household, sending Paul's "Ma" Matilda her share of linen and goods and her son's manuscripts and books. Now in need of a job, she applied for a teaching position at the M Street (later the Dunbar) High School, the best secondary facility for blacks in the city, but there were no vacancies.[64] (Angelina Grimké began teaching at M Street in 1907.) At the same time, she was helping to find work for her sister, Leila. James Young and Leila had also separated, leaving her, their four small children, and Mother Patricia without an economic mainstay. By the fall, both Dunbar-Nelson and Leila had secured employment in Wilmington's Howard High School, an institution that principal Edwina B. Kruse was doggedly building into a fine educational establishment for blacks in Delaware. 1008 French Street, located in a pleasant downtown neighborhood, became home for all of them. By September 12, Matilda Dunbar was writing Dunbar-Nelson at her new address to say that she was glad Alice had found friends, was doing well, and was happy (although she herself was still heartbroken about Paul and Alice).

Circumstances had given a decidedly gynocentric character to Dunbar-Nelson's domestic life. It continued thus, with Alice, her sister, Leila, their mother, Patricia, and Leila's four children (three of whom were girls) forming a household core. They added on husbands and other children as their life choices dictated, but always remained together. Functioning as an economic and emotional unit, the women were crucial to one another's survival.

From 1902 to 1920, Dunbar-Nelson was an important part of Howard High School, first as teacher of English and drawing and then as head of the English department. She executed her often tiresome duties well, teaching, supervising, procuring funds, directing class-night plays, writing the history of the school, assisting the administration, and so on. Though her quick tongue, haughty carriage, and near-white complexion sometimes provoked animosity, Alice maintained working—and, in a few cases, closer—friendships with her coteachers. In activity with the Delaware State Colored Teachers Association, she helped to equalize salaries of black and white teachers outside Wilmington, and at the Association's Third Annual Meeting in Dover, Delaware, on November 10–12, 1921, she delivered an address entitled "English in the Elementary Schools." During the summers, Dunbar-Nelson also instructed in-service teachers at State

College, Dover (now Delaware State College). (She had tried for a summer school position at Tuskegee Institute in 1905.[65])

Some professional publications emanated from her work. For example, in 1908, the journal *Education* printed her "Training of Teachers of English,"[66] a seven-page guide for producing a perfectly prepared language and literature instructor. And the *Educational Review* of Columbia University accepted her paper "The Compensations of a Teacher of English." In a 1920s spirit of rising racial consciousness, her article "Negro Literature for Negro Pupils" advocates a racial approach because for too long Afro-American children have been forced "to believe that they are pensioners on the mental bounty of another race": " . . . for two generations we have given brown and black children a blonde ideal of beauty to worship, a milk-white literature to assimilate, and a pearly Paradise to anticipate, in which their dark faces would be hopelessly out of place."[67] Dunbar-Nelson was also interested in writing textbooks. She corresponded with the World Book Company about doing an industrial training text for them.[68] At about the same time, she proposed "a supplementary reader for the seventh and eighth grades of colored schools" to Doubleday Page and Company. Their rejection is a comment on establishment publication of black works then and now:

> . . . the book should contain a great deal more material of the character of that selection you have given from Booker T. Washington to the exclusion of quite a number of selections you have made. Your own examination of this material in the light of the comparison we have drawn will show you very clearly what we mean.[69]

They were obliquely telling her that they did not appreciate her more militant selections.

Dunbar-Nelson's educational work was paralleled by her own further study. On August 2, 1907, her application for September admission to Cornell University as a special student was approved by the Dean of Arts and Sciences. She had already attended summer school there, concentrating on English literature. She wrote a February 27, 1904, essay on the romantic visionary poet William Blake, which was marked "an admirable paper"; in another assignment for Professor Schelling, "Why I Like Jane Austen," she explained:

> And so, to those who prefer caviare, let us of the plain dinner-table, where the family even perchance uses napkin rings, say humbly that because of Jane Austen's simple style, quiet humor, keen irony, sprightly narrative, mischievous poking into our homely, everyday souls, and gentle

ending of her stories, we like her and them, though they be the Apotheosis
of the Commonplace.[70]

Dunbar-Nelson's thesis on the influence of Milton on Wordsworth was
her foremost scholarly accomplishment. Her major professor, Dr. Lane
Cooper, consulted her about the subject, as did other scholars such as Mrs.
Cynthia St. John and Professor Raymond Dexter Havens, who praised her
valuable study.[71] From it, she published an April 1909 article in the respected journal *Modern Language Notes* on "Wordsworth's Use of Milton's
Description of Pandemonium."[72] The knowledge and love of literature
that all of these facts suggest are evident throughout her corpus in Dunbar-
Nelson's allusions and writing style. Later, in courses at Columbia, the
Pennsylvania School of Industrial Art, and the University of Pennsylvania,
she studied English educational measurements and psychology.

Not surprisingly, Dunbar-Nelson continued to be linked to her famous
husband Paul, who died in 1906. She talked and wrote about him, and,
with the celebrated tenor Roland Hayes, presented a March 21, 1916,
recital called "The Life of Paul Laurence Dunbar Told in His Songs and
Lyrics" at the New Century Club in Wilmington. More concretely, her
lawyer negotiated an agreement with Paul's mother whereby Mrs. Dunbar
received two-thirds of Paul's royalties, and Alice, one-third. These pay-
ments were a welcome supplement to Dunbar-Nelson's modest salary.
Until she died, she relied on them for both necessities and extras. In a
March 3, 1931, diary entry, she cries, "The depression hit my royalties!"[73]

Dunbar-Nelson's current intimate relationships were a potpourri of mis-
matches and marriages. When she arrived in Delaware, she began an
especially amicable friendship with her principal, Edwina B. Kruse, who
apparently took Alice "under her wing." Born in Puerto Rico to a native
mother and German father, Kruse was a self-made, powerful woman who
was alternately feared and respected. "Ned" (as she was called) evidenced
her concern for Alice in the numerous letters that she wrote to her. She
saluted Alice as "Dearest of Sweethearts" or "My little Kid," paid her
expenses and gave her money, helped her family, was full of love and
endearments and jealousy, counted the days until Alice's return, and
signed herself "Your own Ned." Kruse sent long, daily letters full of home,
school, and town gossip when Alice studied at Cornell or taught in Dover,
or when she herself took courses in school management at New York
University.

A three-day series of October 1907 epistles illustrates the correspondence at its warmest. October 5, 1907:

I want you to know dear, that every thought of my life is for you, every throb of my heart is yours and yours alone. I just can not ever let any one else have you.

October 6, 1907:

I *wish*, oh! how I do wish you were here—Alice! I wish I had never let you go away at all. Gertrude and Etta send love and I can't send any because it is all there in Ithaca wound up in you.

October 7, 1907:

I'll be more cheerful tomorrow. How I want you, my love.

These letters display the ardency that Carroll Smith-Rosenberg discovered was common in the homosocial "female world of love and ritual" during the nineteenth century.[74] Given the circumstances and Dunbar-Nelson's later documented lesbian friendships, they may bespeak more. Though still affectionate, later letters (from 1908 to 1910) are not as warm. A characteristic one of June 11, 1908, is also indicative of Alice's extensive social involvement. Kruse writes:

Well, we will all be glad to see you when you do come but I thing [sic] the people on French Street, at 1008, I mean will not want you out of their sight so I have schooled myself to expect to see just a very little of you. Then too, French is all alive with people all of the time and I think it will keep you pretty busy to see them all . . .

Alice and "Krusie" maintained varying levels of friendship. Even when Kruse became senile in the 1920s, Dunbar-Nelson was dutifully attentive. When Kruse died on June 23, 1930, she wrote in her diary a moving personal obituary:

My mind goes back over the years when we were closer than sisters—till first Arthur [Callis], then Anna [Brodnax] broke up our Eden—and then to 1920 with our semi-friendship. Those first seven years! Well, she passed away. . . . her life spelled more romance than will ever be told. A friend she was—and paradox of paradoxes—one of my worst enemies. Let her soul rest in peace. I loved her once. Twenty years ago, her death would have wrecked my life.[75]

Dunbar-Nelson tried to chronicle the romance of Kruse's biography in a novel of 595 typewritten pages that she wrote shortly before her own death.

"This Lofty Oak" is a *roman à clef*—often thinly veiled—where Godwin equals Howard High School, Wilton is Wilmington, Millville is a working class neighborhood analogous to the black community, the Clearwater is the Brandywine River, and so on. The characters also have their real-life prototypes, but, as Dunbar-Nelson says in the foreword, they are "so mixed up, added to, subtracted from, and coalesced that there is no one who is a complete personality"—except the inimitable Fredericka. Dunbar-Nelson herself is partially incorporated into a Julia from Washington, D.C., whom Fredericka meets and who eventually comes to Wilton to marry a physician. It is noteworthy that she gives herself so small a part in the book. She also includes nothing of the intense relationship she and Kruse shared—although, near the novel's beginning, she mentions that Fredericka had more than one too close, "unhealthy" friendship with another girl. However, this motif is dropped.

Instead, the novel concentrates on Fredericka's meteoric rise to power and its attendant hardening of her into a Nietzschean figure, who, nonetheless, has her private woes and affections. Beginning in Puerto Rico, where Fredericka's mestizo mother is apparently concealing the identity of her own black mother, the book moves to Knickerbockean New York City, where Fredericka is orphaned and must begin to make her own way. It also includes her one and only love, for the husband of a family where she boarded. This consists of one afternoon's consummation, then eternal renunciation. All subsequent proposals she refuses in favor of her teaching, for which she has to remain unmarried. Fredericka keeps the principalship of her school and her vast power at whatever cost.

Stylistically, "This Lofty Oak" is readable, primarily because Dunbar-Nelson writes good English prose. The narrator adopts the device of retelling what Fredericka had told her in recollections about her life—for example, "As Fredericka used to say. . . . " This reminiscent tone seems more than appropriate for a work that, in a sense, is the posthumous final word on Kruse, as well as Dunbar-Nelson's own last literary effort. It would probably have been more effective as biography or as autobiographical narrative, since casting it as a novel raises expectations of plot and style that are not fulfilled. (In a September 29, 1933, letter to Mr. Frank Dodd, Dunbar-Nelson herself confesses that the work is "really a biography, thrown in novel-shape.")

A voluminous correspondence of rejection for "This Lofty Oak" exists in Dunbar-Nelson's papers. From 1933 to the end of 1934, it was refused by Harcourt, Brace; Doubleday, Doran; Macmillan; William Morris; Little, Brown; E. P. Dutton; Harper and Brothers; Dodd, Mead; Bobbs-Merrill;

Longmans, Green; Farrar and Rinehart; and Houghton Mifflin. Some publishers acknowledged its "merits," "interest," and "pleasant and readable" style, but they all seemed to feel—in the words of Bobbs-Merrill's August 14, 1934, letter—that it was not "quite outstanding enough to justify our taking it on in these highly competitive times." As late as 1951, Dunbar-Nelson's niece, Pauline A. Young, was still attempting to market the book, but it remained unpublished.

During her early years in Wilmington, Dunbar-Nelson was involved in another relationship that made of her a "dear little girl." It was with a retired U.S. Army sergeant who called himself Major C. A. Fleetwood, and was conducted principally by mail since Fleetwood, who was considerably older than Alice, lived in Washington, D.C. He gave her advice, loaned her money, bought her clothing, and confessed that he would have loved to have her for his wife, but "I am like the child who while wanting the moon, has learned that it cannot be reached, and has contentedly settled down to recognize existing circumstances and admire it at a distance."[76] Fleetwood was a stickler regarding details and expected instant compliance with his wishes and directives. His letters—which rarely ran to less than eight pages—often take on a scolding, paternalistic tone, albeit in gentle, well-turned words. All in all, he seems a bit insufferable; but the fact that Alice maintained close contact with him reveals something about her personality and needs and about the forms of black male-female relationships during that time.

The Arthur Callis who "broke up" Dunbar-Nelson and Kruse's "Eden" was more significant. Alice met him at Cornell, where he was finishing a baccalaureate degree, before he came to teach English at Howard High School in 1909. Reversing the pattern of the other two relationships, she was twelve years older and more established. For reasons that remain a mystery, Dunbar-Nelson married him on January 19, 1910, but kept the union an absolute secret. Perhaps she was ashamed of the difference in their ages and social standing. Perhaps she required marriage to engage in physical intimacy, but later thought differently about the whole affair. Perhaps she decided that it really was not the best life choice for either or both of them. Piecing together the little available data yields only a puzzling picture.

A November 7, 1911, letter that is apparently from Callis to Alice details his troubles of the past eighteen months with a Myra, who drained him of $700 in mental sanitarium costs and subsequently denigrated him. He says, "She has no idea of what really occurred last year, but wrote me 'I only had a nervous breakdown such as you have had several times.'" Is this simply a malicious barb, or can it be taken to mean that his marrying Alice was really some kind of mental aberration? Years later, when Dunbar-Nelson saw Callis at a 1930 ball in Washington, D.C., the two of them danced together and she wrote: "He has not forgotten. Rather intense." The next day, after dining at his home, she and her current husband, Robert, laughed at the clandestine irony of "the gentleman and his wife entertaining his divorced wife and her husband."[77] Though cryptic, the fullest comment occurs in a June 4, 1931, diary entry, where Dunbar-Nelson records a conversation between herself and Callis:

> When we were driving down to the office . . . Arthur said—well, it was not much, the four years of our romance, the jewel around which his whole life was built—and a bit more and I haltingly replied that it was a beautiful thing that I hated to destroy. Yet I knew that destroy it I must—to save him. Ruthless I was—but it was best for him. And he told me again something of his desperation in Chicago, and how he never hated Robert—how could he help loving me!

Having saved money from teaching at Howard, Callis went on to receive his M.D. degree in 1921 from Rush Medical College, University of Chicago. He married a woman named Pauline, to "spite" Alice in 1913,[78] and had two daughters born in Chicago in 1916 and 1917. Then, on September 2, 1927, he married Myra Hill Colson. In 1930, Callis came to Washington, D.C., where he taught at the Howard University Medical School and maintained a private practice. A founder of Alpha Phi Alpha fraternity (the first one for black men), a productive doctor, and a busy, civic-minded man, Callis died well respected on November 12, 1974. His fraternity-sponsored biography, *Henry Arthur Callis: Life and Legacy* (1977), briefly mentions that he and Dunbar-Nelson "became friends and the friendship continued until they were married."[79] This is the only public statement of their union.

After all of her faux pas, Alice Ruth Moore Dunbar (now almost forty-one years old) finally entered a lasting union with Robert J. Nelson (b. 1873) on April 20, 1916. A journalist and widower from Harrisburg, Pennsylvania, he had been left with two small children when his wife died of tuberculosis. Dunbar-Nelson helped to raise them until first Robert Clash, "Bobby" (b. 1905), and then Harriet Elizabeth (b. 1903) died on April 18, 1918, and February 15, 1924, respectively, of respiratory ailments. It is interesting to note that even though Dunbar-Nelson had no biological children of her own, she did a share of mothering—of these two, as well as of her sister's four. However, two of the latter also died young—Leila Ruth on January 17, 1921, and Ethel Corinne on October 7, 1930—periodically

diminishing the Young-Nelson household and leaving only Laurence Theodore (b. 1901) and Pauline Alice (b. 1900) as survivors.

Dunbar-Nelson became well acquainted with Robert when they worked
together in publishing the *Masterpieces of Negro Eloquence* (1914). The 1913
letterhead for the Douglass Publishing Company, Harrisburg, Pennsylvania, carries him as president and her as editor-in-chief. This partnership
in racial-political-journalistic activity set the pattern for their entire relationship. From 1920 to 1922, they published the Wilmington *Advocate,* a
liberal black newspaper that kept them embroiled in controversy and partisan politics. Dunbar-Nelson also provided him with copy for the Elks
newspaper, the Washington *Eagle,* which he edited from 1925 to 1930.
Robert was, it seems, a salutary influence on her. Being more solidly in
touch with ordinary black life and also being a "race man," he broadened
her racial understanding. His mild calmness and practical sense also balanced her high-strung nature. From this point onward, they were engaged
in mutual, supportive struggle to live comfortably and work productively.

World War I proved stimulating for Dunbar-Nelson. After some national
debate about whether black people should fight abroad while suffering
racism at home, she—like the majority of Afro-Americans—"rallied
'round the flag." She did so literally, organizing a massive June 14, 1918,
Flag Day parade-demonstration that netted her much publicity. With participation from 6,000 blacks, it was hailed as "the greatest day in the
history of Delaware colored people," "where the loyalty of the Race to the
American flag was the gist of the many brilliant and patriotic addresses."
Dunbar-Nelson was personally lauded as "the originator of the idea."[80]
Even though Georgia Douglas Johnson and Angelina Grimké also had
social consciousness and aided worthy causes, this was a type of attention-
garnering civic labor that neither of them would have undertaken.

Further, Dunbar-Nelson founded a local chapter of The Circle for Negro
War Relief. Her ultimate ambition was to go overseas. On February 20,
1918, the Philadelphia *Public Ledger* informed her that "it would be impossible for this newspaper to assume the responsibility of another correspon-
dent in France." She even considered traveling as one of four black female
canteen workers in France. Eventually, she toured the southern United
States as a field representativae of the Woman's Committee of the Council
of National Defense (August–October 1918) to further war work among
black women. Correspondence to her from Hannah J. Patterson, the
Washington resident director, reveals that Dunbar-Nelson acted independently and was lax about keeping receipts for the reimbursement of her
expenses. In Mississippi, she had to be reminded of the committee's policy

of not endorsing other groups when she became involved in a movement by domestic workers to build a labor union.

These experiences constituted a basis for her article "Negro Women in War Work," published in Emmett J. Scott's *Official History of the American Negro in the World War* (1919). Scott, who later became secretary of Howard University, served as special assistant for black affairs to the secretary of war. He and Dunbar-Nelson formed a liaison, for she reveals in her 1921 diary that she wrote a "Dream Book" to commemorate the romance, "though I would never give it to the public, only the fragments which I did give—the sonnet 'Violets,' and the one or two others, for which E.J.S. has never forgiven me." She continues:

> I was much amused . . . to see him slip the Army seal ring around on his finger so that only a band showed—afraid doubtless that I had on the counterpart, and that it would be noticeable. When I saw him doing this surreptitiously, I made a point of showing both my hands . . . so that he could see that I no longer wear his ring.[81]

As she grew older, Dunbar-Nelson indulged more freely her taste for such sexual adventure.

Burgeoning political activity further characterizes this period of Dunbar-Nelson's life. In fact, her role in Republican party work lay behind the loss of her position at Howard High School.[82] She had traveled to the Social Justice Conference of the then Senator Harding at Marion, Ohio—despite the nonsupport of the school administration. When she returned to her classes the following Monday morning, Principal Ray Wooten (who had succeeded Ms. Kruse) had locked her out of her room for "political activity" and "[in]compatibility." The Board of Education said it would sustain Wooten's action, a stance tantamount to firing her. Dunbar-Nelson, countering, stated that, regardless of the board's decision, she would not return to the classroom because her usefulness as a teacher had been impaired. Wooten, a young man, had only been principal for nine days, and it seems that he felt threatened by Dunbar-Nelson's presence and importance. Although he said he was acting on his own, he may not have been, or at least he knew that his lockout of her would be welcomed by those unfriendly to her.

At the time, Dunbar-Nelson was a member of the Republican State Committee, the first Afro-American woman in the country to be named to such a political post. As chairman of the League of Colored Republican Women, she had directed the 1920 campaign among black women in the state. In 1921, she was chairman of the publicity committee of the National

League of Colored Republican Women. That same year, she enjoyed recognition as a member of the delegation of prominent black citizens who presented racial concerns to President Harding at the White House in September. Even more controversially, she headed the Anti-Lynching Crusaders in Delaware, who were fighting in 1922 for congressional passage of the Dyer Anti-Lynching Bill. Her 1924 article "Politics in Delaware" conveys her political astuteness in its sharp critique and analysis.[83] She condemns Delaware for being the only state where "the colored man may not practice law"; "colored people have not had one of their race serve on the jury"; "there are no colored policemen"; the Ku Klux Klan is controlled by and in turn controls the party in power"; and where "in the past several years three colored women and girls have been raped by white men." Though rape is a capital offense, "not one of the men charged with the heinous crime has been punished as the law provides." These grievances, aggravated by the congressmen not supporting the Dyer bill, fueled a defection to the Democratic party. Thus Dunbar-Nelson found herself spearheading the 1924 Democratic political campaign among black women from the party's New York City headquarters.

As these facts indicate, much of her political activity focused on women. During the campaign for equal suffrage, she worked diligently, serving in 1915 as field organizer in the Middle Atlantic States (which were striving for state constitutional amendments). She held office in the Delaware chapter of the Federation of Colored Women's Clubs and appeared at other national chapter functions. Together with members of the National Association of Colored Women such as Mrs. Mary Church Terrell of Washington, D.C., and Mrs. S. Joe Brown of Des Moines, Iowa, Dunbar-Nelson helped draft a "Platform of the Colored Women of America" when they met at Tuskegee Institute, July 12–16, 1920. A highly political document—as the statements of black clubwomen during that critical time were wont to be—it encourages their women to "fit themselves" for exercising the newly acquired franchise, recommends racially relevant educational improvements, protests mob violence, and so forth.

Dunbar-Nelson's concentration on educational and political matters is reflected in her writing. As has been noted, she usually maintained a separation between her "real" life and her creative literature. However, during this period, her outside world and her writing come smoothly together in occasional and functional literature, while strictly belletristic work languishes. Grimké also paid attention to racial issues throughout her writing career; the only difference is that she espoused them in the traditional fine arts genres.

Dunbar-Nelson's essays and articles address miscellaneous topics.[84] In "Hysteria," she upbraids the Negro race for being easily led by sentimental oratory. "Is It Time for the Negro Colleges in the South to Be Put into the Hands of Negro Teachers?" answers the question with an indignant affirmative. Her two-part *Messenger* monograph, "People of Color in Louisiana," is scholarly history replete with footnotes. It and another informative essay, "Delaware: A Jewel of Inconsistencies," are still valuable references. Oratory comes to the fore in two speeches, "Lincoln and Douglass" and "A Life of Social Service as Exemplified in David Livingstone." These utilize classical techniques and a balanced eighteenth-century style.

In this excerpt from "David Livingstone," the mode is frankly declamatory:

> The finding of the poles, north and south, is no greater feat than his. For, after all, what is it to humanity that the magnetic pole, north or south, is a few degrees east or west of a certain point in the frozen seas and barren ice mountains? What can humanity offer as a reward to those whose bodies lie under cairns of ice save a barren recognition of their heroism? What have their lives served, beyond that of examples of heroism and determination? Bronze tablets will record their deeds, but no races will arise in future years to call them blessed. Cold marble will enshrine their memory; but there will be no fair commerce, nor civilization, nor the thankful prayers of those who have been led to know God. (Pp. 191–92)

It strikes a contemporary reader as ironic that Dunbar-Nelson is here lauding the opening up of Africa to white colonization and exploitation. Very often, her tone in these pieces is rhetorical, exhortatory. She can also make good use of both sarcasm and figurative language, as in this sentence from "Hysteria": "Then everyone went home, saying what a wonderfully fine meeting it was, and the Great Man departed, followed by John the Baptist, and a timid aureole of prominent citizens, fawning for a glance, or a word of recognition" (p. 125). Finally, these occasional writings display a breadth of knowledge and a serviceable, sometimes even graceful, style that combine to make them rather engaging reading.

Dunbar-Nelson's involvement with oratorical tradition culminates in two volumes that she edited—*Masterpieces of Negro Eloquence* (1914) and *The Dunbar Speaker and Entertainer* (1920). She began soliciting material for *Masterpieces* in the summer of 1913 with a form letter that explained the venture: to publish "the greatest speeches delivered by members of our race at such a popular price as to put the book into the hands of every patriotic, race-loving Negro in the country."[85] The hope was that the volume would be "an inspiration to the rising generation by causing them to reflect on the eloquence of their own great men." Arthur Schomburg, the noted bibliophile, aided her immensely by referring her to possible inclusions and loaning her books from his unrivaled private collection. Whether because of the work of editing or general fatigue, in the middle of production, Dunbar-Nelson fell ill, but she continued to "sneak to the type-writer, and read proof in bed" and respond with spleen to " 'sassy' letters from the office about proof not being promptly returned, copy being late, dates not in order, etc."[86]

Though *Masterpieces* was a handsome book, it was apparently not profitable. While wishing Schomburg success on his bibliography in 1918, Dunbar-Nelson moans: "I know—yea verily do Mr. Nelson and I know about $2000 worth of know—how apathetic is this race of ours—apathetic and *pathetically* so on matters literary."[87] Dunbar-Nelson seems not to have thought of it, but the war may have negatively affected sales.

Like *Masterpieces,* the *Dunbar Speaker and Entertainer* capitalized on the Dunbar name and her literary-journalistic training. It consisted of both prose and poetry, assumed a somewhat lighter tone, and was also meant to function as a school reader. Both volumes attest to the Afro-American oral tradition, whether folk or literary. At Sunday School, church, school, community center, etc., black speakers need readily available material for the "speeches," "pieces," "talks," "poems," and "addresses" that are a staple ingredient of most programs. Furthermore, from her own experience, Dunbar-Nelson was conversant with the demands of platform oratory, especially before black audiences who expected their information and entertainment to come with flair. Throughout her life, talking to groups— even at what she called "dinky," "backyard" affairs—was one of the major ways she kept herself and her reputation alive. She routinely shared platforms with such figures as Alain Locke, A. Philip Randolph, Mary Church Terrell, and Thomas Elso Jones. Though she was an effective speaker, she occasionally wished to be more arousing in the "fire and brimstone" manner. Near the end of her life, she developed a fresh, anecdotal style, which she liked.

Her sole foray into fine literature during this third period was a one-act play, *Mine Eyes Have Seen,* published in 1918 in *The Crisis;*[88] but even it is literature with a purpose or, one may say, propaganda. Its blatant intent is to persuade black people to support the war. The young draftee Chris asks: "Must I go and fight for the nation that let my father's murder [by whites] go unpunished? That killed my mother—that took away my chances for making a man out of myself?" (p. 272). American injustices are further highlighted by the older brother Dan, who was crippled, "maimed for life in a factory of hell!" and by the family's having been burned out of the South and into the bleak poverty of the North because "niggers had no business having such a decent home." Chris also points out that black men shed blood in 1776, 1812, 1861, and 1898 only to be denied freedom and recognition of their valor. The debate goes so far as to draw in a Jewish boy who declares that "there isn't a wrong . . . your race has endured that mine has not suffered, too" and an Irish matron, Mrs. O'Neill, whose husband died in the fighting. A muleteer from the front brings trench horror and atrocity stories ("They crucified children"). After a speech of Christian charity by Dan, sister Lucy sums up the turning tide: "Chris, we do need you, but your country needs you more. And, above that, your race is calling you to carry on its good name, and with that, the voice of humanity is calling to us all—" (p. 274). Swelling to the strains of "The Battle Hymn of the Republic," the play ends with an awakened Chris, whose eyes have seen the glory, and a "martial crash."

The Jewish character and interracialism accorded with the current thrust of the National Association for the Advancement of Colored People and its organ, *The Crisis,* as well as with Dunbar-Nelson's own integrationist ethics. One also notes that the Socialists are blamed for poisoning Chris's mind. In tone, the play is almost jingoistic—a fact that might suggest a possibly satiric reading. Ironically, ten years later, Dunbar-Nelson is earning her living denouncing war and espousing international peace. Like many Americans who had supported World War I, she favored pacifism over a second major conflict. Yet, it is also true that she—sometimes opportunistically—attuned her public utterances to the pulse of the times. If its intense pitch can be forgiven, *Mine Eyes* is a fairly good play. Certainly dramatic, it presents a tight situation, a variety of characters, and interesting dialogue. After reading the play in *The Crisis,* Caroline Bond of The Circle for Negro War Relief pronounced it "splendid."[89] On April 10, 1918, Dunbar-Nelson granted the Dunbar High School in Washington, D.C., permission to stage the work.

The night-and-day difference between *Mine Eyes Have Seen* and her little 1900 playlet, *The Author's Evening at Home,* illuminates how completely Dunbar-Nelson's focus has shifted.[90] Published in *The Smart Set,* the earlier piece belongs in the category with her slight, airy short stories—although it is very slickly ("smart"-ly) done. An author in his library cannot write because of his fidgety, petulant wife, who demands attention. Both she and his mother ostensibly attempt to maintain quiet, while constantly disrupting him with idle chatter and distracting him with noisy movements and sighs. The play is sophisticated and, by the standards of the time, amusing. Dunbar-Nelson can also be commended for her economy of form and dialogue. Though she is obviously drawing on her domestic situation with Paul and his mother, as was her custom, she changes it from real-life black to literary white, even throwing in a maidservant named Mary, who says "Yes, mum."

Except for one or two school pageants, no other drama by Dunbar-Nelson exists, although a 1928 newspaper article states that "she has written a number of plays for amateur producers."[91] The article continues:

> . . . she prefers to write plays. She believes that the stage is the best medium for exploiting ourselves; that we must break away from propaganda per se and the conventional musical comedy that starts on a plantation and ends in a cabaret, and present to the American public all phases of Negro life and culture.

Here, Dunbar-Nelson is criticizing the popular 1920s black musicals such as *Shuffle Along* and *Chocolate Dandies*, while echoing the Harlem Renaissance hope for an indigenous Afro-American theater. During this same period, Georgia Douglas Johnson had sidelined poetry and begun her successful writing of such plays as *Blue Blood* and *Plumes*. Whether or not she actually wrote drama, Dunbar-Nelson's interest in the genre was keen until she died. Her diary shows that she saw, enjoyed, and critiqued every play possible (something made easier by her ability to casually "pass" for convenience in public accomodations). Remaining in her papers are clippings and programs from performances at the Philadelphia Walnut Street Theatre, Academy of Music, Chestnut Street Opera House, Forrest Theater, etc., ranging from Jane Cowl in *Art and Mrs. Bottle* to Lew Leslie's 1930 *Blackbirds*. After moving to Philadelphia in 1932, she headed the Paul Laurence Dunbar Theater Guild, which aimed to foment a dramatic revival in the Philadelphia black cultural community.

More documentation exists for Dunbar-Nelson's attempts at producing screenplays, a medium allied to stage drama and one that, in its social and practical dimensions, also reflects the general character of her writing during this period. Apparently, she was fascinated with the new motion pictures. From year to year, she watched the films advance in scope and technology, becoming an inveterate movie addict who devoured all types of shows. She sneaked into cheap movie houses on her lunch hour and devoted pages of her diary to comparing each "big picture" with the last. Sometime between 1909 (when the family moved from 1008 to 916

French Street) and 1916 (before she married Robert Nelson), she typed up a seventy-six-page "Motion Picture Play in Eleven Episodes," entitled "Nine—Nineteen—Nine ('9—19—'09')." The plot runs as follows:

> Hope Dudley, and her little sister, Jeanette, are left penniless by the death of their father. . . . In their extremity, they appeal to their uncle . . . , a wealthy curmudgeon with a spite against humanity. Dying, he dreads to leave his money so that it will benefit anyone, so devises a freak will which he thinks will wreak all the harm possible. He has seen how Hope despises Morton Hollis, his villainous secretary. In his will he leaves all his fortune to Hope and Jeanette. . . . But Hope must marry Hollis at once [which she does on September 9, 1909]. Immediately after the ceremony, she and Hollis must separate and remain apart for 19 months, she to retain occupancy of the grim old mansion. At the expiration of that time, if Hope has succeeded in keeping . . . the marriage certificate, she is to be free, the marriage annulled . . . and the fortune will be her's [*sic*] and Jeannette's. If, on the other hand, Hollis succeeds in obtaining the marriage certificate, Hope must be his wife, and the fortune will be his.

In the ensuing struggle—which features stalled trains and hired assassins and ranges from the Middle Atlantic states to Mardi Gras in New Orleans—Hope is aided by her real lover, Robert Neils, the hero of the story. "Just at mid-night, on the last night of the 19 months, the plot is cleared up," and the lovers triumph.

This is unabashed melodrama of the *Perils of Pauline* type popularized by movie serials (which began running in 1915). She pulled out this "despised serial" (her words) in 1921, when she was planning the making of a film with a young man who worked for the *Advocate*. At about the same time, she was angling for a joint venture with Oscar Micheaux, novelist and pioneer black filmmaker. Her September 16, 1921, diary entry records: "Micheaux and Wade [his assistant] came into the office on Wednesday afternoon, were introduced, and settled themselves to talk. . . . I gently hinted to Micheaux that I'd like to collaborate with him, showed him 'The Goodness of St. Rocque.' He did not bite so readily, however."[92] Three days later, she is writing out "a plot for a five reeler," based on her story "By the Bayou St. John" from the *St. Rocque* volume. Since the story is essentially a mood piece that only hints at an ill-fated romance between two warm-blooded lovers, it is hard to imagine how she extrapolated it into a film scenario. Apparently, however, she used her old stories as one source for plot ideas.

What resulted did not suit the market. The Realart Pictures Corporation had agreed to consider her work but returned one play and was "anxious about the serial" because they were "not distinctively colored enough."[93] When she viewed what she deemed a "mighty good" Realart film, *The Burden of Race*, on Thanksgiving Day 1921, she understood her shortcomings: "I see now what kind of stuff the Real people want, and I realize that I can hardly hope to come up to their standard as long as I have the kind of thing in hand that I have." Yet it does not appear that she expended much effort to produce what they required. This suggests that her interest in the genre was ephemeral and perhaps motivated by her constant need for money. Dunbar-Nelson mentions that she wrote "at white heat" a scenario called "The Coward," "a sizzling drama" of 3000 words about which nothing else is known. A three-page synopsis with scenes, entitled "Love's Disguise," also survives among her papers. It tells the story of Agnes, whose face was one-half beautiful, one-half disfigured. She is eventually made normal by a medical doctor who had hired her to nurse his mother when no one else would. Afterward, they marry. Neither of these scripts was ever filmed. After all of her disappointments, Dunbar-Nelson apparently abandoned the notion of writing motion pictures and contented herself with being an avid consumer of other authors' talent in this form.

The Dunbar-Nelson who ends this period is considerably different from the one who began it. Twenty years older, she has established a stable, lifetime relationship and devised for herself a workable mode of interpersonal behavior. Though she did not produce much creative writing, her articles, speeches, and club and educational work kept her name before the public. When the Harlem Renaissance swings into high gear, she will not be forgotten. In fact, these years can be viewed as a bridge between the exciting periods on either side.

iv

Throughout her life, Dunbar-Nelson wrote poetry to release private feelings and commemorate special occasions, but she did not elevate it to her primary mode of expression. However, her activity in this genre increased sufficiently during the 1920s to make her one of the many lyricists of the Harlem Renaissance. Even though she was forty-five years old in 1920 and clearly not one of the brash young voices, Dunbar-Nelson shared in the literary upsurge. As a respected writer of the older generation, she was sent copies of newly published books and asked to judge contests. As a still-active contemporary, she herself entered competitions and contributed work to magazines, journals, and anthologies. Her basically traditional style did not undergo a radical transformation, yet some modernization in her subject matter, voice, and technique can be detected toward the end of the era.

After the juvenilia of *Violets* (1895), Dunbar-Nelson concentrated on short fiction and prose instead of poetry. The few poems that she wrote during the early 1900s are poems of love and *joie d'esprit,* which echo the general timbre of her years with Paul Laurence Dunbar. In 1902 *Munsey's Magazine* published a drinking song by her with a bonny Scots flair. It begins:

> Oh, drink thou deep of the purple wine,
>   And it's hey for love, for I love you so!
> . . . .
> The sea lies violet, deep, and wide,
> My heart beats high with the rushing tide;
> Was it fancy, beloved, the seagulls cried:
>   "Sing loud for love, for I love him so"?[94]

That same year, "Summit and Vale," a brief six-line lyric that compares life's brightness to mountain sun and its sorrow to the misty plain, appeared in *Lippincott's Magazine.* Like the short stories of this agent-aided period of professional authorship, these two poems found an outlet in slick, mainstream magazines.

Dunbar's influence can be felt in a lilting lyric in ballad stanza about a little bird singing the bliss of nature and love:

> He lilts and he tilts and he sways in the leaves,
> For the sun is a-shine, and a gold fabric weaves . . . [95]

"A Common Plaint" is another lighthearted poem, but it carries the serious undertone of not gaining publication, which Alice voiced in her letters to Paul. The author wishes to write a thrilling tale and has her "pot on the fire." Furthermore,

> A check looms large into my sight,
> And here, I scribble rhymes;
> No editor will heed my plight,
> I've proved that scores of times:
> Oh, hero, gallant, come bedight,
> A check looms large into my sight.

She gives up, deciding she "cannot write" and would "rather dream than work." This poem is labeled *Smart Set,* but whether this means it was submitted or published there is not clear—although it is sufficiently well written in that magazine's style to have merited acceptance.

Finally, two unpublished poems from 1902–1909 (and probably closer to the earlier date) seem to reflect the turbulence of her separation from Dunbar. "Still from the Depths" cries the anguish of one soul calling over distance to another, now that it is

> Freed from the power of passion assuaged,
> Freed from the depths of self-love ungauged.

"Sorrow's Crown" has as its epigraph: "A sorrow's crown of sorrow is remembering happier things." It tells the tale of a perfect couple who are divided by another woman. Since there seems to be no actual basis for the plot (other than Alice's possible grief/regret), "Sorrow's Crown" may be the poetic equivalent of her sad, little love stories.

From about 1917 to the mid-1920s, Dunbar-Nelson's poetry mirrors the public activism of her life during this period. Some works also emanated from private experience artistically rendered. These poems—traditional in form—represent her at her best. Among this group is "Violets" (almost her signature poem), which was first published in the August 1917 *Crisis*. Given what Dunbar-Nelson revealed in her diary about its origin in a "Dream Book" of her romance with Emmett J. Scott, it could not have been written very long before that date. The title recalls the name of her very first book as well as the fact that these were her lifelong favorite blooms. After viewing the spectacular Philadelphia Flower Show in 1931, she wrote: "Azaleas and orchids and everything but violets. Such a few wild ones . . . but I would have welcomed a profusion."[96] Considering how much she loved them, it is fitting that she should be best remembered by a poem that bears their name.

"Violets" is a flawlessly executed Shakespearean sonnet that begins with the announcement:

> I had not thought of violets of late,
> The wild, shy kind that springs beneath your feet
> In wistful April days, when lovers mate
> And wander through the fields in raptures sweet.

The second quatrain presents the speaker's corrupted idea of violets as a florist's creation for jaded night life, until the next four lines return the flowers to their rightful place:

> So far from sweet real things my thoughts had strayed,
> I had forgot wide fields, and clear brown streams;
> The perfect loveliness that God has made,—
> Wild violets shy and heaven-mounting dreams.

Having clearly set up a sharp contrast between the natural and the artificial, the poem concludes by celebrating the natural in a subtle linking of nature, violets, spiritual aspiration, and the lover (here introduced for the first time), who receives a dramatic apotheosis for his motivating role:

> And now—unwittingly, you've made me dream
> Of violets, and my soul's forgotten gleam.

The poem's sweetness of theme (conveyed in universal symbols), logical neatness (a corollary of its form), accessible though literary diction, and easy iambic meter all combine to make it pleasing.

Because of their romantic subjects and sonnet forms, three poems published in the July 1925 *Opportunity* magazine seem to date from—and may in fact be further works from—this "Dream Book." "Communion" recounts one holy day spent reliving "irridescent" memories of a past love. An Italian sonnet, it concludes: "Yourself denied, what better could I ask / Than to commune with memories alone?" "Music" begins with an exclamation and description of various instruments:

> Heart-break of cellos, wood-winds in tender frets;
> Orchestra, symphony, bird-song, flute;
> Coronach of contraltos, shrill strings a-mute.

It then proceeds to a catalogue of classic and operatic scores that confirms Dunbar-Nelson's impressive knowledge. The final three lines of heightened feeling equate music with the loved one in a manner reminiscent of "Violets," though here it is far more straightforward. Finally, "Of Old St. Augustine" is a well-wrought poem in which the speaker rejoices that "those whose earthly form is held in thrall" may still live with their souls "unscathed—untouched—far from alarm." The imagery throughout is martial and religious. Dunbar-Nelson shows that she can employ meaningful ambiguity when she speaks of besieged nuns "despoiled / By knights, who battered at the peaceful fold." As a comment on the reality of racism (one of the ways it can be read), the poem posits a personal and idealistic "solution."

Other poems of the early 1920s are more topical and occasional. "The Lights at Carney's Point" is almost unique in Dunbar-Nelson's poetry because of its precise reference to man-made aspects of twentieth-century industrial life.[97] Carney's Point, New Jersey, which is located just across the Delaware River from Wilmington, was a DuPont Company industrial site. Alluding to the company's manufacture of gunpowder (a lucrative activity during the recently ended war), the poem asks: "Is it peace you dream in your flashing gleam, / O'er the quiet flow of the Delaware?" The lights change from white to red to gold in metaphors of bloodshed, death, and commercialism. Finally they turn gray

> ... in the ash of day,
> For a quiet Aurora brought a halcyon balm;
> And the sun laughed high in the infinite sky,
> And the lights were forgot in the sweet, sane calm.

In characteristic Dunbar-Nelson fashion, nature and the natural triumph over human sordidness (a triumph encoded in the tripping anapests of the poem). But this is willful forgetfulness—especially if one thinks past the conclusion of the poem and remains mindful of the negative realities that have been presented in it.

Written for the 1921 Philadelphia *Public Ledger* "Woman in History" contest, Dunbar-Nelson's Italian sonnet "To Madame Curie" is notable for its brilliant allusiveness to Keats's famous "On First Looking into Chapman's Homer" and its fine literary style.[98] "To the Negro Farmers of the United States" baldly announces its topic—a tribute to these peaceful "brave ones of the soil" for their agrarian simplicity and their "gift supreme to foil / The bare-fanged wolves of hunger." This sonnet is reminiscent of Georgia Douglas Johnson's honorific race poems in *Bronze*. Last among this group of works is "I Sit and Sew," which has recently been revived for its feminist spirit. A war poem published in 1920, it is spoken by a woman who chafes against the "useless task" of sewing while more important fighting is needed:

> My soul in pity flings
> Appealing cries, yearning only to go
> There in that holocaust of hell, those fields of woe—
> But—I must sit and sew.
>
> The little useless seam, the idle patch;
> . . . .
> It is no roseate dream
> That beckons me—this pretty futile seam,
> It stifles me—God, must I sit and sew?

A sharp distinction is made between the world of men (which is referred to in a heavier diction: "martial tred," "grim-faced," "stern-eyed") and the slighter, confined world of women (typified by the repetitive sewing). Rhythmic disjunctions in the poem's iambic meter reflect this distinction, as well as the speaker's resulting agitation. The question of war's desirability aside, one woman's complaint about her specific "uselessness" be-

comes an impassioned commentary on the narrowness of culturally defined sexual roles.

The poetry that Dunbar-Nelson wrote in the late 1920s is, on the whole,
not as successful as these earlier poems. An attempt to refurbish her style
for the new age is signaled by her adoption of free verse and a more vivid,
ingenuous persona. Her use of the breathless, ejaculatory, exclamation-
marked style of the youthful poets can be seen at the beginning of "Forest
Fire":

> And I have seen a forest fire;
> God, it was an awful thing!
> It crept with scarlet tongues,
> Fire!
> Higher.[99]

As the poem proceeds, Dunbar-Nelson reverts to the less colloquial, more
discursive and literary manner—including rhyme—that came more naturally to her:

> It flung orange and black
> Scarves to hang in a mocking wrack,
> . . . .
> Turning the gold of foliage to dross,
> Till the forest, panting in shame,
> Gave its virginal beauty to the flame . . .

Interestingly, this poem remains essentially descriptive without any of the
racial symbolism that Harlem Renaissance poets often embedded in poems
of this type to give them thematic significance. This same observation can
be made about "Snow in October," with its emblem of a strong, young
autumn tree "bending beneath a weight of snow" but thrusting through its
"crested leaves," "defiant, glowing." Instead of homing in on the racially
applicable mood of defiance (as other poets of the period would surely
have done), Dunbar-Nelson turns the whole into a personal symbol of
premature aging.

Her practice in these poems proves that Dunbar-Nelson adhered to a
basically romantic concept of poetry, and really did wish—as she told
Dunbar years earlier—to maintain separation between race and imaginative literature. This is almost as obvious in her poems of the New Negro
1920s as it was in her short stories at the turn of the century. "April Is on
the Way," which was published in *Ebony and Topaz* in 1927, is ostensibly
the monologue of a hunted man who is seemingly about to be lynched for

protecting his beloved from violation by white men. However, the situation is so obliquely handled and so enmeshed with contrasting scenes, philosophizing, and nature description that it is almost lost. (Dunbar-Nelson may have believed, though, that the counterpointed contexts would serve to add poignancy.) The net result is a rather confusing work.

Counterpoint was one of her favorite techniques in these late 1920s poems. In fact, ironic juxtaposition seems to be her way of handling social commentary. "The Proletariat Speaks" (*The Crisis*, 1929)[100] is built on the contrast between the "beautiful things" the heroine loves and the "proletariat" realities of where she works, what she eats, and how she rests. Among the things she loves are "carven seats and tapestries, and old masters / Whose patina shows the wealth of centuries"; "pale silver, etched with heraldries"; "rose shaded lamps and golden atomizers." All these are true to Dunbar-Nelson's taste for gracious living. Some contrasting realities—presented in alternate stanzas—are a dusty office overlooking a squalid alley; lumpy gobs of cafeteria food; and a hot tenement room. The diction of the two worlds also contrasts, and the tone is ironically humorous, partly because of the speaker's wryly resigned acceptance of her condition. Lastly, "Harlem John Henry Views the Airmada" is an intellectually demanding work that features a black protagonist who questions war against a juxtaposed background of black spirituals and folk songs. Her June 10, 1931, diary entry discusses its genesis: " . . . I was inert until about three [P.M.] when words leapt at me from somewhere and I began and finished 'Harlem John Henry Views the Airmada,' a poem in blank verse, with spirituals running through. A weird thing, five pages long, which left me in two hours' time as limp as a rag." The poem was speedily rejected by white magazines such as *The Bookman, Atlantic Monthly, Harper's,* and *Mercury,* until the January 1932 *Crisis* featured it as "An epic of Negro Peace to which we give the whole of our poetry page."

Dunbar-Nelson did not write very much poetry. What she wrote improves markedly from her juvenile verse to the mature work of the 1920s. Overall, she is a fairly good poet who is particularly competent in rhymed and metered forms and is at her best when these forms are combined with traditional, yet sincerely felt, poetic subjects. Dunbar-Nelson's bent as a writer was more discursive than poetic, especially if "poetic" is viewed in the modern sense as abbreviated concentration of expression. Her facility with language fostered in her a torrential habit with words. For example, diction of all kinds—from colloquial to learned to literary—sprang easily from her huge vocabulary. Such facile composition may not have been best for her poetry. Because it did not encourage or seem to require rewriting,

Dunbar-Nelson was not given to revising her work. However, in at least one instance, she rushed out of bed to tinker with a line: to change a preposition in "Harlem John Henry Views the Airmada" from "And that wild wonder *of* a soundless world" to "And that wild wonder *at* a soundless world." After doing so, she asked herself, "Now which is better?"[101] Undoubtedly this instance says less about her usual compositional method than it does about the compulsions that her general perfectionism could trigger. Further, there is no evidence of her reworking her poetry, such as drafts and contemporary remarks (as there are for her stories).

It seems that had Dunbar-Nelson devoted more time to her poetry, she would have produced even better work, but apparently it did not absorb her to that extent. In addition to not being her predilection, deliberate concentration on writing a poem did not accord with her concept of poetry. Essentially romantic, it caused her to reserve poetry for intense emotion and other special occasions. Given how she hoarded the "Dream Book," it is apparent that she sometimes saw poetry as too private to be publicly shared. This dichotomy helped to foster her attraction to the ideal versus real, natural versus artificial theme that she used as the base for both the content and form of many of her poems. Her romantic concepts also account for her stock of nature imagery. That she wrote poetry—even to the degree that she did—ultimately proved to be a boon for Dunbar-Nelson. It suited the Harlem Renaissance emphasis on verse and found space in the books and magazines of the period, thus helping to ensure her niche in literary history.

That her reputation became fixed as a poet results also from the fact that the little formal critical attention given her usually focuses on her poetry. She is included in James Weldon Johnson's landmark anthology, *The Book of American Negro Poetry* (1931), and in Robert Kerlin's helpful compilation *Negro Poets and Their Poems* (1935). Kerlin called her "Violets" "a sonnet . . . to which . . . Mrs. Browning or Christina Rossetti might have appended her signature without detriment to her fame." Sterling Brown devotes one paragraph of his *Negro Poetry and Drama* to her. Commenting on her "many poems," he notes only that they "echo the romantic themes."[102]

In addition to her poetry, Dunbar-Nelson's participation in the Renaissance is documented in other, nonliterary ways. As an indication of the resurgent scholarly interest in the Afro-American past, she worked with the noted black historian Carter G. Woodson on a textbook. She also attended the many conferences, meetings, and conventions that functioned as occasions for race work and networking. As they traveled from city to city, many individuals stopped at one another's homes because of the Jim

Crow dearth of accommodations. Dunbar-Nelson entertained Langston Hughes, Walter White, and others and was, in turn, housed by Bessye Bearden and the numerous other hostesses who boarded her when she traveled professionally. In such circumstances, collegiality and friendship easily combined. After returning to Washington, D.C., from a conference in North Carolina, Dunbar-Nelson and W. E. B. DuBois made breakfast with Georgia Douglas Johnson before continuing on their journeys. Even more social was the late-night partying and cabaret-going in Harlem–New York City. Her August 15–18, 1928, diary entry records visits to the Venetian Tea Room, the "Dark Tower," the Cotton Club, and the Mexico, in addition to attendance at a formal ball and a large, "messy," private party "staged" by one Jay Clifford. Dunbar-Nelson naturally aligned herself with the older, more genteel crowd, yet she wrote in 1929 that she found "a curious selfishness on the part of the Jim [James Weldon] Johnsons and the Walter Whites and have my usual loneliness in the crowd. Oh, so pitiful!"[103]

All of Dunbar-Nelson's moving about contributed to her effectiveness as a journalist, a genre that occupied her considerably during this period. She wrote three different columns—"Une Femme Dit" for the Pittsburgh *Courier* from February 20, 1926, to September 18, 1926; "As in a Looking Glass" for the Washington *Eagle* from 1926 to 1930; and "So It Seems—to Alice Dunbar-Nelson," again for the *Courier* from January to May 1930. Some of these columns and other features were syndicated by the Associated Negro Press. Long before this, Dunbar-Nelson had entered the field of professional journalism. A 1902 article declares that "she won her spurs in daily journalism, and that in Chicago, on the *Daily News*." Another source mentions that she "served her apprenticeship as special writer on the New York *Sun* and Chicago *Record-Herald*."[104] In her position as associate editor of the struggling Wilmington *Advocate*, she provided editorials and much routine copy for the paper (which, unfortunately, have not been preserved).

From 1913 to 1915 she also served as associate editor of the *A.M.E.* [African Methodist Episcopal] *Church Review*. One of her last efforts, in spring 1931, was the launching of an unsuccessful news column, Station K-A-D-N, which she had hoped would be picked up by the papers. She explained her scheme in a letter of solicitation to Hannah Clothier Hull of the Women's International League for Peace and Freedom:

> I am about to start a news bureau, weekly releases to the 170 odd Negro newspapers. . . . My thought was to have just about a column of stuff, a

> book review, some short paragraphs on timely topics, something personal, some propaganda, so disguised as to be subtly appealing. . . . I do not intend to charge the papers for the service, for the reason that most Negro newspapers are swamped with [free] releases. . . . So the news bureau . . . would have to depend for its existence on the payments of those who wish their message put across.[105]

Apparently, she did not raise sufficient backing and newspapers did not use her test column, for on May 11, she declares the idea "a failure."[106] But this disappointment came after a lifetime of successes in the age of journalism, when H. L. Mencken, George Schuyler, and lesser-known figures like herself flourished amid the rising newspaper chains.

Dunbar-Nelson's work in journalism represents thousands of words of writing, so it was good that they came so easily to her. Perhaps the task of "producing literature" by-the-word, by-the-week influenced the way she wrote in imaginative genres. Clearly, the time and energy that she devoted to newspaper writing made of her a working, professional journalist who was recognized as such. In "A Survey of the Negro Press" in *Opportunity* magazine (1927), Eugene Gordon wrote of her: "In my estimation there are few better column conductors of her sex on any newspaper. I should like to see her on some influential daily where her unmistakable talents would be allowed full exercise."[107] A 1930 article about her in the *Courier* is headlined: "Bernice [Dutrielle, *Courier* reporter] Interviews America's Greatest Woman Columnist."[108] It is significant that Dunbar-Nelson was not a typical female-stereotyped columnist who specialized in society doings or strictly women's news. What she wrote is a far cry from the gossip of Geraldyn Dismond, who was columnist and managing editor of *The Inter-State Tattler,* "Afro-America's most frivolous newspaper," and was awarded first place among Negro press society writers in 1927. Her proper motto was "Wherever Society Moves Geraldyn's 'Snap-shots' Follow."[109] Dunbar-Nelson's columns are also superior to Gwendolyn Bennett's race-conscious, but chatty "Ebony Flute" contributions in *Opportunity* magazine.

The journalism that Dunbar-Nelson practiced was indeed a man's profession. Not only did she write serious columns and editorials, but she also did routine reporting and news features. Once, in February 1899, she was to have covered a Tuskegee conference for the Boston *Transcript* but finally could not attend because her sister fell ill. However, her husband Paul went and promised to mail some notes to her. But, in a February 25 letter to him, she writes:

> I concluded not to wait for your letter to write my article for I was afraid Clemens [the editor] might squeal 'too late,' so sitting by Leila's bedside

two [?] evenings, I delved into my imagination and evolved 2600 words, glowingly descriptive of the whole affair and sent it in yesterday. I put in a few reports about the storm damage, expiated [*sic*] on the bad roads caused by the snow melting and lied around generally. Lord, I hope it'll go.

As it turned out, her account, as she said later, "wasn't far off." She had even given a brief résumé of Booker T. Washington's opening address that was "strangely true" to Paul's report. Her intuitive reporter's sense had stood her in good stead, and though she was too careful generally to revert to it for copy, in this one instance, it enabled her to keep an assignment that meant so much to her both professionally and financially. She tried to do overseas reporting during World War I, and her diary often shows her writing and sending news while away from home.

Dunbar-Nelson participated wholeheartedly in this man's world (comparable, in ways, to her delving into partisan politics). Not surprisingly, her gender did not help her. This is especially evident in the early depression 1930s, when, her excellent credentials notwithstanding, she could not secure a desperately needed position of any kind in black journalism. Her situation in a male-dominated profession is suggested by an exchange that occurred between her and Ira F. Lewis, manager of the Pittsburgh *Courier*, about payment for her "So It Seems" columns. Addressing her (sarcastically) as "Dear Madam" in an April 12, 1930, letter, Lewis denies that the paper agreed to pay her ten dollars per column and continues insultingly:

> But despite the fact that you stated that your "stuff" was worth more now than it was four years ago (which I doubt, ha! ha!) we thought we would write you so we could have an understanding and not expect too much of each other. [They had sent her fifty dollars in March and planned to send another fifty dollars at the end of April.]

Interestingly, Dunbar-Nelson pens a very cool reply to him three days later. Midway through the letter, she writes:

> I understand that business is tight, that you have a heavy obligation on you to get your new equipment paid for and all that, and being an old newspaper woman myself, am prepared to be reasonable and all that— provided you deal with me as man to man, as if I had some common sense, or at least the intelligence of a twelve year old.

As she realized, whatever misunderstanding there may have been, Lewis was not dealing with her "as man to man." She reminds him in detail about their agreement and says that throwing up smokescreens about her worth deceives no one:

> Now that being all clear, I am prepared to accept your apology for
> thinking I am so dumb as you pretended to think I am. And will appreciate
> something on acount in time to get myself an Easter bonnet—which means
> return mail.

Thus, she concludes this potentially ugly business in a dignified way that
combines her toughness and her femininity. Women in nontraditional
roles have often been forced to operate in this fashion.

Two drawbacks to journalism for Dunbar-Nelson were that it did not
pay reliably well (even though it was more dependable than creative writing), and that it is ephemeral writing that does not make posthumous
literary reputations. She would have fared better had she landed a position
like that of her friend Bessye Bearden, who was paid fifty dollars per week
for her Chicago *Defender* page, or if she had written for some of the more
enduring journals, such as *Opportunity* or *Crisis*. Yet Dunbar-Nelson's
achievements in this field gave her considerable visibility in the black
world.

Her first major column of the 1920s, "Une Femme Dit," had as its
subtitle "Crisp, Bright Opinions of Current Happenings From a Woman's
Point of View." This description could practically serve for all of her weekly
columns, if one adds the understanding that the woman is Afro-American
and that the bright tone occasionally shades into seriousness. Five representative weeks of "Une Femme Dit" can illustrate her material and
tone.[110] She discusses the current state of black theater, commends a progressive churchman for keeping abreast of modern life, applauds the admission that juvenile courts are racially prejudiced, deplores the pseudo-
scientific approach to studying black people, praises the work being done
to foster race pride and higher education by the black Greek sororities and
fraternities, and opines that American politics are a joke, in a display of
Toni Cade Bambara-like rhetoric:

> Now that the smoke and dust of battle have cleared away, and the spell-
> binders, ward workers, directors, political sharpsters, high-ups, senators,
> congressmen, cabinet officers, women's clubs, sob-sister[s], repeaters, old
> timers, I-knew-him-whenners, big guns and small fry have lain them down
> to rest after six or seven weeks' strenuous campaigning, the like of which
> has not been seen since the good old days before the late war—the mere
> voters can heave a sign of relief and go about their daily occupations again,
> and the housewife may clean up the mess of campaign literature, and use
> the innumerable booklets to light the kitchen fire.

She teases men for their election excitement versus the voting calmness
of newly franchised women: "Canute tried to sweep back the ocean with a

gesture. That is the apotheosis of futility. Multiply it by ten and raise it to the n'th power, and you have the futility of trying to squelch the Man and Brother who has elected himself to lead the campaign." In the same five columns, Dunbar-Nelson chides temperance zealots for their inflexibility, laughs at "upper ten" blacks who lie about not being born in the South, discusses the presidencies of black colleges as a Gaston-and-Adolf affair (a reference not generally familiar today), comments on a public figure denying that he is a Ku Klux Klansman, explains America's love of black music, revels about the two weeks of summer vacation (coining the word "scanties"), and replies to three letters she ostensibly received from "Anxious Young Persons."

Her "As in a Looking Glass" columns were similar to these. However, Dunbar-Nelson drew more of her matter from articles that had been published in current magazines, and she also reviewed more books. Among these were: Julia Peterkin, *Black April;* Alain Locke, editor, *Four Negro Poets;* Dr. E. C. L. Adams, *Nigger to Nigger;* W. E. B. DuBois, *Dark Princess;* Esther Hyman, *Study in Bronze* (A West Indian novel); Georgia Douglas Johnson, *An Autumn Love Cycle;* and Vera Caspary, *The White Girl* (a white author's story of a black girl passing). These reviews show Dunbar-Nelson functioning as literary critic, often displaying a great deal of insight and judgment. Speaking of James Weldon Johnson's reissued *Autobiography of an Ex-Colored Man,* she writes: "The tale itself in the light of present day accomplishment sounds almost late-Victorian. But the manner of telling, in its bald, terse, cold, almost impersonal clarity reminds one involuntarily of Booker Washington's 'Up From Slavery.'" She was delighted with Nella Larsen's *Passing,* saying that, when the denouement comes, it is

> so surprising, so unexpected, so startling, so provocative of a whole flood of possibilities, so fraught with mystery, of a "Lady or Tiger" problem, that you are suddenly aware that you have been reading a masterpiece all along, and that the subtle artistry of the story lies in just this—its apparent inocuousness, with its universality of appeal. (May 3, 1929)

She waxed poetic about Larsen's style: "It is compact and terse; stripped of non-essentials of language or incident or description. It is hardly more than a bare outline. But it etches itself on your memory, like stark trees against a wintry sunset."

In addition to reviewing books, Dunbar-Nelson also critiqued stage shows, plays, and films—for example, Franke Harling's *Deep River,* billed as "a native opera in jazz"; *Black Boy,* the story of Jack Johnson, with Paul Robeson; *In Abraham's Bosom; Joan of Arc,* which she called a "perfect film," and *Noah's Ark,* which she dubbed the "world's worst." Obviously, this heightened culture was an aspect of the Harlem Renaissance. The era is further reflected in her columns by such things as her coverage of the 1927 *Opportunity* dinner, her acerbic comments about the unsightly knees of stage-show chorines, and her almost satirical portrait of downtown whites at uptown nightclubs:

> To my mind the funniest thing about the so-called black and tan cabarets of Harlem is the fact that they are not black and tan at all—but mostly white, filled largely with middle-aged Jews and flossy ladies of certain and uncertain ages, weirdly dancing with their own race, and looking all the while as if they are saying to themselves—"My what a wicked thrill I am getting?" (May 13, 1927)

In 1929, she noted that one Sunday's *New York Times Book Review* section was "dark-hued," and agreed with George W. Jacobs's comment in the *Nation* that black literature depicting the seamy side of Harlem does not delineate Negro life: "It is time that someone protested against the 'sewer literature' which has offended the nostrils of those to whom literature is a beautiful dignified mistress and not a strident, dishevelled gutter-snipe" (June 4, 1929). Clearly, she classes herself with that group.

What caught Dunbar-Nelson's attention covered an extremely wide range. She deplored the U.S. press glorifying Marines shooting down Chinese citizens; told her readers what Roland Hayes and Paul Robeson earned each night; imparted the news that Sylvia Chen, "the girl dictator," was half-black and half-Chinese; wondered about America's preoccupation with Charles Lindbergh; and congratulated Henry Ford on his cessation of anti-Semitic attacks, even though his motives may have been mercenary. Of course, black people and racial problems were important, perennial topics. She forgave individuals who suffered segregation to see a brilliant theatrical performance, but chided those who would buy a box of candy at a discriminating drug store. Her ken extended to Africa, about which she made a still-resonant remark:

> All writers it seems latterly, who discuss the Dark Continent are unanimous in sounding the word of warning to white Europe about the dangers lurking in this land of mystery and magic. But the white man . . . blunders on somehow. . . . But he is never going to relinquish gold and diamonds and ivory and rubber and oil and mahogany and ebony without a struggle to the death. (January 13, 1928)

She always pointed out racial milestones and Negro "firsts," and likewise struck out indignantly and angrily at continuing racism. The famous

Boston, Massachusetts, Farmers Cookery School drew particularly heavy fire for its reply to an application from a Howard High School Domestic Science teacher. She called their racist response "one of the most ingenious tracts on race hatred, segregation, and cracker pussy-footing that has ever been written or printed" (May 20, 1927). Attention to women, especially black ones, is inherent in her columns. Occasionally, she makes topical, specific references, declaring, for example, that women know the economy better than financial experts because of their real experience, and painting a liberated picture of a train car of decent, sophisticated women smoking their cigarettes (which she herself did).

Though they closely resemble these "As in a Looking Glass" columns, Dunbar-Nelson's 1930 "So It Seems" pieces are not quite as compelling. One suspects some diminution of verve and interest. Segments are choppier, and the tone more perfunctory. Perhaps the veteran columnist was tiring, or her work may simply have been betraying the troubled nature of her life at this point. Topics she touched upon were Amos 'n' Andy, Countee Cullen's book *The Black Christ,* and the woman who originated Friendship Week. Her American Inter-Racial Peace Committee tour of the South also provided her with copy.

While she was producing these weekly columns, Dunbar-Nelson was still writing editorials and occasional magazine articles. Important essays focusing on black womanhood appeared in the *Messenger* during the first half of 1927. The June 1927 essay "Facing Life Squarely" took its title from the ritual of the Girl Reserves, a group for which Dunbar-Nelson served as leader. She wishes "every Aframerican woman in this country" to face race issues boldly:

> And the women of our race must realize that there is no progress in sobbing with joy over the spectacle of two or three ordinary Southern white women sitting down to talk with several very high class black women over the race problem. We are deluding ourselves if we feel we are getting anywhere by having conferences, when hundreds of black women are wringing their hands because their men have been driven over the crumbling levee to certain death [during the Mississippi Flood], while white men stand out of the danger zone.

She could be just as racially sharp and gender-specific in her editorials. One of the best of these, "The Ultimate Insult," appeared in the Washington *Eagle* on October 26, 1928. The infamous Mississippi governor Theodore G. Bilbo accused Republican presidential candidate Hoover of calling upon and dancing with a colored woman. Hoover's assistant, George

Akerson, responded by declaring that the statement was "unqualifiedly false," and "the most indecent and unworthy statement in the whole of a bitter campaign." It is this slur which incensed Dunbar-Nelson:

> It is safe to assert that there is not a colored woman in the United States who would want to dance with Mr. Hoover, or would feel herself honored in so doing. But every woman of color feels her soul flame into a white heat of insulted rage at the characterization by Mr. Akerson, as "an indecent and unworthy statement." . . . any Negro who would vote for Mr. Hoover after this gratuitous insult to the womenkind of the race is unworthy of the trusting faith of a sister, the loyal love of a wife, or the tender self-sacrificing devotion of a mother.

Reading these kinds of writings by Dunbar-Nelson makes one wonder what novel, play, or story she might have developed if she had held a non-ivory tower concept of creative literature and had not maintained so rigorously the separation between her real life and daily concerns, and her art.

Dunbar-Nelson's journalism shows her as literary critic, political analyst, social commentator, race theorist, humorist, stage and film critic, etc. (One compares Georgia Douglas Johnson's much slighter foray into weekly journalism as a "homely philosopher.") She generally adopted the urbane, yet opinionated, tone favored by columnists, but also—as was necessary for maintaining freshness—used a variety of moods and modes. One does not know if readers rushed to her column each week; however, reading it would usually have been informative and entertaining. Her work reveals a breadth of educated knowledge, which she seems less given to displaying in her later, more straightforward pieces. Clearly, too, she was exceptionally well informed about the events of her day—in both the white and black worlds. Overall, her journalism deserves a more promi-nent place in the consideration of her as a writer. When placed alongside her other work, it enhances her stature.

Even though Dunbar-Nelson spent a good portion of her time writing, she simultaneously maintained the other aspects of her busy life. This included continuing, committed participation in the black women's club movement, which was doing so much to combat negative sterotypes about Afro-American women and to aid the overall betterment of the race mate-rially and spiritually. For Dunbar-Nelson, this work entailed such activities as attending local executive and full membership meetings; cooperating with other clubwomen and the public to carry out official duties, tasks, and projects; planning state, regional, and national conventions. She held of-fice in the Federation of Colored Women's Clubs and was also involved with the Delta Sigma Theta sorority (for which she wrote the lyrics of their official hymn) and the Daughter Elks, the "sister" auxiliary to the Improved Benevolent and Protective Order of Elks, the Black Elks, for whom her husband Robert worked as editor of their Washington *Eagle* newspaper. Her affiliation with this last group is especially notable because it was a less "hoity-toity," more grassroots women's movement centered in fundamentalist churches and neighborhood lodges. For the Elk Daughters in 1928, she conceived and directed an amateur cabaret theatrical named the "Club Ritz-Carlton." In Dunbar-Nelson's life, her club movement activity was the widest extension of her black female support system.

In conjunction with the Delaware State Federation, Dunbar-Nelson helped to found in 1920 the Industrial School for Colored Girls in Marshalltown, Delaware, a facility for delinquent and homeless female juveniles. Luckily for her, this enterprise yielded her employment after the loss of her Howard High School teaching position and the demise of the Wilmington *Advocate* newspaper. From 1924 to 1928 she conducted its public school department, a demanding job that meant teaching mixed-grade classes, attending court parole sessions, and directing musical and dramatic presentations. On the extracurricular side, it meant encouraging the promising girls to seek further education and taking an active interest in the general welfare of all the young women (placing them in private homes, counseling necessary abortions, buying small presents, and so on).

Because this enterprise did not satisfy her, Dunbar-Nelson was elated to secure the newly created position of Executive Secretary of the American Inter-Racial Peace Committee (AIPC), a subsidiary organization of the American Friends (Quakers) Service Committee. After she assumed the full-time, paying position on June 1, 1928, the change that it made in her life proved her initial hunch that this job would pan out "big." It gave her the chance to promote not only the work of the committee but also herself. The aim of the AIPC was "to develop and enlist the active support of the Negroes of America in the cause of Peace," while fostering equality and understanding between races and the general idea of international peace.[111] Dunbar-Nelson worked out of the Friends' headquarters at 20 South Twelfth Street, Philadelphia, so each weekday saw her "battling trains" for her commute from Wilmington. Her role involved not so much routine office tasks (although answering letters, writing reports, etc., were necessary) as calling on people, attending meetings, speaking at conferences, sponsoring programs, and similar outreach strategies.

Her first year featured a mass launching at the Broad Street Theater; her second was highlighted by the supremely successful 1929 National Negro

Music Festival; 1930 was the year of her triumphal cross-country tour, which in ten weeks took her not only through the South (and a host of small black colleges) but as far west as California, then back through the Midwest. The most impressive engagement of this 10,000-mile speaking trip was a March 11 presentation by the Los Angeles Civic League, where she addressed a large, enthusiastic audience on "The Negro and International Peace." This lecture, described by one newspaper as "easily a masterpiece in oratorical elegance and logic,"[112] is indeed striking.

Dunbar-Nelson begins by saying that black people have heretofore fallen in step with America's war program, but now a new note has crept in:

> The Negro begins to see that what affects humanity of the darker skin everywhere, must affect him here on this continent. The sufferings of Gandhi in India; the struggles of the natives in South Africa for economic independence; the cry of the Filipinoes for self-determination; the woes of Haiti and of Nicaragua . . . —all these must be part of his thinking. These are his people, bone of his bone, flesh of his flesh, bound to him by that chain which the white world has forged—the chain of color, and those black and heavy links, hammered out on the anvil of prejudice, may not be broken, but must ever be welded stronger, as hatred closes in around them.

Because of a heightened consciousness,

> Clear-eyed, the Negro stands now and sees war for what it is,—an economic conflict. Greed and capitalism, reaching out to acquire more and yet more—and the little ones of the earth, the peasant and the proletarian— and the mass of Negroes is both—but the infinitesimal grains of black powder which fire the big Bertha of commerce.

The radicalism of this speech is interesting. First, it contrasts markedly with her 1914 propaganda play, *Mine Eyes Have Seen,* suggesting that Dunbar-Nelson has altered her views to accommodate her own personal changes and changes in the sociopolitical climate. Second, it extends the theme of Third World awareness that is obvious in her newspaper columns. Third, it distinctly sounds the Marxist, proletarian note of the 1930s. Dunbar-Nelson never went so far as to embrace Socialism-Communism, but she occasionally, as here, utilized the rhetoric and some applicable tenets. Finally, in its solid alliance of Dunbar-Nelson with the mass of ordinary black people, the speech demonstrates the not-uncommon dual set of values that has always been evident in her behavior. Looking at the race from within it, she often made critical and disparaging remarks that suggest a kind of personal alienation. However, when she was mindful of the larger, social contexts, she was militantly pro-black.

Dunbar-Nelson's three years with the AIPC were rewarding—especially
in giving her salaried work that utilized her many skills in a unique, public
manner. The job, however, had its harrowing aspects. She had to cooper-
ate with the chairman of the committee, Leslie Pinckney Hill, principal
(president) of Cheyney State Normal School (College), Pennsylvania. Too
many times, he was uninterested, unavailable, or vaguely unsupportive.
Intraoffice politics were also fraught with rivalry and personality clashes.
Doing her work in the field, Dunbar-Nelson confronted racism and sexism,
but it was more crucial and demoralizing for her to encounter such attitudes from the Friends themselves, whom she once referred to sarcastically
as "sweet Quakers." Finally, despite some gains, the AIPC was not a grand
success. It was difficult to assess its impact, but the financial problems were
easy to see. When the parent body decided to abolish the Inter-Racial
Peace Committee in the spring of 1931, Dunbar-Nelson herself was re-
lieved to close this chapter of her life. In his April 10 letter of farewell
commendation, Clarence E. Pickett, executive secretary of the American
Friends Service Committee wrote:

> From the personal point of view, it has always been a deep satisfaction to
> me to have you in our office and to feel that through you we had a visible
> connecting link with members of your race. . . . I can only hope that in due
> time we shall find it possible to undertake some further work with members
> of the negro [*sic*] group.

Her AIPC activity had capitalized on her famous name. The Dunbar link
also helped maintain her speaking engagements before high schools, clubs,
and other civic groups. When she visited Bermuda October 12–24, 1931,
the stellar affair of her sojourn was "An Evening with Paul Laurence
Dunbar," which she presented. The "woman angle," too, continued to be
her specialty. In reply to an invitation to speak at an April 25, 1931,
Conference on the Economic Status of Negroes, she responded: "Perhaps,
since you have so many men on the program, and they will of necessity be
more interested in men than in women, I had better talk about the exploitation of Negro women in the labor field."

One piece of information exists regarding how Robert Nelson felt about
his wife keeping her celebrated ex-husband's name. It appears in Nahum
Daniel Brascher's "Random Thoughts" column in the Chicago *Defender* on
September 28, 1935—ten days after Alice's death. In a section headed
"Alice Dunbar-Nelson Passes On," Brascher writes:

> Talking with Robert (Bob) Nelson in a Washington hotel once, he told
> me of the cheerful chiding he frequently received because of Alice Ruth

> Moore Dunbar Nelson dropping all of her other names except Alice Dunbar
> Nelson. In his fine native Pennsylvania cultured way Bob said: "I regard it
> an honor for my wife to retain the name of the great Paul Laurence Dun-
> bar."

This anecdote and Brascher's brief description indicate that Alice's Bobbo
was basically a fine man, especially when the report is placed alongside
other evidence about him. Self-assured about his own worth and life, he
never tried to hinder his prominent wife, although he could on occasion be
jealous and domestically sexist. A good example is contained in this May
25, 1929, diary entry, written after the National Negro Music Festival, an
event that Dunbar-Nelson had planned, arranged, carried out, and worked
on day and night just before its occurrence:

> Nearly cracked when I got home a wreck, and Bobbo asked me if there was
> anything to eat in the ice-box. It was too cruel. But when I got off my shoes,
> into nightie and bathrobe, and went down into the kitchen to eat the
> sandwiches he had cooked (fried egg) and a high ball, did not feel so near to
> tears. I might have bawled him out a plenty.

This entry also highlights the troubled interface between work outside and
work inside the home, and reveals the role expectations that women like
Dunbar-Nelson had to reconcile.

Unfortunately, very little of the correspondence that they may have
shared is extant. On December 18, 1928, he wrote her a brief note appended to an announcement: "Alice:—This might be a good chance to get
over your peace propaganda. Bobo." This easy familiarity and terse help-
fulness seem characteristic of their relationship. Though the sober, practical
aspects of their union stand out, it also had a warmer side. In a sweet but
unaffected and down-to-earth tone, Bobbo forestalled a quarrel with Alice
on December 8, 1931: "I don't know why you think I will hit the ceiling
when you want me to come home [from his Elks' work in Washington,
D.C.]. The only reason would be the cost but I have never hesitated to do,
or come home, when I felt that I could afford it. Don't be like that!" He
ends "with lots of love and kisses I am now and evermore shall be, thine
own," and signs himself "Loving / Bobo your Heart / Husband." A July 1,
1932, letter is also revealing. Bobbo salutes her as "My Love Paramount,"
and concludes, "Come let me hug and kiss you as I tell you how much I
love you and that I shall evermore be, thine own. . . . " Perhaps instead of
simply mellowing, their relationship blossomed with age. Undoubtedly,
Dunbar-Nelson knew better than posterity could ever guess why she

counted her blessings like this on Thanksgiving Day 1930: "And yet I have a lot to be thankful for. Bobbo, first, last and always, the best of all."

Dunbar-Nelson was clearly a sensuous woman whose passion could not always find expression. Her situation was further complicated by the fact that she apparently needed multiple and varied channels for her erotic energy. During this period of her life, it becomes unequivocal that these included romantic relationships with women. In her 1928 diary, Dunbar-Nelson mentions that a friend of hers tells her to "look over" a Betty Linford, and that a "heavy flirtation" between two clubwomen friends of hers puts her "nose sadly out of joint" (July 25, August 1). She also makes overt reference to homosexual individuals and reads Radclyffe Hall's lesbian classic, *The Well of Loneliness,* in 1929. Finally, in 1930, she hesitantly tells the story of her tempestuous affair with Fay Jackson Robinson, a younger newspaperwoman and socialite whom she encountered during her stay in California.

Fay, whom Dunbar-Nelson called her "little blue dream of loveliness," was a member of the executive council of the Los Angeles Civic League. The mother of at least one daughter, she secured a job as a journalist with the California *Eagle* after eventually separating from her husband, John, under scandalous circumstances. As Dunbar-Nelson read the situation: "She [Fay] has left her husband and it looks like a hell of a mess to me. Privately, I think they were both after Tesse and John won."[113] Dunbar-Nelson was ecstatic about their connection, but it also proved to be "a hell of a mess" because of Fay's prior relationship with another woman, Helene Ricks London, an artist who was likewise interested in Dunbar-Nelson. (In fact, Dunbar-Nelson visited her in Bermuda in 1931.) The three of them corresponded feverishly after Alice's return to Delaware, and her emotions vacillated between friendly pleasure and disappointed distress regarding the affair. Distance—as much as misunderstandings and miscommunications—separated Fay and Dunbar-Nelson, who could yet sigh in her diary on March 18, 1931: "Anniversary of My One Perfect Day . . . And still we cannot meet again."

Dunbar-Nelson wrote Fay a number of poems that, regrettably, are unavailable. These would have been notable additions to the store of lesbian poetry by Afro-American women, especially earlier writers. Only one poem and the first-line titles of half a dozen others are recorded in her diary: "I had not thought to ope that secret room"; "Pale April, decking her hair with daffodils"; "I could not even dream—"; "Lest I should worry you if day by day"; "I knew I'd suffer if I let love come"; and a final one,

which she describes on April 12, 1930 as "a sonnet on my feverous condition [she was ill], likening Fay to a cool lake, a cool flower." The extant
poem, which for some reason she copied or wrote into her April 3 diary, is
a rough, ten-line lyric that emanates more from emotion than artistry. The
first half reads:

> You did not need to creep into my heart
> The way you did. You could have smiled
> And knowing what you did, have kept apart
> From all my inner soul. But you beguiled
> Deliberately. Then flung my poor love by . . .

It concludes on the same note of reproach at having had "the golden
dream I reared" cruelly smashed.

Almost ten years earlier, Dunbar-Nelson had written a poem entitled
"You! Inez!" (her exclamations and italics) that, in retrospect, can be identified as another lesbian work. Signed only with her cursive initials and
dated February 16, 1921, it exists as a heatedly scrawled scrap among her
papers:

> Orange gleams athwart a crimson soul
> Lambent flames; purple passion lurks
> In your dusk eyes.
> Red mouth; flower soft,
> Your soul leaps up and flashes
> Star-like, white, flame-hot.
> Curving arms, encircling a world of love.
> You! Stirring the depths of passionate desire!

The imagery here is reminiscent of similar lines by Angelina Grimké, who
also wrote submerged, woman-identified poetry during the early twentieth
century. Given that these poets did not labor over this work, which they
knew was clandestine and unpublishable, one wonders what quality poetry would have resulted if they had wedded technical polish with such
inspiration and strength of feeling.

Dunbar-Nelson's experience reveals the existence and operation of an
active black lesbian network. All of these women were prominent and
professional, and most had husbands and/or children. Somehow, they
contrived to be themselves and carry on these relationships in what most
surely must have been an extremely repressive context. Could it be that
Paul's "vile story" about Dunbar-Nelson—for which she left him in
1902—was somehow related to her sexuality? And might the extreme
need for self-protective secrecy have prompted her subsequent inflex-

ibility? Dunbar-Nelson's bisexuality certainly makes of her an even more fascinating woman, whose complex life galvanizes new thought and new questions.

Her diary was the only place where Dunbar-Nelson could even begin to discuss her sexual relationships and other personal privacies. She kept it from July 29 to December 31, 1921, then from November 1926 to December 1931, and probably also for additional months that have been lost. Of necessity, this work became a repository for psychological clues and other general information about her. It serves, especially, to illuminate what it meant to be a black woman/writer in earlier twentieth-century America, while providing the accompanying background and contexts. Finally, Dunbar-Nelson's diary is one of her most significant writings, a literary document that may be her penultimately enduring one. She expressed a prescient knowledge of its worth when she wrote in it on September 21, 1928: "Put in most of the day at the office making up my diary. Seemed an awful thing to do just to spend that time, but my diary is going to be a valuable thing one of these days." This diary is only the second book-length one available by an Afro-American woman.[114] Because of Dunbar-Nelson's sophisticated literary background, she was familiar with the form and traditions of English diary-keeping, which somehow suited her needs. She used her journal as a place to vent her thoughts and emotions and disrobe her inner self. Clearly, it was important to her. She railed against it as a weight on her heart and could barely find the time that it required, but she managed to keep it up. The diary charts the contours of her life over the years that it covers, revealing in its style and type of entries her kaleidoscope of moods and activities.

The diary also presents Dunbar-Nelson's strongest and most distinctive voice. Three representative passages are illustrative:

Her physical description of President Harding—

> The president remained standing, partly facing Johnson, three quarters away from us. I watched his face closely. It was heavily impassive, as you would expect it to be. He is a trifle thinner than this time last year. I suppose playing golf has been better for his health than sitting on the porch at Marion receiving delegations. His complexion is changed. . . . It is no longer swarthily sallow, but swarthily ruddy, which makes him appear fairer. He still affects the short coat, which is rather surprising in such a big man, and I was really astonished at the size of his feet, for I did not get a chance to see them last year. His eyes, excessively little, are surrounded by firmer flesh than last year, but they still have that look of brilliant intelligence found in the eye of an elephant, with something of the same stubborn implacability. Remarkably small eyes. (September 30, 1921)

One evening on her rooftop—

> Here I sit on a pile of cushions on my roof, and all the lovely panorama of the eastern side of the city is spread before me. . . . It's much better to be out here on the roof with the white moon hanging in the opalescent twilight sky than down-stairs on the crowded front porch . . . It is clear and peaceful and true up here. Mama calls, and I invite her out. She could no more clamber thru that window than fly. (August 15, 1921)

A fit of ire—

> When I left Washington five months ago in August I vowed I'd not come back soon. When I leave this time, I'll stay away five years. Washington is a changed place to me since Bobbo came to live at the Wilsons. He nor they have neither social flair nor social contacts and my old friends have fallen away from me. It is humiliating. Bobbo feels that he has adequately entertained me and given me the proper setting when he has allowed me to sit around in that filthy pig pen he calls an office, and share his barren little room. Mrs. F. [Mrs. Wilson] when she has given me a greasy meal in her cluttered kitchen. Disgusting. And outside of Narka—no one invites me anywhere. So I am quite bitter when Bobbo gets snippy with me. (December 18, 1928)

Dunbar-Nelson was really her own best character. Some instinctive sense of this must have led her to dramatize her life in the diary. She had qualities of individuality and flamboyance comparable to Zora Neale Hurston. Hurston, however, made the world and what she wrote her stage. Dunbar-Nelson fully stars only in her diary.

Through spotlighting her, her private chronicle illuminates crucial concerns. Some of these—such as work, sexuality, writing, female supports— have already been discussed. A few other issues are notable. Money, for example, was a critical problem for Dunbar-Nelson, as it was for many others like her. Financial stresses for her and Robert were often acute. As a black woman writer, her economic foothold was perilous, and his position as a black man was far from the secure sufficiency that would have allowed her the luxury of leisure or a carefree mind. Therefore Dunbar-Nelson's so-called middle-class position was based more on breeding, education, culture, looks, and manners than on money. She resorted to such stratagems as pawning her rings and earrings to pay the water bill, and borrowing cash from a disreputable loan shark to survive after she lost her American Inter-Racial Peace Committee secretaryship. Her aristocratic bearing also obscured the fact that she was a genuine, down-to-earth person, who, when she allowed herself, enjoyed all types of activities and people, such as drinking black-market Italian wine and playing cards with her "rough-necky" friends.

Health is another area that generally remains hidden. However, in a daily record, it would receive proportionate attention. Though she seemed physically robust, loved to cook and eat, and operated at a high energy level, Dunbar-Nelson was beset by a host of ailments ranging from hypertension and indigestion to "fatigue, blues and leucorrhea." Much too often, she was, as she put it, "profoundly in the D's—discouraged, depressed, disheartened, disgusted" (August 2, 1930). Qualities that enabled her to survive were her strength of mind, spirituality, and psychic power.

Viewed as literature, Dunbar-Nelson's diary is not like the self-consciously and laboriously written documents of Virginia Woolf and Anaïs Nin. Kept in the ordinary way, it has the expected virtues (spontaneity, daily disclosure, etc.) and limitations (flatness, repetition, loose writing, etc.) of the prototypical—not to say classic—diary form. Even though she never regarded the journal as a vehicle for creative literary expression, its style has interest, merit, and tonal variety. However, in terms of its posthumous value, the diary (like her journalism) was an unfortunate genre in which to pour so much time and effort. Such noncanonical forms are not highly prized, and neither are the many women who write in them.

For most Harlem Renaissance figures—Dunbar-Nelson included—the 1930s was a waning period. There were still some small recognitions. For example, when the James Weldon Johnson Dinner Committee was planning its appreciation fête, Chairman Arthur Spingarn wrote her "to ask the honor of using your name as one of the General Committee under whose auspices the invitations may be issued."[115] She continued to have the satisfaction of being treated with respect and camaraderie by some important colleagues. She had been corresponding with writer George S. Schuyler about a newspaper that he proposed to establish. On May 22, 1930, he wrote her to say that there was nothing definite regarding the "still non-existent newspaper," but "do come by to see us while you are in Gotham by all means . . . that isn't the only subject under the sun that intelligent people can discuss."

However, at this point, Dunbar-Nelson could not be purely interested in intellectual chat. Money had become a desparate problem. She was casting about for employment and trying to generate income-producing schemes. For instance, in 1931 she devised a series of lectures called "Romances of the Negro in American History" and even printed a glossy publicity brochure. Lester A. Walton, a newspaperman and impresario with whom she wanted to work, pronounced her "a good drawing card" and the idea "an excellent vehicle to carry you to financial and artistic success." But in his April 29, 1931, letter, he regretted that it was too late to begin booking a summer tour. Furthermore, her past accomplishments and reputation were not materially aiding her on any other fronts.

To make matters worse, her attempts at writing and publication were ill conceived. The most blatant example is a horrible 8400-word story entitled "No Sacrifice," Dunbar-Nelson's poor imitation of a confessional pulp romance. Interestingly, it is a deracialized and faintly sensationalized version of her relationship with Paul Dunbar. In an almost totally expository style, the heroine Aline traces the ups-and-downs, downs-and-ups of her marriage, separation, and reconciliation with Gerald Kennedy, famous poet and novelist. She begins:

> Stories usually end with the marriage, the chime of the wedding bells, and the "and so they lived happily ever after." Mine begins with the wedding, or rather the engagement. I had met Gerald in a rather romantic fashion. He saw my picture in an amateur magazine, which published some of my verses, and a brief biographical sketch. He wrote me in my southern home, and I was thrilled to the very center of my being when the letter came. . . . That he would condescend to notice the amateurish out-pourings of a little small-town southern school-girl seemed incredible. I answered his letter, and a correspondence grew up, more or less clandestine. My mother had old-fashioned ideas about correspondence with strange men, and I did not take her entirely into my confidence as to the number and length of our letters. Nor of the ardent verses which he sent me—and afterwards sold to magazines, for Gerald was a poet as well as a novelist.

At the melodramatic conclusion, when Aline renounces a fortune to nurse Gerald, who has been reduced to attempted suicide by drink, debauchery, and sickness, she pronounces her action "No sacrifice, darling, but glorious happiness": "And the glory of the sunset covered us as our lips touched in a holy communion."

The fact that Dunbar-Nelson harks back thirty years to her ill-fated relationship with Paul (whom she scarcely mentioned otherwise) for elements of this fictional romance says more about her artistic pragmatism than it does about the mellowness of her heart. Also, her handling of personal reality is again reminiscent of what Patricia Beer notes about nineteenth-century women novelists in England: that their writing "reveals a network of discrepancies . . . between what the novelists thought in real life and the views they set forth in their novels; between what they accepted for themselves and what they accepted for their heroines."[116] Even in work that Dunbar-Nelson took much more seriously than this cynically written story, one sees her operating in this way. Aline would give up the world—and herself—for love; but Alice never would.

Dunbar-Nelson sent the story to be professionally critiqued. On December 3, 1930, she writes in her diary: "A big envelope from Lichtnauer dismayed me this a.m. Returned "No Sacrifice" with four pages of criticism. I paid $8.00 for the worst panning I ever got. I can't write—no use trying. Can't even do a 'True Story.' No money this a.m. . . . " The abrupt juxtaposition of not being able to write this True Story and "no money" suggests that financial exigency had prompted her to make the attempt. Dunbar-Nelson should also have been demoralized at being treated as a "new writer" and "unknown" by August Lenniger, a literary agent to whom she submitted two of her short short stories in early 1931.[117] But she herself invited the indignity. Finally, beginning in June 1930, she wrote 1000, 1300, 1700 words per day, producing a satirical novel called "Uplift," which was so unsatisfactory that she allowed it to die a natural death early in 1931.

Dunbar-Nelson had also tried her hand at pseudonymous writing and publication. An early instance is her poem "April Is on the Way," which won honorable mention in the 1927 *Opportunity* contest under the name "Karen Ellison."[118] This use of pen names by the coterie of Renaissance writers has been viewed as a sign of the deterioration of the period. Later, she more understandably adopted a pseudonym for a highly revealing personal essay, "Brass Ankles Speaks," which she seems to have written sometime early in 1929. In the current hubbub about race, a Brass Ankles raises her voice:

> It seems but fair and just now for some of the neglected light-skinned colored people, who have not "passed" to rise and speak a word in self-defense. I am of the latter class, what E. C. Adams in "Nigger to Nigger" immortalizes in the poem, "Brass Ankles." White enough to pass for white, but with a darker family background, a real love for the mother race, and no desire to be numbered among the white race.

From a miserable southern childhood, when she was tormented and ostracized by the darker children in school as a "Light nigger, with straight hair," she moved north to college, where she came "up against a dead wall of hate and prejudice and misunderstanding" for the same reason. Even her good friends laugh at her when she says that she has nevertheless not been able to develop a "color sense":

> . . . but there is always a barrier, a veil—nay, rather a vitrified glass wall, which I can neither break down, batter down, nor pierce. I have to see dear

friends turn from a talk with me, to exchange a glance of comprehension and understanding one with another which I, nor anyone of my complexion, can ever hope to share.

At her first teaching job, she and the other "half white" teachers are dogged by "spite" and "unreasoning prejudice":

But when we began going about together and spending our time in each other's society, a howl went up. We were organizing a "blue vein" society. We were mistresses of white men. We were Lesbians. We hated black folk and plotted against them. As a matter of fact, we had no other recourse but to cling together.

Thus, her whole life has been spent between the Scylla and Charybdis of intra- and interracial hell.

Many of the references and anecdotes in this autobiographical piece are recognizably Dunbar-Nelson's own. It seems that she is saying here what she would not express in any other written form, for as the essay noted, "To complain would be only to bring upon themselves another storm of abuse and fury." The ten-page typescript is signed Adele Morris at the South Twelfth Street address of the Friends Service Committee. Dunbar-Nelson sent what must have been this work to *Plain Talk* magazine. The editor, G. D. Eaton, replied on April 4, 1929:

Dear Miss Nelson:
I like this piece very much, but I don't want to run it anonymously. Yet I realize the danger to you if you put your name under the title.

Five days later, he writes to say that he also objects to running it pseudonymously: "After all, your document is a personal one, and that is the more reason it should carry your own name." But Dunbar-Nelson would never appear so naked in public print. "Brass Ankles Speaks" remained another unsuccessful attempt at publication. While working in Philadelphia she also experimented with urban description under the name "Al Dane" in a brief piece, "By Paths in the Quaker City."

Generally, during 1930 and 1931, Dunbar-Nelson weathered a personal slump as acute as the general depression that gripped the country. Yet she managed to end her 1931 diary hoping on New Year's Eve "for prosperity for all, and happiness distributed everywhere."

Snapshot (July 1934): A glitteringly bejewelled Mrs. Robert J. Nelson is "among the Philadelphians who went to New York to attend the first performance of the Aeolian Opera Company." The previous fall-winter she had presented several artists at "a series of Sunday evening parties at her home." Snapshot (October 1934): Derby-hatted and spectacled, Dunbar-Nelson stands with five distinguished-looking black gentlemen, her dark, "dress for success" outfit blending evenly with their ties and three-piece suits. The group addressed a preelection "rally held in the courthouse by the Harrisburg Colored Republican Club."[119]

Dunbar-Nelson is now "living life." In January 1932 her husband Robert had finally been appointed to the Pennsylvania State Athletic Commission by Governor Gifford Pinchot. A just reward for dedicated political labor, it was their long-awaited salvation from precariousness to prosperity. As one of their friends indelicately put it, they are now "in the money."[120] Dunbar-Nelson has her own fancy personalized stationery and her own comfortable, well-appointed home, about which the same friend noted: "You are to be especially complimented for the marvelous harmony portrayed in the fittings and furnishings in your wonderful home." When she invites Arthur Schomburg to speak before the Philadelphia chapter of the Association for the Study of Negro Life and History, she brightly tells him, "I'll pick you up in a plane and deposit you on my front porch."[121] In addition to the association, she now belongs to the West Philadelphia Charity Bridge Club, the Mercy Hospital Service Club, and the Sophisticates and Board of Trustees of the Douglass Hospital. In January 1934 she serves on a committee to distribute relief among unemployed Philadelphia blacks.

Playing the role of philanthropic society matron did not totally occupy her. True to her activist history, she spoke at a mass demonstration protesting the unjust sentencing of the "Scottsboro Boys." Under a subheading "Thank God," the April 22, 1933, Philadelphia *Afro-American* reported:

> "Thank God for the Scottsboro case," said Mrs. Alice Dunbar Nelson, one of the speakers at the meeting, "because it has apparently aroused the Negroes. I'm glad that something has happened that has brought all Negroes, regardless of denominational or political views together here."

More partisanly, she delivered an October 18, 1934, campaign speech, "Point of View of Women," in which she addressed women about escalating food prices and whacked the New Deal policies. In the literary area, she gave reviews to her Pierian Book Club; and it was during these final three years of her life that she wrote her twilight novel about Edwina Kruse ("This Lofty Oak"), discussed earlier. The last available work she saw in print was a small, homiletic piece entitled "Try Golden Rule Next," which appeared in the June 1, 1935, New York *Amsterdam News.*

On September 18, 1935, she died of heart trouble in the University of Pennsylvania hospital. In her sixty years, she had been busy enough and successful enough at her business to make three distinguished lifetimes. Not the least of these is her work as an earlier black woman writer whose important place in the Afro-American female literary tradition is only now becoming clear. A creditable romantic poet, an interesting—if uneven— short fictionist, an essayist and speech writer, a renowned journalist, and a marvelous diarist, her legacy is large.

Rhapsodizing about the sea, which she loved, in her July 19, 1929, diary, Dunbar-Nelson wrote:

> But the water! I came here for it. Weeks I dreamed of it. Here it is. No inconvenience too great for the love of it—even these hot days when it was calm as a mill pond and none too clean—I could wait. Lovely, luxurious, voluptuous water. Howe was right when he spoke of drowning as "the gentlest death the gods gave to man." To float on and on and on into sweet oblivion. What a temptation.

However, her fate was a "massive mahogany casket" banked with dahlias and roses (no violets),[122] then cremation in Wilmington because no Philadelphia establishment would perform that service for a black person. But her final wish was honored by the waters of the Delaware River when her husband scattered her ashes to "the four winds, either over land or sea."

CHAPTER III

Angelina Weld Grimké (1880–1958)

Unlike what is true of Alice Dunbar-Nelson and Georgia Douglas Johnson, no mystery surrounds the birth and parentage of Angelina Weld Grimké, although she too comes from a heritage of mixed blood. Because of her name, she is likely to be confused with her famous white abolitionist-feminist aunt, Angelina Grimké Weld. The relationship between them is yet another example of the web of race and miscegenation that tangles so much United States family history. Grimké herself was well informed about her interesting background and indeed recounts it in a biographical sketch of her father, Archibald Henry Grimké, which she wrote in 1925.[1]

Grimké begins with a striking "pen picture" of her paternal grandmother, Nancy Weston Grimké, who "was a slave by birth, but a most remarkable woman":

> I knew her for the only time, the last year of her life (she lived to be eighty four) and though I was a child, then, I can remember her perfectly. She spent her days, sitting in a large rattan rocker in her sunny room on the second floor back of my uncle's Washington home. She moved about seldom and then with the greatest effort, leaning on a cane; but there was something unconquerable, indomitable in that bent, gaunt body and in that clean-cut, eagle-like face. If she yielded to age it was only inch by inch. Her keen old eyes could flash and I never heard her speak in uncertain tones. . . . Some-time, somewhere, that spirit must have lived in the body of a great queen or an empress. How else explain her? But the most beautiful thing about her was her motherly love.

Angelina Weld Grimké as a young woman. (Photo courtesy of the Moorland-Spingarn Research Center.)

Angelina Weld Grimké in her middle years. (Photo courtesy of the Moorland-Spingarn Research Center.)

Before Emancipation, this vital woman had lived on a plantation, "Cane-acre," thirteen miles outside of Charleston, South Carolina, and borne three sons for the master, Henry Grimké, a member of the Charleston aristocracy. The eldest of these, Archibald, became Angelina's father.

While Archibald was a student at Lincoln University, Pennsylvania, he and his brother Francis attracted the notice of Sarah M. Grimké and Angelina Grimké Weld, the two Grimké sisters from South Carolina who could not tolerate conditions in the South and came north to fight for abolition and women's rights. Living in Boston, they saw an article in the *Anti-Slavery Standard* that mentioned the remarkable achievement of the two young men. According to Grimké, their surname "immediately riveted" Angelina's attention:

> A correspondence began between her and the two boys and, in their junior year [1868–69], accompanied by her son, Stuart, she came to visit them. She now did a thing that seems well nigh unbelievable. Becoming convinced that these boys were her brother's children, she acknowledged them as her nephews!

Thus began an intimate association between them. When the boys graduated, they visited the sisters in Hyde Park, Massachusetts, and later, after he had finished Harvard Law School in 1874, Archibald set up practice in Boston. In 1879, he married Sarah E. Stanley, described by the Boston *Sunday Globe* in 1894 as "a white woman who belonged to one of the best known families in this city."[2] That same year, Aunt Angelina died, and when Archibald and Sarah's daughter was born the next year on February 27, they named her Angelina Weld in memory of her great aunt. Near the end of her life, Grimké "spoke with much pleasure of being Angelina's namesake."[3]

Only one biographical area, the situation with her mother, presents something of a puzzle. Since Grimké was reared by her father, it is clear that the two parents separated. In 1887–88, Grimké received nice, affectionate letters written by her mother and the Stanley grandparents from Detroit. The correspondence with her mother apparently continued, for in 1897 Angelina's father replied to her: "No, dear child, I don't object to your writing to her [her mother] if she write to you first. In that case I should be very sorry if you failed to answer her letter. I do not wish you ever to forget that she is your mother and your duty to her as her child."[4]

Her mother's sister, Emma Austin Tolles, seems to have been even more genuinely concerned that Grimké would not forget her mother. She spoke freely to Angelina about her and even mentioned ways that the two of them were alike—for example, their having the same physical measurements.[5] Tolles wrote one of her most explicit letters to Grimké on October 1, 1898, about five weeks after Sarah Stanley had died. She announced her passing, and then said of her:

> She was hoping to see you once more and was trying so hard to make a little home to which you could come and visit.
>
> She never ceased to love you as dearly as ever and it was a great trial to her to have you go away from her . . . but it was the only thing to do.
>
> I have had several letters from the people who took care of her. She had every thing done that could be done. . . .

Tolles called her sister Sarah "one of the most wonderful souls that ever came to this planet," and referred to the world as "a scorching fire through which she has passed." She ends her remembrances with:

> Her book—"The Light of Egypt" is the most wonderful book of modern times though she says it will be one hundred years before the world will recognize it. She nearly lost her life in writing it but her soul never flinched from a duty. She had two or three friends who have stood by her from first to last, who have considered it a privilege to do so.

Though Angelina said she was accustomed to not having a mother, she thought of her, recalling as late as August 25, 1914, that this was the sixteenth anniversary of her mother's death.[6] It is psychologically interesting that in her literary works, motherhood is a major theme, and all of her girls have loving mothers or mother surrogates.

Biographically speaking, Grimké attracts attention because of her colorful family background and life, and what they teach about the American black experience of the late nineteenth and early twentieth centuries, especially of black women, of cultured, comfortable blacks, and of those whose family trees had more white than black roots. From early childhood Angelina was reared by her father in the liberal, aristocratic society of old Boston. Through his aunts, Archibald had come to know outstanding people like Lucy Stone, Judge Sewell, William Lloyd Garrison, Charles Sumner, Wendell Phillips, Elizabeth Peabody, Lewis Hayden, Frederick Douglass, and many more. Angelina grew up in an environment with some of these same people and, of course, the Welds, the family of Angelina's husband, Theodore D. She "was frequently cared for in the Weld home," and when she was thirteen years old, wrote a poem "To Theodore D.

Weld—On His 90th Birthday," which appeared in the *Norfolk County Gazette*.⁷ Thus she lived in an atmosphere of religious, feminist, political, and racial liberalism.

Undoubtedly, this background influenced the direction of her talent. Its gentility encouraged her to concentrate on the "talented tenth" and to produce work that was correct, conservative, and highbrow, and poetry that was conventionally "poetic." To an undeterminable extent, her background also probably contributed to a kind of personal unhappiness that impelled her toward themes of dejection and loss. Angelina also felt the psychological pressure of having to live up to family name and standards, exaggerated by the "we must prove ourselves" syndrome that operated among educated blacks. In a photograph taken of her class at Fairmount School, Hyde Park, when she was ten years old, she stands unobtrusively in the middle of the picture—the only black child, a tiny, East Indian-looking girl with large, sad eyes.⁸ When her father was in Santo Domingo from 1894 to 1898 as United States consul, practically every letter he wrote her was filled with exhortations to be good, study hard, be a lady, make him proud of her, and so on.⁹ But most importantly, Grimké's heritage of social activism helps account for the propagandistic nature of her fiction and drama.

This direction becomes evident very early, for, like Alice Dunbar-Nelson, she began writing as a young girl. Three of her juvenile short fictions are "Black Is, As Black Does," a moral dream-tale about a lynched black man who finds favor with God while a self-righteous white man is damned; "The Revery of a Violin," a pathetic little sketch about a formerly happy violin-playing woman who is now sunk into poverty and misery; and "Evangaline, A Novel." She also wrote at least one story that is clearly about white characters, "The Laughing Hand." It concerns the blighted love affair of Ellen Erroll, age thirty-five, and Phil, an artist who has his face mutilated by cancer. "Black Is, As Black Does" was published in *The Colored American Magazine* in 1900.¹⁰ Around this same time, she also attempted to place another work about which her father wrote in a June 12, 1899, letter to her: "I am indeed sorry that Miss Blackwell considered your story not available for the *Woman's Journal*." The rest of these pieces exist only in manuscript as do, of course, the dozen or so stories that she left unfinished—"Blind Alley," which she may have planned as a novel; "The Handicapped," a "race" story; and "The Ear," among others.

This youthful fiction notwithstanding, Grimké's initial writing and publication were in verse. The earliest poetry in her scrapbooks dates back to

February 15, 1891, a few days before her eleventh birthday. Her first published poem appeared in the Hyde Park, Massachusetts, Norfolk *County Gazette* on May 27, 1893. It was a fourteen-stanza Memorial Day tribute to a forgotten soldier called "The Grave in the Corner." The next year on July 22, the Boston *Sunday Globe* printed her "Street Echoes," a social protest poem:

> And I say can this be right,
> The poor in darkness, the rich in light?
> Health and joy, the rich man's pride,
> Mis'ry e'er on poverty's side.

Adults encouraged her in her verse making. After reading "Nana's" (her lifelong nickname)[11] "Grave in the Corner," Louise I. Guiney, who was connected with the *Gazette*, wrote Mr. Grimké: "I should think, without rashness, that the child shows promise, and is on the right track. This little poem sounds as if it came from a young mind which had fed on literature, and not merely on books promiscously [sic] chosen."[12]

Her poetry during this time is typical juvenile verse. The pieces have titles like "A February Day," "The Last Grasshopper," "Three Angels," "The Blooming Flowers," "Moonlight on the St. John," and "Rest." They are rhymed and metered and display the expected features and faults of juvenile poetry—occasional metrical roughness, a precocious sensibility, imitative or romantic themes, and standard poetic diction—for example, from "Rest":

> All alone she lay unheeded
> With her sunny golden hair
> And a smile it lighted up
> Her face so wan and fair.

Grimké continued to write throughout her school years. The period between 1900 and 1902, immediately before she began teaching in Washington, D.C., was particularly fruitful. Her poems began appearing in *The Boston Transcript*, still a newspaper but one with a national circulation and reputation. Most of these were innocuous lyrics about such subjects as the coming of spring, the death of a "fair enchantress" named Phyllis, and the aspirations and struggles of the individual soul.[13] However, she once submitted a poem called "Beware Lest He Awakes" about a strong but quiescent black man who would one day erupt into violence. The editor, Charles S. Hunt, rejected it in a January 2, 1902, note of explanation:

I am sorry to send this back, but it is not from lack of literary quality. So far as that is concerned it is all right, and the indignant spirit in which it is written is all right. But it is the implied threat of a bloody rising on the part of the negro. God knows the negro has suffered enough in the past to warrant a good deal. But the worst of his evil days are over. . . . Fifty years ago your poem would have had an excuse for being, but those days are past.

Perhaps criticism of this sort may have discouraged Grimké from attempting militant—even overtly racial—poems. However, this particular poem was accepted by *The Pilot* and published in its May 10, 1902, issue. Another one of her early poems called "Then And Now" also has obvious racial reference. It begins:

> They knew, those gone, bent backs, the lash's cut
> On crimsoning and shudd'ring flesh, and thirst
> And hunger and all weariness . . . [14]

During this period, Grimké tried to write dialect poetry à la Paul Laurence Dunbar (who was then at the height of his fame), which she never published. Two of these jingles she titled "Lil' Gal" and "Ma [My] Cayoline." The first stanza of "Lil' Gal" (February 4, 1902) reads:

> Lil' Gal! Lil' Gal!
> Don' you keep on shakin' so!
> Dere! Dere! Don' you cry no mo'!
> Hyars a place to res' you head
> And to hide does eyes so red
> Don' you neber neber fear
> When you knows dat I am near
> Lil' Gal!

"Ma Cayoline" (March 22, 1902) begins:

> Some gals am mighty sassy
> An' some am mighty pert
> An some Oh Lawd a Massy!
> Seems lak dese made to flirt.

But, despite the varied excellence of other girls, the speaker concludes that "Fo eyes dat spark and shine / An ways ez sweet ez honey / Gib me ma Cayoline."

Here Grimké is obviously trying her hand at a then almost obligatory type of black poetry. But she had no innate affinity for it and, given her background, was ill equipped to succeed. Dunbar-Nelson also attempted dialect during these same years, when she was married to Paul. She wrote an unpublished comic dialect tale, "The Delegate from Adamsboro," about a country bumpkin with political pretensions who goes to Washington, D.C., has his illusions shattered, and then comes back to his good wife's steaming cornbread.[15] But this story is not even as effective as Grimké's dialect verse. That women as removed as Dunbar-Nelson and Grimké from a dialect milieu essayed literature in this form further attests to the popularity of the genre. Furthermore, in its most derivative manifestations, dialect work connoted a masculine persona and tone—notwithstanding the excellent female effects achieved by an original poet like Frances Watkins Harper.

Throughout this period, Grimké's father, whom she always apprised of her writing activities and sent copies of her poems, cheered her on—as in this letter of October 22, 1905:

> Your verses, my dear, are real poetry. They have . . . "the authentic fire." I like them much. I see no diminution of your ability to make real poetry. All you have to do is hold on in the course in which you are now sailing with such favoring winds and you will be sure to arrive at your destination. Do not let the reception or rejection of your verses by the magazines discourage you in the least.

In 1909, she received the grandest of her early recognitions, also in the *Transcript*. "The Listener" column for October 27 recalled "the singularly poignant note" of her elegiac poetry and then printed her "El Beso," calling it "as perfect as an antique gem in its genre," and concluding the notice with the statement that "any of the greater poets might have been proud to add such a flower to the modern English anthology." "El Beso," one of her better earlier poems, shows her approaching the style and virtues of her finest poetry:

> Twilight—and you,
> Quiet—the stars;
> Snare of the shine of your teeth,
> Your provocative laughter,
> The gloom of your hair;
> Lure of you, eye and lip,
> Yearning, yearning,
> Languor, surrender;
>   Your mouth
> And madness, madness
> Tremulous, breathless, flaming,
> The space of a sigh;

> Then awaking—remembrance,
> Pain, regret—your sobbing;
> And again quiet—the stars,
> Twilight—and you.[16]

Answering a letter of appreciation from her on November 1, 1909, E. H. Clement of the *Transcript* expanded on the column's praise: "I do really believe you are possessed of a peculiar & wonderful gift & shall always be interested to see it develop & fructify. Do send me more of your work as it comes to you—I would not force it though. There is plenty of time for you & it." Apparently, though, she also had her detractors. In a very interesting letter written on November 12, Mr. Grimké, who was himself ebullient about her success, gives his candid assessment of his daughter's black critics and summarizes some additional favorable reaction to "The Listener" article:

> [The] colored gentry . . . are not worth bothering your head about. For they are for the most part [?] eaten up with envy and jealousy of one another. . . . All the same your verses are appreciated as witness the Sunday Globe which I sent you and which had copied El Beso. Today Lottie Lampson is to read your verses and the Transcript's comments to the Book Lovers. . . . Mrs. T. [Mrs. Molly Terrell ?] writes from Washington that El Beso is a gem and hopes to see your verses in Book form at no very distant day. Prof. [?] writes that the Transcript has given just enough of your poetry to give a taste for more and Prof. Miller [Kelly Miller, Howard University Dean] expresses his pleasure at the "fine [?]." And last but not least in praise of it and you comes Roscoe Bruce [Superintendent in charge of Washington, D.C., Negro schools] who says: "Your daughter is one of those few teachers who can and do actually write English as well as teach it. She has rare and high gifts of imagination and passion. I think Miss Grimké ought to develop these gifts to the fullest extent by the constant exercise of them."

As these letters suggest, Grimké's father and his opinions meant a great deal to her. She emphatically said so in her 1912 diary:

> My father . . . is so much a part of me he is so all and all so absolutely necessary that I am taking him I find as a matter of course. This is wrong. I wonder, though, whether when some people are as one there may not be some little excuse. This I know now and I have always known it and felt it. I have no desire absolutely for life without him.

It seems that her father was, in a strange way, the motivation for much of what she achieved. He was a very exacting, though obviously lovable, parent and at first was not proud of his daughter. On February 22, 1899, he wrote her a crucial letter, in which he confessed:

> I do hope and pray my dear that I shall yet see you entirely different from what you are that I could truly say that you are a comfort to your fond old papa. But I cannot say it, and I now begin to fear that I shall never be able to say so truthfully, for all you care about is self, and all the things which interest you in life are full of self, self, self. Although a woman you neglect the good, and earnest, and useful things of life, and are given up to thoughtlessness, pleasure, idleness, allowing all the golden opportunities for self-improvement, for fitting yourself for a life of usefulness to slip away. I supposed once that you had talents for intellectual pursuits, but I think so no longer. I should be but too glad if you did anything well, if you care to do anything well, but I know that you do not.

Henceforward, Angelina began to send him copies of poems and stories that she was writing. In a November 5, 1900, letter to him, she voices a reason why: "Well, I must close now as I am anxious to mail all this stuff to you, if only to prove to you that I really did try to do something."[17] Apparently she resumed her writing as one means of redeeming herself in her father's eyes. Yet her extreme emotional dependence on him probably contributed to psychological problems that became critical later in her life.

Grimké's writing was aided by sound education of a type that was not uncommon for an advantaged black woman of her times. In addition to the resources that her father could provide, her schooling was assisted by Theodore Weld, who, in his will, "assigned a bequest to 'my nephew,' Archibald Grimké, for the education" of Angelina.[18] She attended the grammar schools of Hyde Park, Massachusetts, and Washington, D.C. (1887–94), then received her secondary education (1895–98) at the Carleton Academy, Northfield, Minnesota; Cushing Academy, Ashburnham, Massachusetts; and the Girls' Latin School, Boston. At these places, she was probably the only black student (or one of a very few). Certainly she was the only black child during some of her grammar years in Hyde Park. It is likely that this was also the case at these excellent white secondary schools. And later, at Harvard, the same circumstances prevailed, for, on July 10, 1909, she wrote to her father, "I am virtually the only one again in my class this year, although there have been visitors."[19]

She earned good grades, maintaining averages in the high eighties and low nineties (except for one "D," which she received in Bible Study at Carleton). Subsequently, she attended the Boston Normal School of Gymnastics (which later became the Department of Hygiene of Wellesley College), from which she received a degree in 1902. Thus far, her choice of a college course is the one unexpected detail. Grimké may have selected it partially because her mother was interested in physical culture[20] and partially because she did not choose to exert herself in any other field. From 1904 to 1910 she took summer courses at Harvard, this time in English, a more likely field. They included "Anglo-Saxon," "English Poets of the Romantic Period," and "18th Century English Literature" with Henry Milner Rideout. In them, she performed passably well.

Again, not surprisingly, Grimké took up a career as a teacher. She began in physical education at the Armstrong Manual Training School in Washington, D.C., in 1902, but changed to English. This precipitated a mild scandal that surrounded her tenure in the Washington, D.C., schools. Apparently, she was not happy at Armstrong and finally requested a transfer to the M Street (later named the Dunbar) High School. Much correspondence and influence mongering surrounded this 1907 move. As early as October 6, 1905, Grimké's father wrote her that he was "sorry that things at the school continue in such an unsatisfactory state. But knowing that fellow who is at the head of it as we do, a change cannot be expected to take place just yet." He advises her to do her work well and not let on when she is hurt or humiliated, and then continues: "But if things at the Armstrong become intolerable to your sensitive nature go to Mrs. [? Probably Anna J. Cooper, M Street principal] and ask her to transfer you to the M Street High School. Don't mention the fact to her that I suggested this to you however." Later on, he himself visited Superintendent Roscoe Bruce.

At Armstrong, the principal, Dr. W. B. Evans, who did not think well of her work, had given her poor evaluations, averring that she had been hired to teach physical education but was, through covert maneuvering, changed to English. He said further that she had an "unfortunate temperament" and was "unfitted by attitude to teach in a school of this kind" since she personally did not like industrial education. Though she was not granted a raise and had been slated for termination, she was hired at M Street. The situation troubled her, but her father enjoined her not to worry because his enemies were using her to vex him.[21] After the transfer, her ratings markedly improved, indicating, among other things, that she probably was better suited to teach in an academic rather than a trade school. There, she gave her composition classes topics like "My First Love," "On Being Colored," and "Vanity."

Overall, these first thirty years of Grimké's life seem to be a long period of adolescence, both personally and artistically. Coming from a cultured, biracial background (and a "broken home"), which was economically stable but emotionally disquieting, she acquired habits of shyness, diffidence, and dependency (especially upon her classically patriarchal father). Encouraged to achieve, she began developing herself as a writer. Most of what she produced was juvenile apprentice work, but it—especially the poetry—shows promise and also indicates her future themes.

ii

After the success of her 1909 poem "El Beso," Grimké received even more widespread attention for *Rachel,* a problem play that was first staged in 1916 and published in 1920. She has moved from poetry and fiction to drama, a genre that will claim a considerable amount of her literary effort. *Rachel* is Grimké's best-known work. It is also her most prominent piece of literary propaganda. In fact, the play program advertised: "This is the first attempt to use the stage for race propaganda in order to enlighten the American people relative to the lamentable condition of ten million of colored citizens in this free Republic."[22]

Grimké intended to achieve this enlightenment by showing how American racial prejudice blighted the lives of a good, upstanding, attractive black family. The action centers on Mrs. Loving, a middle-aged widow living in "a northern city" during "the first decade of the Twentieth Century," and her teenaged children, a son Tom and daughter Rachel.[23] On the day that the play begins, Mrs. Loving tells them, after ten years of silence, that it is the anniversary of their father's and stepbrother's lynchings down south because of the father's fierce denunciation of the hanging of an innocent black man. Four years later, Rachel and Tom have met additional prejudice in their own lives. He, an electrical engineer, cannot find a suitable job. She, a graduate in Domestic Science, can secure no position teaching school. In addition to this, Rachel learns of the evils suffered even by little black children in a racist society. After her seven-year-old adopted son comes home traumatized by being called a "nigger" and having stones hurled at him by some older white boys, she renounces motherhood and sends away her sweetheart John—despite the fact that she has been portrayed throughout as a young woman born to have and nurture children.

In an article about her drama, Grimké explained the motivation behind this story: "Now the purpose was to show how a refined, sensitive, highly-strung girl, a dreamer and an idealist, the strongest instinct in whose nature is a love for children and a desire some day to be a mother herself—how this girl would react to this force [racial prejudice]."[24] Grimké's choice of this central plot was dictated by her desire to appeal to white women, whom she wished to awaken from their conservatism: "My belief was, then, that . . . if their hearts could be reached even if only a little, then, perhaps, instead of being active or passive enemies, they might become, at least, less inimical and possibly friendly."[25] This was idealism. In 1917 she had asked one of her friends, another black woman, what she thought of "the attitude of the white mothers as regards the race question."[26]

Her secondary purpose was to counter the stereotype of "the darkey" by presenting "the best type of colored people," whom she describes in this way:

> Certainly colored people are living in homes that are clean, well-kept with many evidences of taste and refinement about them. They are many of them well educated, cultivated and cultured; they are well-mannered and, in many instances, more moral than the whites; they love beauty; they have ideals and ambitions, and they do not talk—this educated type—in the Negro dialect. All the joys and sorrows and emotions the white people feel they feel; their feelings are as sensitive; they can be hurt as easily; they are as proud.[27]

The degree to which Grimké's play achieved her purposes cannot, of course, be measured. However, according to Arthur P. Davis, *Rachel* was "the first successful stage drama to be written by a Negro."[28] Based on the effort that Grimké put into it, the play should have been a success. She started it at least as early as 1914 (and possibly before then), for she was circulating it in manuscript for criticism in January 1915. The drama began with the title *The Pervert*, then became *Blessed Are the Barren*, and proceeded through many revisions and rewritings to eventually emerge as *Rachel*. In all but the final version, Rachel is called Janet and this change of the heroine's name to suggest her biblical counterpart seems to have been a last-minute inspiration. As late as August 16, 1916 (after the play's Washington, D.C., premiere), she wrote from Massachusetts to her father in Washington about this change: "You can explain to Helen [the typist] (can't you?) about the change throughout the play of 'Janet' to 'Rachel.' That is the only change."[29] In keeping with Janet's rechristening, Grimké had deleted some phrases at the end of the drama that echoed her earlier title: " 'Blessed are the barren!'—Blessed are they.—'Then shall they say to the mountains—fall on us;—and to the hills—cover us.' " She also added an epigraph, taken from Matthew 2:18, which reads: "In Rama was there a voice heard, lamentation, and weeping, and great mourning, Rachel weeping for her children, and would not be comforted, because they are not."

The majority of Grimké's revisions involved cutting the manuscript. In most instances, too, she seems to have followed her own inclinations about her work, despite the fact that she solicited advice from other people. One such person was Dr. John G. Underhill, United States–Canadian representative for the Society of Spanish Authors, who gave her specific suggestions that she rejected. For example, Underhill thought that Mrs. Loving's indictment of herself before she tells Rachel and Tom how their father and brother died in Act I impeded the movement of the dialogue and broke its force. He even went so far as to rewrite the speeches,[30] but in the printed version, Mrs. Loving still procrastinates.

Apparently, *Rachel* was not presented many times as a stage play. It was first performed in Washington on March 3–4, 1916, under the auspices of the Drama Committee of the District of Columbia branch of the N.A.A.C.P., next at the Neighborhood Playhouse in New York City on April 26, 1917, and then in Cambridge, Massachusetts, on May 24 under the sponsorship of St. Bartholomew's Church. In all three instances, the actors were amateurs or semiprofessionals, the original company under the direction of Nathaniel Guy boasting the most talent (Guy himself, Zita Dyson, Rachel Guy). No other records of its performance have been found, although in 1924 the Colored Branch YMCA of New Castle, Pennsylvania, requested her permission to stage *Rachel* for publicity and fund-raising;[31] and one can assume that there were other less important amateur productions of the work. In 1919, there also seemed to be some talk of a professional staging. On August 25, Grimké wrote to her father: "That is certainly cheering news you gave me about Mrs. Henderson and 'Rachel.' George Gliss [?] is one of the leading American—or is he English?—actors. It would be wonderful if he could be made interested."[32]

For the most part, reaction to *Rachel* on stage appears to have been favorable. Naturally, Grimké's friends were enthusiastic and told her in the warmest, most personal terms how much her play had affected them. For instance, Meta Warrick Fuller, the famous sculptor, wrote her a letter the night after seeing the Cambridge performance. She quoted lines from the play and spoke movingly of her love for her own baby boy as a means of communicating to Grimké "how thoroughly you reached me." She said further: "There was so much that appealed to me most strongly for it was strong to the point of bitterness and to oppose its bitterness there was an underlying current of sweetness and delicacy—it was beautiful—terribly beautiful—all the more terrible because of its beauty."[33] Another acquaintance, Montgomery Gregory, assistant professor of public speaking at Howard University, expressed his "sincere appreciation of your artistic achievement in laying bare the real *soul* of our race and in depicting with cruel accuracy its daily agonies."[34] Reviewing the Washington, D.C., performance for the *Washington Post,* Ralph Graves noted its sincerity and flatteringly compared it to a Brieux play: "In the sincerity of 'Rachel' there is much the same note of pessimism which the great French dramatist, Brieux, has embodied in 'Blanchette' the drama in which the central figure, educated above her normal social station, finds herself in hopeless conflict with her family and her surroundings."[35] He concluded with a statement that is interesting for what it subtly reveals about Grave's own racial assumptions: " 'Rachel' is surcharged with danger if presented on the stage indiscriminately before audiences of subnormal powers of differentiation and analysis, but if published it would have a wide field of missionary usefulness."[36] The play's New York engagement also attracted "considerable comment."[37]

However, it required publishing *Rachel* to make it the consciousness-raising instrument that Grimké wished it to be. Even though she aimed her appeal at white women, not many of them could have seen the play. Maud Cuney Hare, the celebrated musicologist, who was also a member of the Cambridge audience, said that there "was a fine audience—a large one with at least fifty persons present," and mentioned that another viewer "wished a large white audience could see the play." She herself added: "But those present could not help but catch the story and the seed will grow."[38] Yet the number of whites at the performances, which took place in school auditoriums and a small art theater—albeit in large cities—could not have been great. Furthermore, one wonders just how vulnerable this segment of Grimké's audience was to her message. Again to quote Meta Fuller:

> . . . while it [the mixed audience] was sympathetic, I do not believe it arose to the high tention [*sic*] of the plot in every instance.
>
> Some of the finest points failed to "get across;" this was due not to the play nor to the actors but to that part of the audience which failed to look beneath the surface—I say in my humble judgment, so much the better for the play and for the actors.[39]

And at least one white woman told Grimké outright that she did not find Rachel's tragedy convincing. Writing to her on January 19, 1915, after reading the play, May Childs Nerney, secretary of the N.A.A.C.P., put it this way: "I have no doubt that many young colored women feel and act as Janet [Rachel] is depicted as doing—it is the great tragedy of the problem—but somehow your play doesn't convince me of this."

Like Georgia Douglas Johnson and many other black women writers both before and after her, Grimké resorted to self-subsidized publication for her drama. In a "Memorandum of Agreement" with the Cornhill Company dated August 14, 1919, she was to "assume as her share of the publishing risk" $300 and was to receive 25 free author copies, 50 percent of gross receipts up to 700 copies and 20 percent of gross receipts thereafter.[40] As a book, *Rachel* commanded considerably more attention. The most sensational criticism of the work seems to have been that it advocated genocide. It was this charge that prompted Grimké to explain her real purposes, for she begins her vindication by saying: "Since it has been understood that 'Rachel' preaches race suicide, I would emphasize that that was not my intention. To the contrary, the appeal is not primarily to the colored people, but to the whites."[41]

The other major criticism of the play was that Grimké had overdrawn—if not misrepresented—her characters' problems. The *Grinnell Review* (Iowa) wrote: "Exaggeration spoils this play. Had Miss Grimké's negroes been less shabby-genteel, their tragedy would have been more convincing."[42] Other reviews noted that the play was "pitched in a highly emotional key,"[43] that it was "morbid and overstrained,"[44] and that, despite instances to the contrary, it "pictures the negro's life as sad and his efforts to rise as unavailing."[45] Furthering this line of comment, the Wilmington, Delaware, *Every Evening* declared: "Many who are familiar with colored people en masse will hardly incline to sympathy with the severely drawn picture presented in this play, as it is too radically at variance with the evidence so largely in view in communities throughout the northern part of the country where the Negro population is numerous."[46] The Washington, D.C., *Star* carried this criticism of Grimké's material to its highest point, suggesting, in effect, that she should have written another play entirely:

> Perhaps another standpoint on the part of the author would have produced a more helpful drama. For instance, one that would cover the splendid half century of growth made by the colored race since its emancipation in the United States. Or possibly, one based on the progress of the individual, with that progress as his full compensation.[47]

Apparently, some reviewers found Grimké's subject matter unpalatable and preferred not having their attention directed to the deplorable conditions that the play indicts. The Grinnell critic admitted that "we are made to feel [the black race's tragedy] with sufficient force to be thoroughly uncomfortable."[48]

However, most of the nearly fifty reviews and notices published as of April 1921 were favorable. The bulk of these repeated *Rachel*'s subtitle, "A Play of Protest," observed that "all the characters are colored," and praised the author for vividly portraying "the black man's burden." The more sympathetic of them should have pleased Grimké since they indicated that her message had hit home. For example, the *Catholic World* printed: "As a protest against white prejudice it makes its mark, and its closing scene rises to the dignity of a masterly (and pathetic) climax. Miss Grimké has sustained her indictment and scored heavily."[49] The Buffalo, New York, *Courier* went even further: "There is a terrible tragic note throughout the three acts of this little play, which compels one to think, and if possible to lend aid to try and remove the prejudice against the colored race."[50] The longer articles recounted the plot, and a few critics even assessed the artistic merit of the work: "It is well written and full of pathos. . . . "[51] "It is a work of real literary value as well, and cannot help but win a place for itself among recent publications along things dramatic."[52] "As a piece of literature, the play is done with vigor and certainty; its dialogue is crisp; its tenderness and its pathos ring true."[53] H. G. Wells, who received a review copy of the book but published nothing about it, told Grimké in a personal note that her play was "a most moving one that has stirred me profoundly. I have long felt the intensity of the tragedy of the educated colored people."[54]

In more recent times, *Rachel* has not received much notice. In what is probably the harshest judgment of the play, Sterling Brown pronounces: "There is no conflict and little characterization; the propaganda depresses rather than stirs."[55] While a contemporary reader is likely to agree that the play is somewhat lacking in interest and that its propaganda is not uplifting, it probably succeeded in 1920—as it does now—because it is a novel and competent treatment of an important topic.

Like closet drama, *Rachel* reads better than it acts. There is not much action and its interest comes from discerning the characters' inner pressures and juxtaposing their situation with the social reality outside the play. Some of the speeches are long, and in Act III, Rachel tells Jimmy a bedtime fairy tale that runs to four pages. However, most of the lengthy deliveries are set propaganda speeches, as when Tom declaims:

> Today, we colored men and women, everywhere—are up against it. Every year, we are having a harder time of it. In the South, they make it as impossible as they can for us to get an education. We're hemmed in on all sides. Our one safeguard—the ballot—in most states, is taken away already, or is being taken away. Economically, in a few lines, we have a slight

show—but at what a cost! In the North, they make a pretence of liberality: they give us the ballot and a good education, and then—snuff us out. Each year, the problem just to live, gets more difficult to solve. How about these children—if we're fools enough to have any? (Act II, p. 49)

For a beginning playwright, Grimké evidences considerable skill in dramaturgy, a fact that Dr. Underhill, her critic, noted: "I may say, at the outset, that I understand that it is a first play, and though I have read many such, if that is the case it is the best that I have read."[56] Particularly notable is her handling of exposition, elapsed time, and pacing. She fills in the four years between Acts I and II efficiently and varies the mood and movement of her action by interspersing two songs and including lighter, domestic scenes among her weightier ones (though these "playful" interludes seem forced). Equally as commendable is her dialogue, which is natural and smooth-flowing—except for her occasional failure to use subject-verb contractions, her self-conscious incorporation of slang and colloquialisms, and her not knowing children well enough to make the little boy and his prattle realistic. In the matter of language, it is quite obvious that Grimké was being very, very careful to present her "best type of colored people." She even has them making Latin puns, a fact that says a great deal about her motives and her anticipated audience as well as reveals her years of study at the Boston Girls' Latin School.

The biggest faults today's reader is likely to find with the play are its sentimentality and characterization—especially in regard to Rachel. Even though one may be sympathetic toward Grimké's heroine and, of course, convinced of the truth of her message, Rachel still comes across as "extreme." Perhaps she is too sensitive, too good, too sweet—almost saccharine. She is also sentimental to the point of being melodramatic. Talking to her mother about little black children in Act I, she "buries her head in her mother's lap and sobs" and later "faints in her mother's arms." Her speech after she has sent John away, which concludes the play, is the best example. Its last half reads in part:

> And my little children! my little children! (The weeping [of Jimmy] ceases; pauses). I shall never—see—you—now. Your little, brown, beautiful bodies—I shall never see.— . . . Little children! No more need you come to me—weeping—weeping. You may be happy now—you are safe. Little weeping, voices, hush! hush! (The weeping begins again. To Jimmy, her whole soul in her voice) Jimmy! My little Jimmy! Honey! I'm coming—Ma Rachel loves you so. (Sobs and goes blindly, unsteadily to the rear doorway; she leans her head there one second against the door; and then

stumbles through and disappears. The light in the lamp flickers and goes out. . . . It is black. The terrible, heartbreaking weeping continues). (Act III, pp. 95–96)

A provocative question that Rachel's characterization raises is the degree to which she may be autobiographical. Aside from the external similarities between Grimké and her character, one deeper parallel is certain. Grimké, like Rachel, made an early decision not to marry and have children. This fact is documented by her first diary, which she kept from July 18 to September 10, 1903, when she was twenty-three years old. In her entry for September 6, Grimké writes, after having spoken several times of a friend of hers and her new baby: "I shall never know what it means to be a mother, for I shall never marry. I am through with love and the like forever. . . . " Exactly why she resolved this is not clear, but it is probably related to the disastrous love affair that the diary records. The diary is taken up with her spilling over about her heartbreak and unhappiness because of an unnamed lover. She steeps herself in pain and misery and near the end of the diary, though the sharpness abates, she confesses that she still loves and desires the person. She decides that she will never marry, never know the joy of children, but will instead occupy her life with her father and her writing. Details about the lover and the relationship are sparse (they enjoyed some recreation and visits together, she and her father discussed them), and the few that do exist give no insight into why the liaison ended so tragically. One can only speculate.

At any rate, for reasons personal to her, Rachel's depiction may not have been as improbable to Grimké as it seems to others. And her possible emotional involvement in her heroine's plight may account as much as literary and stage convention for the sentimental fervor of Rachel's characterization.

Lynching and the sorrow of having children are again the twin subjects of Grimké's second and last, unpublished drama. Also, like *Rachel*, the play is centered on a young black woman, and is related to a biblical story by its title "Mara" and a scriptual epigraph: "Call me Mara for the Almighty hath dealt very bitterly with me," Naomi's cry of bereavement in Ruth 1:20. The drama exists as a large manuscript box of holograph text. There are numerous drafts and revisions, and one final, complete handwritten copy of approximately 190 pages. Judging from this, Grimké worked rather arduously on the play, but precisely when is difficult to determine. It should probably be dated sometime in the early to middle 1920s, after the success of *Rachel* and before the latter part of that decade, when her sick father required her constant nursing. There is no indication that Grimké ever attempted either to stage or to publish it (not even a typed copy). This is unusual, considering the time she put into the work and knowing that, as a rule, she made the most of her writings and sought to get them into print. Perhaps the waning of enthusiasm for black writers and drying up of publishing outlets at the onset of the depression was a relevant factor. In some ways, "Mara" is a better play than *Rachel* and is definitely interesting as a second dramatic work by Grimké.

The four-act play is set in the South at the turn of the century. The characters are Richard Marston, "a retired physician"; Ellen Marston, "his wife"; Mara Marston, their daughter; Lester Carewe, "a young southern aristocrat"—the only white character and the villain of the piece; Joanna Jessups, "Mara's nurse and the Marston's maid"; and Jasper Jessups, "Joanna's husband, the Marstons' gardener and general utility man." All of the action takes place at "The Cedars," the Marstons' home, in July.

Act I begins with Jasper and Joanna talking, mostly about the strange young white man whom Jasper had seen lurking about the premises earlier that afternoon. If Jasper has identified him correctly, he belongs to the family that had flogged to death Dr. Marston's mother. The doctor, who was five at the time, was made to listen to her screams. Even though Dr. Marston hates the family, he has now retired to his home vicinity for his health. The reader learns throughout this act that their estate is lovely, yet it is surrounded by a ten- to twelve-foot wall and a locked gate; and the doctor, already an expert marksman, occupies his time with target practice and the acquisition of more revolvers.

Like Rachel, Mara is depicted as an enigmatic, dreamy, sensitive yet playful and impetuous girl. She has spent this, her birthday afternoon, as usual—lying in the hammock listening so hard to the passersby outside the gate that she can see them and feel the kind of people they are. She tells her mother that only one of them has frightened her, a young white gentleman who rode by the past two days. Hearing this, Jasper obviously thinks she means Carewe and shivers violently. Mara has also spent this particular day pretending that she was dead to see how it felt, and has concluded that death is beautiful. There are other ominous foreshadowings: Mara's puny-looking birthday bush that Jasper is to plant, the queer sun and sky that Mrs. Marston notices, the continual questioning about Mr. Marston's late return from town, and so on.

At the end of the act when the gate is flung open, Mara looks longingly out and wonders how something as lovely as the world outside can also be evil. (Her mother had explained that this was why they were enclosed.)

Mrs. Marston also suspects that Mara wishes to venture out though she says she is content and knows it is her beloved father's wish that they remain inside.

In Act II, Dr. Marston returns. There is much affectionate banter and embracing among the three of them, especially between him and Mara. Mara is told for the first time that she is not their only, but their seventh child. The first six died between the ages of thirteen and eighteen—hence her name, which means "bitterness," and their custom of planting a birthday bush as a sympathetic growing, which began when she was thirteen. Now that she is eighteen, this bush will be the last. Dr. Marston gives Mara an opal for her present, a gem that Mrs. Marston believes is bad luck unless it is a birthstone. The doctor informs his wife that some of the Carewes have returned to their homestead and she, in turn, recounts what she had learned earlier from Mara about the passerby she feared.

Mara dresses for the special family dinner and then comes back outside. In a very pretty moonlight scene, she thanks God for her happiness and renders him a dance—in the midst of which Carewe appears. After Mara notices him, she comes over to the wall and they converse. During their exchange, she is naïve and childishly frank (even telling Carewe that he is beautiful), he reticent and seemingly puzzled though obviously fascinated by her. By questioning her, he finds out all about her and her family. He also promises to return if she does not reveal to anyone that he has been there. Finally, she agrees. As Carewe rides off, Mara recognizes him as the man she feared. The scene ends with her noting the mournful hoot of an owl.

The next act is certainly the climactic one. On a night one week later, Mara dresses up in her birthday finery to go into the yard after teasing her parents about a delicious secret she has, which she promises to tell her father upon her return. A fierce thunderstorm swiftly rises. They call and search for Mara—but in vain. Eventually, she blows in, wet, torn, haggard. She has obviously been raped (though this comes out only by inference and indirection), and her mind has completely gone. She asks for God in his house and brokenly speaks of someone (herself) who died outside. Her father, a light-skinned man, frightens her. The whole scene is highly charged and dramatic, with pitiful, crazed Mara, her weeping mother, and tense old father.

Finally, Mara faints after trying to escape, and they get her to bed. Jasper has meanwhile discovered a rope ladder concealed against the wall, and tells Dr. Marston that he has just seen Carewe ride away. The Marstons then discuss their lack of lawful redress in the South. The doctor intimates that he will seek revenge. When Mrs. Marston reminds him of God, Dr. Marston renounces him and forbids the name to be spoken in his house ever again.

In Act IV, Dr. Marston is seen waiting for Carewe as he has been for the last three nights. Mara is still deranged—beautiful, ethereal, laughing an elfin laugh, and still not knowing herself or anybody. During her appearance, she warns that "he" is coming, the sound of two horses' hooves is heard, Dr. Marston goes outside, fires two shots, and reappears saying, "He—will—not—return—again!" In the second scene, a mob comes, carries the Marston family out, and apparently lynches them: "No one is left in the house. Suddenly the screams without increase in tenor in anguish. In the midst of a scream there is an abrupt silence. After that there is no sound."

This plot sounds like Gothic melodrama. Nevertheless, *Mara* holds attention better than *Rachel* does, is fairly exciting and more imaginative, and free enough of lapses so that the reader is not unpleasantly jarred by them. Also, the reader's patience and credulity are not taxed by an excess of preciousness and sentimentality. The material may have done well—may in fact be better suited for—a novel or novelette. The entire second scene of Act IV, with the exception of a few words, is text. And throughout the play, the reader's sensation is more one of watching action unfold than listening to dialogue. Furthermore, the play's setting and effects would probably be somewhat difficult to stage. It also seems to be too long for a stage play—though the lengthy passages of description and scene directions may be deceptive.

Viewed autobiographically, Grimké's drama reflects her extremely close relationship with her father in the love that exists between Mara and Dr. Marston. When the doctor enters in Act II, "his eyes go dark with a certain fierceness and tenderness toward Mara. They exchange a long look of welcome." "Mara runs to him, throws her arms around him and kisses his shoulder. With his free hand he pats her head and then puts his arm about her." Though Mara loves Mrs. Marston, it is clear that the mother is a third person where she and her father are concerned. Not having grown up with her own mother, Grimké knew and felt more about the father-daughter than the mother-daughter relationship. In one of her diaries, she once remarked that she needed a mother, but that she was accustomed to the lack.[57]

As a playwright, Grimké has matured some in "Mara." The mood is tense and dramatic when it should be, and she has learned how to set scenes and then let events happen as swiftly and naturally as they should.

Obviously, Jasper and Joanna, who are stock, dialect-speaking figures, are meant to provide variety and comic relief. He is "a small black man" in "denim overalls" and a "faded cap," who has "deep-set, kindly and humorous" eyes. Joanna is a "huge elderly woman" who wears an apron and a "knotted bandanna handkerchief." Sometimes, however, the scenes between the two of them are overly prolonged.

There is more variety in the types of characters and in their characterization. Small conflicts exist between them—such as the gentle clashing of the doctor's rationalism with his wife's superstition—which, though not subplots, provide that kind of interest. Even Mara's childish sweetness is easier to take here, since the fact that she has been shut in all her life gives it plausibility. (Could this cloistering be Grimké's objectification of her situation? Certainly, it echoes the "closing door" motif in other works of her own and in those of Dunbar-Nelson.) One might think that the play's southern setting would provide even more opportunity for Grimké to score propaganda points, but this is not the case. Only the exchange between Mr. and Mrs. Marston in Act III approaches being an overt message. It seems that in this play, Grimké is more interested in the characters and their story than in "the problem." Hence, these legitimate dual wellsprings of her work are better balanced.

It is not unusual that Grimké chose to write about lynching and racial prejudice. But it is novel that she does so through these dramas that feature fragile young women like herself whose fine, ethereal natures unfit them for life in a modern racist society. Unfortunately, material and cultural conditions—united with Grimké's gender and her isolation—did not favor the production of a work like "Mara." In the plays that she was writing during the mid-1920s, Georgia Douglas Johnson was also exploring Afro-American problems such as rape and miscegenation, poverty, and lynching from a black female point of view. And she, too, focused on women characters to convey her racial message. However, unlike Grimké's long, unpolished, essentially closet drama, Johnson's finished one-act works gained access to the public through Harlem Renaissance contests and their suitability for publication and easy staging.

Lynching, the core subject of Grimké's plays, also preoccupied her in her most important short stories. It is linked, as in *Rachel* and "Mara," with children in "The Closing Door," which appeared in two parts in *The Birth Control Review* of 1919. The story was initially used in an early draft of *Rachel,* and Grimké may have lifted it from the play so that she could make it a separate work.

The narrator, Lucy, is a young black girl who describes herself like this in the first sentence of the story: "I was fifteen at the time, diffident and old far beyond my years from much knocking about from pillar to post, a yellow scrawny, unbeautiful girl, when the big heart of Agnes Milton took pity upon me, loved me and brought me home to live with her in her tiny, sun-filled flat."[58] Agnes and her husband, Jim, are joyously happy, and when Agnes becomes pregnant, it seems that this child will complete their bliss. However, after she conceives, Agnes decides that they must all "go softly underneath the stars" to protect their too-great happiness. She develops the chilling habit of noiselessly closing herself behind doors. During her pregnancy, the family learns that her favorite brother has died in Mississippi and, when a second brother visits them, that he was lynched after not yielding the sidewalk to a white man. Agnes faints, then becomes hysterical, crying: "I!—I!—An instrument!—another one of the many! a colored woman—doomed!—cursed!—put here!—willing or unwilling! for what?—to bring children here—men children—for the sport—the lust—of . . . mobs. . . . "[59] After her son is born healthy, she refuses to have anything to do with him—all the while fighting her maternal instinct and paining her soul. One night, she steals into the child's room and smothers it, and after a short time in a mental institution, mercifully dies herself.

Grimké wrote "The Closing Door" expressly for a special number of *The Birth Control Review,* "The New Emancipation: The Negroes' Need for Birth Control, As Seen By Themselves."[60] It seems somehow wrong that this tale of madness and infanticide would appear in such a journal and even more peculiar that the killing societal reasons for Agnes's misfortune would be used as an argument for birth control among black people. That it does and is so used is probably because of Grimké. The story is not very good, marred as it is by forced romping scenes, sentimentality, overwriting, and an uncertain tone and point of view. Apparently, though, the editors were pleased with it, for in 1920, Mary Knoblauch urgently solicited another story from Grimké.

She obliged with "Goldie," a story with a long writing history that continues her focus on lynching.[61] In a covering letter to the *Atlantic Monthly* Grimké recounts the basis of her tale and indicates her motivation for writing it. The letter is long, but important enough to quote in full:

> I am sending enclosed a story. It is not a pleasant one but is based on fact. Several years ago, in Georgia, a colored woman quite naturally it would seem became wrought up because her husband had been lynched. She threatened to bring some of the leaders to justice. The mob made up of "chivalrous" and brave white men determined to teach her a lesson. She

was dragged out of town to a desolate part of the woods and the lesson began. First she was strung up by her feet to the limbs of a tree, next her clothes were saturated with kerosene oil, and then she was set afire. While the woman shrieked and writhed in agony, one man who had brought with him a knife used in the butchering of animals, ripped her abdomen wide open. Her unborn child fell to the ground at her feet. It emitted one or two little cries but was soon silenced by brutal heels that crushed out its head. Death came at last to the poor woman. The lesson ended.

Last fall, I think it was you printed an article entitled "Can These Things Be?" That was a very terrible arraignment of the Turks. It, of course, did not happen in America.

The fact of the lynching upon which I based my story happened in the civilized U.S.A. in the 20th Century. Was this woman, I wonder, lynched for the "usual crime?" "Can These Things Be?" Even the Turks have been astounded at the brutality and the ruthlessness of the lynchings in this country. Where are these lynchings leading the U.S.A.? In what will they end?[62]

From this incident, Grimké first fashioned a story that she symbolically entitled "Blackness" (exists in holograph). It is so overburdened with framework, exposition, and creating an atmosphere of eerie darkness, that the heart of the story gets lost. The action centers on two lawyers, one of whom tells the tale to his friend just before he, the tale-teller, has to leave town to escape from some southerners because he killed a white station-master who helped with the murder.

Her second attempt at handling this material Grimké called "The Waitin'" (48 holograph pages). This one follows most closely the account given in her letter. In it, Mary, the wife, is the clear center of interest. She is a forceful character, and the story is told from her limited omniscient point of view. Here also, the crusading intent is strongest. The final sentences of the story read: "And that morning the papers flamed with a righteous indignation over Hun atrocities and Bolshevik barbarities. Carefully tucked away was a careless word or two dismissing little Mary Green."

Finally, Grimké seems to have satisfied herself with "Goldie," which she first called "The Creaking." Viewed artistically, it is the best version of the story. She tells it through Victor Forrest, who, at the frantic summons of his sister Goldie, returns home after five years to find her and her husband dead. How they die and the rest of the background essentially repeat "Blackness" and "The Waitin'," and the reader has to independently deduce some of the details. At the end, Victor avenges them by choking to death the lustful white man responsible and is, of course, lynched. Many of the same leitmotifs occur in all three stories—for example, the husband's

love of trees and bird song, and the horrible creaking of the lynch rope
(used also in *Rachel*).

What makes "Goldie" work so well is its point of view and narrative
method. Using her most modern fictional technique, Grimké allows the
story to unfold through Victor's internal monologue and through flash-
backs. The entire time, the reader is inside Victor's consciousness, thinking
over the past with him as he walks to Goldie's through the dark night, and
discovering little by little with him what has happened as he prowls
through the wrecked cabin. Grimké's description, which is one of her
strengths, is also noticeably good in this story. Describing Victor's journey
down the road, she writes:

> He always paused, a moment or so, on one of these islands [of clear space]
> to drive out expulsively the dank, black oppressiveness of the air he had
> been breathing and to fill his lungs anew with God's night air, that, here, at
> least, was sweet and untroubled. Here, too, his eyes were free again and he
> could see the dimmed white blur of road for a space each way; and, above,
> the stars, millions of them, each one hardly brilliant, stabbing its way
> whitely through the black heavens. And if the island were large enough,
> there was a glimpse, scarely more, of a very pallid, slightly crumpled moon
> sliding furtively down the west.—Yes, sharply black and sharply white, that
> was it, but mostly it was black.[63]

It is hard to say exactly why Grimké concentrated almost exclusively on
lynching in her drama and fiction. Certainly, it was a pressing social ill,
with grievously large numbers of black people being lynched in the United
States each year. Trudier Harris notes that "Violence against black Americans is one recurring historical phenomenon to which every generation of
black writers in this country has been drawn in its attempt to depict the
shaping of black lives. Especially compelling has been violence that takes
the form of lynching."[64] She states, further, that black women writers tend
not to graphically depict lynching and burning rituals, and do not nor-
mally use sexual accusation of black males as the primary cause (which is
true of Grimké's handling of this theme).

Grimké's early concern with the problem is indicated by the fact that in
November 1899, when she was only nineteen, she collected signatures for
an anti-lynching petition.[65] Then, too, many of her works on this subject
were written during the post–World War I lynchings and the controversy
over the Dyer Anti-Lynching Bill of 1922, the same piece of legislation for
which Dunbar-Nelson fought so hard. Perhaps since lynching was the
biggest, most glaring social evil, she chose it as her target, drawn as she was

by her background and environment toward writing racially relevant literature. In thanking her for *Rachel,* Montgomery Gregory had admonished her to "please feel that you have a mission to fulfill; and persist in its fulfillment."[66] Apparently, she decided to do so. Still, one wonders about her constant use of so limited a number of plots and situations.

Grimké's racial views can be deduced from these literary works. Her personal utterances augment the impression of her as an individual acutely conscious of her peculiar racial identity and aware of both the intra- and interracial realities. In an undated letter to a woman at Hampton who was organizing a European tour, she wrote: "As you probably know I am the product of both races and as far as I can make out there is little or no choice between them." This sentiment probably reflects her close association with whites and blacks and her affirmation of all people's essential humanity. However, her diary entry for July 31, 1903, indicates her knowledge that the world was not so simple. Speaking of a Miss Randolph's apparently carefree attitude about her dark skin, she writes:

> For as fair as I am I find I am very sensitive. How much harder it must be to be black. God pity them! They not only have the white people's prejudice to contend with [but] the light colored people's too. Light people are very small. What difference does *color* make *anyway* it is *only skin-deep.*

She also made more political remarks. On June 19, 1909, she wrote her father about commencement at Dunbar High School, and informed him that "President Taft was there and made another non-committal speech,—as usual."[67] In an even longer statement to the *Liberator,* she said:

> You ask for money to send speakers etc. But is not one voice to be raised for us? the little ones, the helpless ones in the hands of this "great democracy"? Do you realize that the future of the colored man in this country was never darker, never more utterly helpless than it is today—after this war for the freeing of all peoples?[68]

Grimké's preoccupations in her stories bear out these racial views, except for one completely different story entitled "Jettisoned." The fact that it treats other subject matter may be due to the advice that she received from one of her friendly white critics, Lillie Buffum Chace Wyman, who was a writer of some reputation herself. On November 21, 1922, Wyman counseled:

> Now *may* I entreat you to leave out [of her next work] consideration of the lynching horror, nor give any *great* prominence to outrageous racial oppression. *Don't,* instantly fly off the handle at this suggestion. I make it, because

you have dealt with those things so powerfully and so beautifully, I want
you to show that you can do different things in literature—for your own
sake and, don't you see that it is well for the colored people to have you
show that you have such varied ability?

She continued in the same letter:

One thing I know you can do,—that is, make the characters whom you
describe in your sketch *attractive*. . . . Do it now, with a less tragic background. I want you to do that, this once. I think, such a production of
yours, a paper, which people would read with pleasure, and which would
inevitably arouse in them the feelings of affectionate sympathy for its per-
sonages, would render double effective your *other* appeals in their behalf
and your representations of the wrong and the cruelty of denying to them
the good things of life. Do you see what I mean?

Apparently, Grimké did see what she meant and decided to produce a
somewhat happier, though still humanly poignant, treatment of black life.
The main character of "Jettisoned" is an old black woman named Miss
Lucy, who is introduced to the reader in this way:

Miss Lucy turned westward, at the corner, into the block where the home
of her little room was, a sordid enough, narrow little street in the white
ungracious glare of the sun, but beautiful, now, its darkness veiled over and
about with the lavender and greys of a late fall twilight. . . . But was Miss
Lucy concerned with all this wistful loveliness? She was not. . . . No, she
was concerned wholly and solely with just one thing, or to be more accurate two,—her feet.

She is tired from ironing for a hard white woman all day but is cheered
by a letter from her married daughter in Long Island, New York, who is
passing for white. This daughter invites her for a visit—with the stipula-
tion, however, that she pose as her old "mammy." Miss Lucy, who would
gladly suffer even this indignity to see her daughter and grandson, is dissuaded by Mary Lou, an adorable young black woman who lives in the
same rooming house and is Miss Lucy's closest friend, almost her surrogate
daughter. Aged and saddened, Miss Lucy puts on a cheerful face and
resolves to use her saved-up fare to make life more pleasant for herself and
for Mary Lou, who clearly needs caring for. She is alone in the world,
penniless, jobless, and unhappy, and has attempted what looked like suicide by turning on her gas stove. At the end of the story, she is linked with
Paul, another neighbor, who is a medical student, and the two of them,
with Miss Lucy, form a congenial threesome.

The story is not exactly happy, but is as close to it as Grimké could come. Racial prejudice does not violently obtrude on the characters (though it is an indirect force through Miss Lucy's drudgery, her daughter's passing, Mary Lou's unemployment, etc.), and no one dies or is killed. Too, there is satisfying love and warm domesticity, an aura of quiet acceptance and contentment, and the prospect of greater future hapiness.

Charles S. Johnson, the editor of the Urban League's *Opportunity* magazine who aided and encouraged Grimké, liked the story. He had been asking her to send him a manuscript for the 1925 *Opportunity* contest, but the only one she had on hand, "Jettisoned," far exceeded the five thousand-word limit (being sixty-seven typed pages). Johnson wanted it anyway, and after he had received and read it, wrote her a glowing letter on January 6, 1925:

> I thought I had reached the saturation point on short stories until I picked up "Jettisoned" which left me tingling strangely inside. This note was intended to be critical,—coldly and dispassionately critical, and perhaps I should wait until morning to allow myself to become unwrapt from its fascination. But just now it is as if I had sat in the presence of at least two flesh warm characters—Miss Lucy and Mary Lou. The story is softly, penetratingly tragic; it is magnificent. . . .
>
> You have achieved a rare thing here: that tragedy of life which escapes the melodramatic; characters which are real, unpretensious and lovable; that lurking shadow of the most interesting quirk the racial situation holds at present; good sound humor, no special pleading,—all this with a delightfully competent touch. I salute you.

Because of its length, the story could not be "entered officially" in the contest, but Johnson had all of the judges read it: "My notion was to lead the way to its publication as a novelette."[69] At least two of the judges shared Johnson's enthusiasm for the work. Edna Worthley Underwood, a novelist, ended her written remarks on it by saying: "This story ploughed deep furrows through my heart. I commend it for honorable mention! I hope to see it in book form." She thought "Jettisoned" was very like "the sincere peasant art of the Old World" and possessed "similarities not a few—with the modern story telling art of Russia."[70]

Another judge, Zona Gale, the well-known fictionist and critic, went so far as to mention it in her *Survey* article about the contest even though it was not a prizewinner:

> This ability to look with detachment on the rich field of raw human emotion . . . is exemplified in one of the entries called Jettisoned, its first

third of outstanding power in character and situation. . . . Here is drama of power, too great drama for the tale, and the writer wavers away from it, offering a solution outside the real drama—but the story serves to show the jagged peaks possible to these pioneers who have accomplished the astounding feat of seeing once more the soul of the commonplace.[71]

Perhaps because of the popularity of the passing theme during the Renaissance, both Gale and Johnson regarded the daughter's racial crossover as the crux of the story, but Grimké does not emphasize this aspect. The daughter never appears; and most of the plot involves Miss Lucy and Mary Lou and does not prominently bring in passing as the supreme theme. The title itself refers to the selfish daughter, who is deservedly chucked overboard, or maybe to her "jettisoning" of her mother and race.

Grimké used dialect in "Jettisoned" (as she had in "Mara" and "The Waitin'"). Speaking about its handling here where it is an inseparable aspect of Miss Lucy's characterization, Charles Johnson observed: "Several times I thought the dialect was not convincingly spelt; but it was not often that I could improve upon the spelling."[72] Modern readers share his uneasy feeling about her dialect representation and are equally as incapable of correcting its orthography. Yet, it is obvious from the difficulty that reading it presents that Grimké cannot write dialect as natural, say, as Dunbar's or Hurston's.

Despite all the kind words bestowed upon "Jettisoned," it was never published. Grimké considered subsidizing it, for on May 28, 1925, Johnson wrote: "Really, I am hopeful of finding a publisher for *Jettisoned*, but I had not considered for a second paying anyone to publish it. A story such as this should sell itself. . . . " Apparently, it did not—or maybe Grimké did not do what she should have to market it.

As a short-story writer, Grimké was not especially talented. Her gifts were essentially lyrical and dramatic. Though she wrote stories throughout her life, they are the least significant of her works. Her situation regarding this genre suggests parallels with both Dunbar-Nelson and Georgia Douglas Johnson. Dunbar-Nelson devoted years to short fiction and considered it one of her major forms, although it does not represent her finest achievement, while Johnson projected many short stories and did apprentice work on others near the end of her life. Why Grimké so doggedly attempted the form is indicated perhaps in a brief speech that she made prefatory to reading one of her stories to the Book Lovers literary club. After noting "the staleness of the material and the staleness of plot" that characterize "the stories in the American Magazines of to-day," Grimké expressed her belief that "the white man . . . is about written out" and needs new material, material, she says, which exists in abundance in the lives of black people. Then she prophesied:

> I am not alone in believing that the great American short story of the future is to spring from the lives of colored people. . . . Someday a genius, white or black is coming and he is going to see us, seize upon us, take [us] just as we are, no more, no less, and make himself immortal through us. I hope he is to be black, for certainly, it seems to me, no one can know us as well as one of ourselves.[73]

Grimké hoped to see in the short story what Jean Toomer, Zora Neale Hurston, and Rudolph Fisher accomplished. How much she knew of their work is not clear. But, more admirably than she managed to, these three Renaissance writers achieved her valid and noble goals for the Afro-American short story.

iii

The third period of Grimké's life finds her in her middle forties, sharing in the glory and good fortune of the Harlem Renaissance. It also brings her into focus as a poet. Though she had already been writing poems, they did not receive really widespread attention until this time. The effort that she poured into her drama and fiction notwithstanding, poetry was truly Grimké's major genre. However much she was applauded for *Rachel,* it was as a poet that she retains a valid place in literary history.

During the mid-1920s, her work was frequently published in *Opportunity* magazine. Perhaps because of her allegiance to *Opportunity* or some seeming antipathy that existed between her family and DuBois, only two or three of her poems appear in *The Crisis,* the N.A.A.C.P. magazine edited by DuBois.[74] Every anthology or special magazine issue of black poetry during the period includes her work—Alain Locke's *The New Negro* (1925), Countee Cullen's *Caroling Dusk* (1927), where she is represented by more poems than any other female poet, Charles S. Johnson's *Ebony and Topaz* (1927), *The Carolina Magazine* (May 1928), and so on. The one unexplainable exception is James Weldon Johnson's *Book of American Negro Poetry,* which, in neither its 1922 nor 1931 edition, reprints any poems by her. Grimké even received a request in 1928 from one Dr. Anna Nussbaum for permission to translate some of her poems into German for an anthology of black poetry.[75]

Grimké also tried to widen the journals in which she published and to enhance further her poetic reputation. Earlier, before she had produced her best poems, she had pieces rejected by magazines like *Harper's* and *The Smart Set*.[76] Now, with the aid of Charles Johnson, she looked again for other publishing outlets. On February 6, 1924, he writes her: "I sent some of the poems which you gave me . . . to Clement Wood and he has expressed considerable interest in them. . . . Meanwhile, I am trying out some other of the poetry magazines."[77] He also submitted some of her poems to *Century Magazine* in 1925; they were returned on June 16. Not readily placing her work caused her anxiety, for on June 25, 1925, Johnson is counseling her to "cease fretting for a spell."

Sometime either before or during this period, Grimké was planning a collection of her poetry. She tentatively called it *Dusk Dreams* and set down a list of twenty-three titles that would constitute the book. Oddly enough, only five of these are published poems and the bulk of them do not represent her at her best—suggesting perhaps that the collection was projected earlier in her career. Whatever the case, it never materialized, although if Grimké had taken the poems that she had published in magazines and anthologies by 1928 (which constitute her most mature work) and added some others to them, she could have assembled a very respectable volume. As it turned out, her name as a poet was kept alive after the 1920s by her inclusion in various textbooks and, of course, by editors of black poetry volumes who kept recycling the same poems.[78] Seemingly, she stopped writing altogether. On May 1, 1932, a friend of hers in Philadelphia, the artist Henry B. Jones, playfully—but earnestly—chided her for not using her gift and writing poetry.[79] Furthermore, none of her extant poems appear to have been produced after this date.

For the sake of convenience, Grimké's poetry can be roughly grouped into five general categories: (1) elegies, (2) love lyrics, (3) nature lyrics, (4) racial poems, and (5) philosophical poems about the human condition.

Throughout her career, Grimké eulogized family and close friends, beginning with Joseph Lee, described as "the Boston Negro caterer and hotel-keeper who was long Mr. W. D. Howells's admired host at Auburndale,"[80] and ending with Clarissa Scott Delany, another black female poet who died in 1927 when she was only twenty-six years old. Recalling her poem to Clarissa, one of Grimké's correspondents, Julia Parks, made a relevant remark: "You surely do appreciate your friends—and can give your thought such exquisitely enduring form."[81] However, she wrote her finest elegy for her famous aunt, Charlotte Forten (the only other black woman besides Dunbar-Nelson whose booklength diary has been published). Forten married Grimké's uncle Francis late in her life and died in 1914. Grimké loved and respected her "Aunt Lottie" (although they had some slight difficulty as two women living in the same house);[82] and the poem that she wrote for her, "To Keep the Memory of Charlotte Forten Grimké," reflects her intimate knowledge and appreciation of this gentle woman. The poem begins:

> Still are there wonders of the dark and day;
> The muted shrilling of shy things at night,
> So small beneath the stars and moon;
> The peace, dream-frail, but perfect while the light
> Lies softly on the leaves at noon.
> These are, and these will be
> Until Eternity;
> But she who loved them well has gone away.[83]

Three more stanzas with the same form and pattern ensue, each one repeating as refrain the last two lines. The entire poem—as do all of Grimké's elegies—allays grief by accepting death as a beautiful phenomenon, placing the departed one in the natural schema, and evoking a sense of her/his continuing presence.

The second category of Grimké's poems, love lyrics, constitute one of the largest groups. These poems are, as a rule, very delicate, musical, romantic, and pensive. "A Mona Lisa" and "When the Green Lies Over the Earth," two of her best-known works, probably belong in this category. Practically all of these lyrics are addressed to women. One that she never published is called either "Rosabel" or "Rosalie":

> I.
> Leaves that whisper whisper ever
>   Listen, listen, pray!
> Birds that twitter twitter softly
>   Do not say me nay.
> Winds that breathe about, upon her
>   (Lines I do not dare)
> Whisper, turtle, breathe upon her
>   That I find her fair.
> II.
> Rose whose soul unfolds white petaled
>   Touch her soul, use white
> Rose whose thoughts unfold gold petaled
>   Blossom in her sight
> Rose whose heart unfolds, red petaled
>   Prick her slow heart's stir
> Tell her white, gold, red my love is—
>   And for her,—for her.

In these poems, Grimké was probably not simply assuming the mask of a traditional male persona, but writing from her own true feelings and experiences. In February 1896 one of her school friends, Mamie (Mary) Burrill, sent her a youthful letter, where, mixed in with apologies, school gossip, and church news, she recalled their secret good times together and re-affirmed her love: "Could I just come to meet thee once more, in the old sweet way, just coming at your calling, and like an angel bending o'er you breathe into your ear, 'I love you.' "[84] For her part, Angelina was even more ardent. In a letter written later that year while she was in Northfield, Minnesota, at the Carleton Academy, she overflows: "Oh Mamie if you only knew how my heart beats when I think of you and it yearns and pants to gaze, if only for one second upon your lovely face." With naïve sweetness, she asks Mamie to be her "wife" and ends the letter: "Now may the Almighty father bless thee little one and keep thee safe from all harm, Your passionate lover."[85]

Mamie went on to become a teacher in the Washington, D.C., public school system, an actress, and a playwright. Her 1919 one-act drama *They That Sit In Darkness* concerns a poor black woman with too many children who is mired in childbearing and poverty because the system denies women access to birth-control information.[86] It appeared in the same special issue of the *Birth Control Review* as Grimké's story "The Closing Door." Exactly what happened between Grimké and Burrill is not clear. She may or may not have been the partner in the disastrous love affair mentioned earlier that Grimké set down in her diary, July 18–September 10, 1903 (although it is a bit hard to imagine Grimké speaking forthrightly about a female lover to her father). Later in their lives, Mamie alluded to their girlhood relationship in a brief note that she wrote to Grimké in July 1911 after Grimké had been injured in a train wreck: "If I can serve you at all, for the sake of the days that are a long way behind us both, I trust you will let me do so."

The manuscript poems that Grimké wrote during the early 1900s parallel the diary's story of heartbreak and unhappiness and indicate, further, that the lover was female—either Mamie or some other woman. "If"— one copy of which is dated July 31, 1903—is divided into halves. The first speculates that if every thought, hope, and dream the speaker has of her love became a pansy, rose, or maidenhair, then the world would be over-run with "rosy blooms, and pansy glooms and curling leaves of green." The second part, though, posits that if every look, word, and deed of the lover became ice, sleet, and snow, then "this old world would fast be curled beneath a wintry moon / With wastes of snow that livid glow—as it is now in June." Another poem, entitled "To Her of the Cruel Lips" and ending "I laugh, yet—my brain is sad," was written November 5, 1903. And, on January 16, 1904, Grimké is asking "Where is the Dream?" and "Why do I Love you so?"

Nothing else exists to tell if and whom and how she loved after this. She followed the external resolutions that she made in her diary to forego marriage and children and occupy her life with writing and her father— and probably continued to desire women, in silence and frustration. Un- like Dunbar-Nelson, Grimké does not appear to have acted on her lesbian feelings with continuous and mature assurance. But—perhaps because she did not—they provided greater impetus for her verse.

Her first developed piece, "El Beso" (quoted earlier), reveals one way that Grimké handled in her public art what seem to be woman-to-woman romantic situations. Here, she writes of "your provocative laughter, / The gloom of your hair; / Lure of you, eye and lip"; and then "Pain, regret— your sobbing." Because of the "feel" of the poem and its diction ("sob- bing," for example), the "you" visualizes as a woman—despite the ab- sence of the third-person pronouns and the usual tendency most readers have (knowledge of persona, notwithstanding) to image the other in a love poem as being opposite in sex from the poem's known author. "A Mona Lisa" is similar in tone and approach. It begins:

> I should like to creep
> Through the long brown grasses
> That are your lashes.[87]

As one might predict, Grimké's unpublished poetry contains an even heavier concentration of love lyrics. In these can be found the raw feeling, feminine pronouns, and womanly imagery that have been excised or muted in the published poems:

> Thou are to me a lone white star,
> That I may gaze on from afar;
> But I may never never press
> My lips on thine in mute caress,
> E'en touch the hem of thy pure dress,
> Thou art so far, so far. . . .

Or:

> My sweetheart walks down laughing ways
> Mid dancing glancing sunkissed ways
> And she is all in white . . .

Most of these lyrics either chronicle a romance that is now dead or record a cruel and unrequited love. The longest poem in this first group is "Autumn." Its initial stanza describes a bleak autumn with spring love gone; stanza two recalls that bygone spring, with its "slim slips of maiden moons, the shimmering stars; / And our love, our first love, glorious, yielding"; the final stanza paints the present contrasting scene where "Your hand does not seek mine . . . the smile is not for me . . . [but] for the new life and dreams wherein I have no part." The anguish of the second type is captured in poems like "Give Me Your Eyes" and "Caprichosa," and distilled in lines such as:

> If I might taste but once, just once
> The dew
> Upon her lips

Another work in this group, "My Shrine," is interesting for its underlying psychological and artistic revelations. The speaker builds a shrine to/for her "maiden small, . . . divinely pure" inside her heart—away from those who might widen their eyes and guffaw. There she kneels, only then daring to speak her soulful words. This poem was carried to the typescript stage and, having reached this point, Grimké substituted "he" for "she" where it was unavoidable. In many of these lyrics, the loved one is wreathed in whiteness (even to the mentioning of "her sweet white hands").

Needless to say, most of this poetry is fragmentary and unpolished. One reads it sensing the poet's tremendous need to voice, to vent, to share—if only on paper—what was pulsing within her, since it seems that sometimes she could not even talk to the woman she wanted, let alone anyone else. "Close your eyes," she says in one poem, "I hear nothing but the beating of my heart."

These romantic poems, as well as all the other types of Grimké's poetry, draw heavily on the natural world for allusions, figures of speech, and imagery. However, some of her work can be strictly classified as pure nature lyrics. Perhaps the best of these are "A Winter Twilight" and "Dusk." The latter reads:

> Twin stars through my purpling pane,
> The shriveling husk
> Of a yellowing moon on the wane—
> And the dusk.[88]

She also writes about the dawn ("Dawn," "At the Spring Dawn"), "Grass Fingers," and the "green of little leaves" ("Greenness").

Grimké produced relatively few racial poems. Of her works with racial overtones, the one most often reprinted is "Tenebris," which is about a shadow hand "huge and black" that plucks at the bricks of "the white man's house": "The bricks are the color of blood and very small. / Is it a black hand, / Or is it a shadow?"[89] These poems are indirect and merely suggest the sensitivity to injustice and the political zeal that characterize her prose.

Finally, there are her philosophical poems about life. A varied lot, these treat regret, religious themes, the need for peace, "The Ways O' Men," a "puppet player" who "sits just beyond the border of our seeing, / Twitching the strings with slow sardonic grin,"[90] the "Paradox" of two people who are spiritually closer when physically apart than when "face to face,"[91] and many other subjects of universal human experience. Generally, her first-person observations resonate more broadly, as in these lines from "The Eyes of My Regret":

> Always at dusk, the same tearless experience,
> . . . .
> Over it, the same slow unlidding of twin stars,
> Two eyes unfathomable, soul-searing,
> . . . .
> The same two eyes that keep me sitting late into the
>   night, chin on knees,
> Keep me there lonely, rigid, tearless, numbly miserable,
>   —The eyes of my Regret.[92]

Grimké was not a literary theoretician, but on one occasion, she impressively explained her own creative process. A young man named Adolph Hult, Jr., a senior at Augustana College, Rock Island, Illinois, was studying her poetry as part of a class project in black literature. He wrote her on November 28, 1925, requesting information about her work. Almost immediately, she responded; what she wrote is one of the few self-critical statements that exists from a black writer of the period. It is introspective, sophisticated, even philosophical:

> I think most [poems] that I do are the reflections of moods. These appear to me in clearly defined forms and colors—remembered from what I have seen, felt. The mood is the spiritual atmosphere. Symbolic also. I love colors and contrasts. Suggestion.
>
> Whatever I have done it seems to me is a reflection of some mood which gives the spiritual atmosphere and significance. The mood has a physical counterpart in Nature in colors concrete images brought out by contrasts. Often to me the whole thing is not only a mood but symbolic as well. The

more vivid the physical picture the more vivid the vibrations in the mind of the reader or listener. Each word has its different wavelength, vibration. Colors, trees flowers skies meadows. The more concrete, definite vivid the picture the more vivid the vibration of word in the reader or listener.

And what is word? May it not be a sort of singing in the harp strings of the mind? Then on the principle of sympathetic vibration is there not in nature a harp singing also to be found. . . . [93]

Her theory of composition here is essentially romantic (even more theoretically so than Dunbar-Nelson's). First of all, the poetry arises from within herself; it is, as she puts it, the reflection of a mood. Her "appear to me" suggests the kind of spontaneous coming of a poem that Coleridge, for "Kubla Khan," called a "rising up." As for the romantic poets, nature is also a primary force that, in her case, furnishes the physical analogues for her moods. And nature, as well as the experience of it and the images in which it is clothed, is symbolic. Finally, she states, in the favorite romantic harp image, the sympathetic correspondence that was supposed to exist between the poet's mind and external nature.

Grimké's poetry accords very closely with her theoretical description of how she writes. Being expressions of the moment, her poems are usually brief. They present the scene or thought as swiftly as possible in sharp, concrete images, and then abandon it. This trait causes critics (like Robert Kerlin, for example) to compare her with the imagists. However, Grimké cannot usually refrain from comment, and thus violates the suggestive objectivity that is a part of their creed. Her poem "The Black Finger" is an excellent case in point. Here is its middle section:

> Slim and still,
> Against a gold, gold sky,
> A straight cypress,
> Sensitive,
> Exquisite,
> A black finger
> Pointing upwards.[94]

Those seven lines have the haiku-like, symbolic compression that the imagists prized. However, the poem consists of three additional lines—a beginning statement, "I have just seen a beautiful thing," and two closing questions, "Why, beautiful, still finger are you black? / And why are you pointing upwards?"—which alter considerably its tone and effect by making attitude and meaning too explicit.

Ironically, this predilection for brevity is also the source of one of Grimké's weaknesses as a poet—her occasional over-reliance on fragmentation and understatement. Sometimes, more often in early poems, her lines are too cropped and ejaculatory, resulting in a series of disjunct, giddy phrases. Something of this can be seen in the second half of "El Beso," quoted above.

Without a doubt, Grimké's greatest strength is her affinity for nature, her ability to really see it and then describe what she has seen with precision and subtlety. Take, for example, this stanza from her elegy "To Clarissa Scott Delany":

> Does the beryl in tarns, the soft orchid in haze,
> The primrose through treetops, the unclouded jade
> Of the north sky, all earth's flamings and russets and grays
> Simply smudge out and fade?[95]

Describing nature gives Grimké her freshest, most original and graphic expressions and helps her avoid the trite or threadbare diction that now and then entraps her. As she says in her poetic statement, she loves color and contrast. She handles them well and builds many of her finest effects upon them.

The mood of Grimké's poetry is predominantly sad and hushed (one of her favorite words). Colors—even when vivid—are not the primary ones, but saffron, green-gold, lilac. Sounds are muted; effects are delicate. Emotion—even when intense—is quiet and refined.

> A hint of gold where the moon will be:
> Through the flocking clouds just a star or two:
> Leaf sounds, soft and wet and hushed,
> And oh! the crying want of you.[96]

Grimké's poems are written in both rhyme and meter, and in what Sterling Brown calls "a carefully worded and cadenced free verse."[97] In some poems, she wavers between the two. Related to this metrical uncertainty is her major fault of repeating words, phrases, and lines in a manner that suggests padding. It seems that when inspiration waned, she sometimes resorted to the stock poetic technique of repetition to try to achieve some easy lyricism. Very few of her poems are written in the jazzy, syncopated style that was in vogue with black writers of the 1920s like Langston Hughes and Helene Johnson. One of them which is, "At April," has this rhythmic beginning:

> Toss your gay heads,
> Brown girl trees;
> Toss your gay lovely heads; . . . [98]

Generally speaking, Grimké's excellencies as a poet outweigh her weaknesses—especially in the handful of well-wrought lyrics that secure her literary fame. However, assessing her accurately requires thoughtful consideration of the personal and social conditions under which she wrote. Clearly, her poetic themes of sadness and void, longing and frustration (which commentators have been at a loss to explain) relate directly to Grimké's convoluted life and thwarted sexuality. One also notes the self-abnegation and diminution that mark her work. It comes out in her persistent vision of herself as small and hidden, for instance, and in the death-wishing verses of "A Mona Lisa" and other poems.

Equally obvious is the connection between her lesbianism and the slimness of her creative output. Because of psychic and artistic constraints, the "lines she did not dare" went almost as unwritten as they were unspoken. Being a black lesbian poet in America at the beginning of the twentieth century meant that one wrote (or half wrote)—in isolation—a lot that she did not show and could not publish. It meant that when one did write to be printed, she did so in shackles—chained between the real experience and the conventions that would not give her voice. It meant that one fashioned a few race and nature poems, transliterated lyrics, and double-tongued verses that sometimes got published. It meant, finally, that one stopped writing altogether, dying "with her real gifts stifled within,"[99] and leaving behind the little that managed to survive of one's true self in fugitive pieces. Ironically, the fact that Grimké did not write and publish enough is given as a major reason for the scanty recognition accorded her (and also other women poets of the Harlem Renaissance).

Especially during the culturally active 1920s, Grimké was called upon to write articles and deliver speeches. It does not appear that she did many of these—which is not surprising given her retiring personality. Dunbar-Nelson could rise almost spontaneously and, as a posthumous column put it, "deliver the most brilliant speeches . . . new, vitalizing talks that made you think."[100] Grimké considered carefully—almost to the point of inhibition—everything she did and said that was not prompted by pique or anger. However, a few of her miscellaneous writings are important enough to mention. (These do not include her brief diaries, which do not even begin to approach the literary significance of Dunbar-Nelson's.) The sketch of her father's life that she wrote for the February 1925 *Opportunity* magazine has already been quoted from. Brown, Davis, and Lee include it in *The Negro Caravan* and refer to it as "one of the few intimate biographical sketches in the literature of the Negro."[101] In her characteristically readable prose, she reveals the Grimké boys street-fighting in Charleston and showing up with canes and high silk hats at the Weld's simple Quaker household; she also imparts necessary biographical and personal data about her father. One of her correspondents singled out her "pen picture" of her grandmother, Mrs. Nancy Weston, for special praise.

Grimké also reviewed Lillie B. C. Wyman's historical novel *Gertrude of Denmark,* combining with it information about Wyman and Wyman's family's antislavery activities.[102] On September 27, 1925, she was invited by the Dubois Circle, "a club of women interested in literature and art," to speak about "The Contribution of Negro Women to Poetry." In addition to her remarks about the short story mentioned above, Grimké wrote two other extant speeches, one entitled "Woman in the Home" and the other, "The Social Emancipation of Woman" (holograph manuscripts). The first is unliberated and Victorian. It views home as woman's proper sphere and praises her for her good, calming influence. The other, a longer and more polished essay, jibes more closely with what Grimké's life indicates that she believed. It espouses the opposite position, seeing woman as man's equal and pressing for societal reforms that would allow women to vote, participate actively in worldly affairs, escape the drudgery and subservience of traditional marriages, and not be penalized any more severely than men for "social sins" such as gambling, drinking, and personal indiscretions.

She begins this second essay with a parable about a garden, gardener, and two plants:

> Now it happened one morning in the early spring, he [the gardener] came forth with two seeds in his hand, and not seeing that they were of the same kind (for he was a narrow, short-sighted, old, man) he planted one in the middle of the garden in the fertile soil, where the sun shone, and the rains and the dews fell; but the other, supposing it to need a different treatment and too delicate to stand the rough rains and winds, he planted in a far corner in the gloom and shelter of the walls.

The middle plant flourishes while the sheltered, weed-choked one is stunted—until a storm comes and exposes it to sun and rain, whereupon it blossoms out, to the astonishment of the gardener, who must now decide how he should henceforth tend the plants. The meaning is obvious (with the storm being reform and the gardener public opinion). Grimké concludes her explanation of the parable by asserting that "the one great overmastering power of growth is freedom," and ends the speech with this impassioned peroration:

> I hope that the time may come when the garden of the world may lie wallless, treeless, weedless, that the man plant and the woman plant may grow drinking alike of the same sun, the same rain, and the same dew, that

their blossoms of thought may bloom in transcending beauty, and that their
seed may spring in the coming years into plants so wonderful and flowers
so glorious that all our grander dreams together are not able to match the
reality.

One would have liked to know why Grimké wrote this essay and what, if
anything, she did with it.

These few miscellaneous pieces and her significant body of published
(and unpublished) poetry represent Grimké during this, the second high
point, of her life. Her final years present, by contrast, a disappointingly
blank picture.

iv

Both Dunbar-Nelson and Georgia Douglas Johnson come into sharp
focus as strong, colorful individuals. It is much harder to see who Grimké
really was. Besides writing and teaching, she occupied herself largely with
family activities and reading. One chapter of Anna Cooper's *Life and Writings of the Grimké Family* provides an intimate treatment of the Grimké
family's Saturday and Sunday evening activities and amusements, which
included art study and musical entertainment. In an autobiographical
statement (which exists in an undated draft), Angelina wrote: "I am a
voracious reader and possess something of a private library." She perused
the classics, current books, and periodical magazines such as *The Nation*
and *The New Republic.*

Grimké also sewed, danced, played tennis, and took almost yearly vacations in Massachusetts and Connecticut. Her circle of friends and acquaintances included members of Old Line Massachusetts families such as
Ellen B. Stebbins,[103] as well as many of the prominent black leaders, educators, writers, and artists of the day. She received friendly notes from
Langston Hughes (who wrote nice letters to everybody) on May 8, 1927,
and June 4, 1937. She also corresponded and visited with Hallie Q. Brown,
the noted elocutionist and author, Jessie Fauset, and Georgia Douglas
Johnson. She was particularly close to her sister poet Georgia Johnson,
writing her a charming poem about the things she liked about her and
receiving from her an invitation to visit her in Washington as late as
1955.[104] On a more official level, she acted as an authority on and representative of the Grimké family (both Archibald and Francis) throughout
her life—for instance, helping to dedicate the Archibald H. Grimké School
in Washington on November 9, 1938.

As Grimké mentioned, she was very "light." She was also very small, weighing only ninety-two pounds in 1899 and one hundred pounds in 1912, after she had matured.[105] She was a pretty little girl and an attractive woman, and she dressed well, judging from her schoolday letters asking her father for clothes and her later department-store bills. As a child, her demeanor was solemn, and in succeeding years, her face attained a "haughty sadness."[106] Interestingly enough, she generally made the girls in her plays and stories petite, cute, and dark-haired, like herself.

Her health, though, was not robust. Correspondence between her and her father and close friends frequently refers to her various ailments. She suffered from enlarged glands, nerves, headaches, bone and bilious conditions. In July 1911 her back was seriously injured in a railway accident. The July 3, 1926, document that granted her retirement as of June 30, 1926, states the grounds as her being "incapable of satisfactorily performing her duties as a teacher." And it appears that two years later, she was extremely unwell.[107]

As everything that has been said about her would indicate, Grimké was not an easygoing extrovert. Describing her as a child, Anna Cooper uses the words "sweet" and "sadfaced" and calls her an "undemonstrative intelligent child."[108] Another lady, Lillian Lewis, wrote her a letter on September 5, 1900, congratulating her on her "Black Is, As Black Does" and marveling: "You quiet, demure, little girl—who would think you dreamed such dreams!" Angelina also disliked crowds, saying once "the fewer [people] the better as far as I am concerned."[109] However, by her own admission, she possessed a number of personality traits that made her difficult. A diary entry that she wrote on New Year's Eve 1911 is most revealing. It reads in part:

> . . . My faith in myself is not profound. On this the last day of the year 1911 I am brought face to face with myself. I cannot say I am proud. My hands are not clean. . . . There are so many, many things I could have left undone, unkind thoughts . . . so many times when I have depressed others unnecessarily because I selfishly was blue; and the shadows black of many other disagreeable and disgusting things. Remorse and regret two unpleasant visitors on the last day yet here they are beside me hugging me close and I can do nought but entertain them civilly for they are rightful guests. . . . I am too critical, too impatient about trifles in my friends. Help me to . . . not be a cad. . . .

Perhaps some of what Grimké writes here can be dismissed as New Year's Eve depression. However, a friend of hers named Joseph B. Robinson, with whom she had a personal relationship, says much the same thing in a January 5, 1934, letter to her:

> I don't know of any friend of yours whom you have known intimately over any length of time, that you don't accuse of trying to rob you or that you don't quarrel with on some pretext or other sooner or later. . . . I do wish you would take hold of yourself quit suspecting everybody. You would certainly find life much more pleasant.

It seems that the final illness and death of her father from 1928 to 1930 marked a turning point in her life, with Grimké becoming more irritable, litigious, and possibly neurotic. Certainly, the strain of nursing her father—even with professional help—was severe. This was complicated, too, by their extremely close relationship, which was, it seems, almost incestuous. Lacking a mother for balance, she was doubly (and probably ambivalently) bound to him with the iron of affection and chastisement—even writing literature to prove her worth and win his approbation. Lacking lovers, husband, her own family, these ties grew into an unhealthy, lifetime dependency. Clearly, his loss would have been traumatic.

During this period, she quarreled with her Uncle Francis and threatened to disinter her father from the "demeaning" plot where he had him buried, wrote haranguing letters to their medical doctor about a nurse who had supposedly bilked them, charged that her uncle had called her "crazy," and procured a May 7, 1930, notarized statement from Dr. William C. McNeill that she was "competent of conducting her business affairs."[110] Her friends, among them Dr. Solomon Fuller (Meta Warrick's husband) and Anna Cooper, all counseled her to "keep the upper hand," "get a fresh grip on yourself," and so forth.[111]

After her father died, Grimké moved to New York, ostensibly for her work, but produced little or nothing thereafter.[112] Unlike practically every other black writer of that period, she had not even applied for the prestigious awards in black literature offered by the Harmon Foundation from 1926 to 1930.[113] Anna Cooper wrote in her 1955 book: "It is regrettable that in later years Miss Grimké has not kept up the line of creative work which her earlier successes foreshadowed."[114] Arna Bontemps states that she "spent the last years of her life in quiet retirement in a New York City apartment."[115]

Other factors also help to explain why Grimké stopped writing. The drying up of interest and literary markets after 1930 has already been mentioned. The New York that Grimké moved to was far less encouraging to black writers than the glorious city of the 1920s. Grimké herself reveals an additional factor in the autobiographical statement that she wrote while she was teaching at Dunbar. The document appears to be a response to questions on an application for a short-story course. Grimké wrote:

> I am not in school at the present and shall have more time than otherwise to devote to this course. I wish to take "short story writing" for I am inherently lazy and I believe that if I set myself the task of working under a competent and exacting teacher I shall get back into the routine of writing. I have not written anything besides a few verses for five or six years.

Clearly, for reasons personal to her, Grimké lost the requisite motivation, mentality, and industry for writing and did so at a time that roughly coincided with and was to some extent influenced by the external conditions that ended the Harlem Renaissance.

A few key statements can serve to summarize Grimké and her achievement. From a progressive and cultivated biracial background, she developed into a versatile, socially conscious writer who was particularly concerned with the plight of black people in a racist society and the special problems that faced black women. Her three-act drama, *Rachel* (1920), attacks the evil of lynching with feeling and a fair amount of dramaturgical skill—as does her later unpublished play, "Mara." Her short stories, the least significant of her writings, also confront prejudice. In the poetry that she wrote throughout her entire career but never collected, Grimké is most successful, treating predominantly love and nature themes in compact, sensitive lyrics. Her miscellaneous pieces reveal her interest in topical issues as well as her adeptness at handling occasional prose. In all of her works, she seems to write autobiographically and utilizes material and experiences relevant to herself.

Considered from a personal standpoint, Grimké's position as a comfortable, educated, racially mixed black woman during the first part of the twentieth century was both advantageous and problematical. It buffered her from the harsher indignities of being black in America at that time and allowed her to develop her literary talent. Yet, at the same time, her extraordinary circumstances probably made it more difficult for her to achieve psychic peace and emotional happiness. She had an unusually intimate relationship with her father, and women were of paramount importance in her real life as in her literary imagination. It seems, however, that personal factors contributed in a major way to the loss of inspiration that terminated her writing career more than twenty-five years before her death in 1958.

What Grimké did accomplish is valuable and worthwhile. It earned her participation in the renaissance of the 1920s and insures her lasting fame as a noteworthy figure in black American literary history, particularly as a woman writer and lesbian poet.

On October 22, 1936, Grimké wrote Harold Jackman a letter that provides the last concrete glimpse of her.[116] Vacationing in Massachusetts, she apologizes for not answering him sooner, but confesses, "I am afraid I am still trifling." She informs him of her plans to return to New York and then comments: "I hate coming back also but not because of the dirt [?] as you know [?], but because it probably means a return to loneliness and uselessness." Apparently, there had been talk among her, Jackman, and Georgia Douglas Johnson of her assuaging this "loneliness and uselessness" by marrying someone, for she tells Jackman: "What Drago [a mutual friend] said is interesting. You could have made it even stronger about my desire to marry." Jackman is one of Johnson's homosexual "sons" and Drago one of the neurotic "mixed breeds" whom she nurtured. Grimké is ambivalent about the efforts to match her with Drago and says in her brusque fashion: "I sent him [Drago] a second card and told him I didn't know whether I had anything to say to him or not that, Georgia to the contrary, one could not write to order. I have heard nothing since. Ahem!!!" The conclusion of her letter reads:

> I do hope I see you soon and that I shall see you often this coming year. You are good for me. I am not certain but I feel, now, that I may write again.
>
>   Hoping to see you very soon
>   Nana

Of course, she did not "write again," and from all available evidence, she retreated even further into the almost unimaginable solitariness of her inner-city apartment. How did she spend so many idle hours and empty months? In a December 26, 1944, letter to Jackman, Johnson asks: "Why is it Nina does not write to me. Please tell her to. I hope she is not sick."[117] The earnestness of her statements reflects Johnson's effort to connect with Grimké and to "dig her out," as it were, from her self-imposed isolation. Johnson was no more successful than modern readers who attempt to find this buried woman. One researches and resurrects—but must struggle to reach her, for she had no spirit left to send. Unlike Dunbar-Nelson and Johnson herself, who saw through adversity to triumph and bring courage in the midst of tears, Grimké was torn and flattened. Her obituary in the *New York Times* on June 11, 1958, begins: "Miss Angelina Weld Grimké, poet and retired school teacher, died yesterday at her home, 208 West

151st Street, after a long illness. She was 78 years old."[118] Long before this, she had inadvertently written her own problematic epitaph in an un-published poem entitled "Under the Days":

> The days fall upon me;
> One by one, they fall,
> Like Leaves. . . . .
> They are black,
> They are gray.
> They are white;
> They are shot through with gold and fire.
> They fall,
> They fall
> Ceaselessly.
> They cover me,
> They crush,
> They smother.
> Who will ever find me
> Under the days?

CHAPTER IV

Georgia Douglas Johnson (1880–1966)

Not much is known of Georgia Douglas Johnson's early life. Even her birthdate is uncertain. Traditionally, it has been given as 1886 by most sources, but biographical evidence and obituary statements substantiate 1880 as the correct date.[1] In that year, on September 10, she was born "a little yellow girl" in Atlanta, Georgia, the child of George and Laura Camp.[2] Details are lacking about who her parents and family were, what were the circumstances of her growing up, and so on. Judging from her appearance, her lifelong preoccupation in life and art with the miscegenation theme, and allusions made by others, she was a black person with considerable white blood in her ancestry. Strangely, GDJ herself never mentions her kin—except on one occasion. In a March 31, 1945, letter to Harold Jackman, she tells him that she sent an Easter card to her sister, whose husband had "dropped dead and I knew she was unstabilized."[3]

Georgia attended Atlanta elementary schools, then proceeded to the normal course at Atlanta University. A "class of '93" (the entering year) photograph shows her standing among the other thirteen, mostly female, students, a very mature-looking young girl in winter hat and furs. After completing this course in 1896, she studied music at Oberlin Conservatory, Oberlin, Ohio, and the Cleveland College of Music, taking "special training" in music, harmony, violin, piano, and voice.[4]

Georgia Douglas Johnson during her heyday. (Photo courtesy of the Schomburg Center for Research in Black Culture, The New York Public Library, Astor, Lenox and Tilden Foundations.)

Georgia Douglas Johnson wearing one of the 1920s-style headbands that she adopted in her later life. (Photo courtesy of the Schomburg Center for Research in Black Culture, The New York Public Library, Astor, Lenox and Tilden Foundations.)

At this point in her life, Georgia wanted to write music. Decades later, she revealed this early ambition in an autobiographical statement: "Long years ago when the world was new for me, I dreamed of being a composer—wrote songs, many of them. The words took fire and the music smouldered and so, following the lead of friends and critics, I turned my face toward poetry and put my songs away. . . . "[5] This love of music sings through the lines of her verse, for, as she put it, "Into my poems I poured the longing for music." Critics have never made this connection between her musical bent and her poems. Even her contemporaries do not remark on it—and they knew that, as Glenn Carrington put it, "she set many of her own poems to music, and took pleasure in singing them and playing them on her piano for selected visitors to her home."[6] Toward the end of her career, she found her way back to her first love and collaborated with the noted composer Lillian Evanti.

Returning to Atlanta, GDJ taught school and served as an assistant principal. Music was probably her major subject; however, she mentions in 1931 that she "once taught teachers to write, well I did more than that I did the drawing and illustrating on the choice school papers"[7]—although she does not say when. It may also have been during this period that she met Henry Lincoln Johnson. Born the son of ex-slaves in 1870, he was A.B. Atlanta University (ca. 1888), LL.B. University of Michigan (ca. 1892), and had been Georgia delegate-at-large to the Republican National Convention since 1896. He and Georgia Douglass (as her name was then usually spelled) were married on September 28, 1903. They gave birth to two sons, Henry Lincoln, Jr., and Peter Douglas, within seven years, and in 1910 relocated to Washington, D.C., where "Link" Senior established a law firm.

For the thirty-year-old GDJ, this move to the nation's capital was a turning point. It sharpened the pace of her life and provided immediate opportunity for broadening contacts. She tells it like this in the third-person statement that she wrote for Countee Cullen's *Caroling Dusk* (1927): "Dean Kelly Miller at Howard University saw some of her poetic efforts and was pleased. [William] Stanley Braithwaite was his friend and he directed her to send something to him at Boston. She did so, and then began a quickening and a realization that she could do!"[8] Her first poems—"Gossamer," "Fame," and "My Little One"—appeared in *The Crisis* in 1916[9] (the same time that Angelina Grimké was presenting her pioneering play, *Rachel*). Two years later, her reputation-making volume *The Heart of a Woman and Other Poems* was published by the Cornhill Company.

The Heart of a Woman has been persistently locked into its designation as a book of tidy lyrics that express the love-longing of a feminine sensibility. Read afresh—that is, deeply, autobiographically, and with feminist aware-ness—it becomes much more than that and takes on new levels of interest and meaning.

One of GDJ's early mentors, established poet-anthologist William Stanley Braithwaite, wrote for her work a poetic and strikingly progressive introduction. He begins, "The poems in this book are intensely feminine and for me this means more than anything else that they are deeply hu-man."[10] He then speaks perceptively about how women have not yet been wholly emancipated and how the world is still ignorant of what remains hidden within their hearts "of mystery and passion, of domestic love and joy and sorrow, of romantic visions and practical ambitions." Unfortu-nately, like most critics, Braithwaite concludes by extolling her (woman's/ the poet's) "marvelous patience," "wonderful endurance," "persistent faith," and "sad felicity." But, before he fell into these clichés, he was groping toward something meaningful—the implications of which he may not have wanted to pursue.

GDJ *does* "lift the veil" from some of "woman's" less smiling faces. Clearly, she is aware of the oppressiveness and pain of the traditional female lot. Her title poem, which opens the volume, begins the revelations with its metaphor of a woman's heart as a bird that wings "forth with the dawn" over "life's turrets and vales," then

> . . . falls back with the night,
> And enters some alien cage in its plight,
> And tries to forget it has dreamed of the stars
> While it breaks, breaks, breaks on the sheltering bars.
>
> (P. 1)

The use of "alien cage" and "sheltering bars" is especially notable here. She makes a similar point in "Smothered Fires," where "a woman with a burning flame" keeps it covered through the years, suppressing the baleful light that would perforce arise, and in "When I Am Dead," whose speaker, having "longed for light and fragrance" and yet dwelt "beneath willows," eschews a hypocritical "blooming legacy" on her funeral bier.

She explicitly crystallizes these moods in an iambic tetrameter quatrain entitled "Foredoom":

> Her life was dwarfed, and wed to blight,
> Her very days were shades of night,

> Her every dream was born entombed,
> Her soul, a bud,—that never bloomed.
>
> (P. 39)

Here, and in similar poems, one might play it safe and read "objectively." However, the import and poignancy of the works are intensified if they are viewed as masked autobiographical utterances of the author herself. Often—in fact, too often for chance—there are references to dead hopes and dreams and a living, coupled aloneness ("Omega," "Despair," "Illusions," "My Little Dreams," etc.). Confronted thus, it is difficult not to recall her childhood ambitions and to wonder what other visionary yearnings she may have been forced to renounce, especially when she uses musical imagery, as in this first half of "Dead Leaves":

> The breaking dead leaves 'neath my feet
> A plaintive melody repeat,
> Recalling shattered hopes that lie
> As relics of a bygone sky.
>
> (P. 6)

Many of these poems are quietly seditious. What is missing from them, however, is a spirit of something other than articulate helplessness.

Equally as striking are the glimpses GDJ gives of her mystical, cosmic spirituality—the limitlessness of the soul ("Elevation"), reincarnation ("Impelled"), and the total connectedness and unity of all ("Modulations"):

> The petals of the faded rose
>   Commingle silently,
> One with the atoms of the dust,
>   One with the chaliced sea.
>
> The essence of my fleeting youth
>   Caught in the web of time,
> Exhales within the springing flowers
>   Or breathes in love sublime.
>
> (P. 35)

In terms of GDJ's general themes and subjects, moods and tones, Braithwaite sketched them when he enumerated "nature, or the seasons, touch of hands or lips, love, desire, or any of the emotional abstractions which sweep like fire or wind or cooling water through the blood." One could extend this list of immemorial lyric concerns by specifying sorrow, death, memory, time and aging, poetry, solitude, and evanescent joy. She treats these much-handled goods with feeling and respect, giving her renditions if not original force, then a delicate power.

Reading GDJ's poems, one is impressed by the degree of her poetic literateness. Like Dunbar-Nelson, she obviously perused quantities of classical, neoclassical, romantic, Victorian, and early twentieth-century verse. Her diction is the surest indication of this—for example, "postern gate," "bedight," "long defile of empty days," "attar," "enisled," "gloaming," "vespering," and "lyric rune." Lightly sprinkling words like these throughout her poems is one of her characteristic techniques. Others include her judicious incorporation of conceits and repeating images, playing iambs against the predominantly anapestic measure of a work, and constructing poems whose second half mirrors the first with turns and variations. Overall, as the Cornhill order blurb for her volume states, her "poems are brief, holding much of music and passion in a small cup of speech."[11]

Finally, there are her poems that are perfect song lyrics, making melody in the reader's ear. At least one deserves full quotation:

> The peerless boon of innocence
>   The first in nature's list,
> Is fading, ere the rising sun
>   The world awake has kist.
>
> The early dew upon the grass,
>   The purity of morn,
> The glint that lies in virgin cheek,
>   Frail cobwebs—of the dawn.
>
> ("Gossamer," p. 3)

While she was producing her first book, GDJ's husband, Lincoln, was advancing in his political career. In 1912, President Taft appointed him Recorder of Deeds for the District of Columbia, a post traditionally occupied by a black man since Frederick Douglass. He continued in this capacity until 1916, and might have done so longer had the Senate not refused to confirm his later nomination by President Harding. Nevertheless, he succeeded in maintaining himself as Republican National Committeeman from Georgia from 1920 until his death in 1925.

It must have been rather difficult for GDJ to write. The biggest obstacle of all was probably Link, who "didn't think much of his wife's longing for a literary career": "He tried to discourage the idea, but would quote her poems when making some of his greatest political speeches. The 'Colonel' thought a woman should take care of her home and her children and be content with that."[12] The home and children were certainly also draining. Quite clearly, GDJ's husband and marriage were typically patriarchal. She was the only one of the three writers under study here who had to endure this precise arrangement. Her and Lincoln's situation was further exacerbated by the ten years' difference in their ages, which could have reenforced the "master-child" dynamic of their husband-wife arrangement. Considering these matters and especially his attitude toward her work, there is a taste of bitter irony in the fact that she dedicated *The Heart of a Woman* "To H. L. Johnson." And yet, a rather intriguing, perhaps counterbalancing, portrait of their intimate relationship is provided by Dunbar-Nelson, who was a friend of GDJ's. In a wonderful journal entry, October 1, 1921, Dunbar-Nelson gives this glimpse of their domestic life:

> From the Y, I went to Lincoln Johnson's house. Georgia seemed glad to see me, and plunged instantly into a stream of poetic talk, mixed with hats, finding mine immensely becoming. . . . [She] wanted to know how to put on hats, and I began to teach her. She really did not know how, and I made her practise and practise again and again. Link [who was recovering from a stroke] seemed so glad that I was teaching his wife an essential thing that he suggested luncheon, "Irish potato salad, and some of my tomatoes from the garden, Georgia, so Miss Alice can see how fine my garden is." "Well fix it," said Georgia, and he did. Two dainty plates of salad, little fine slices of bread, tea, and all. Of course, he had to push away papers, manuscript, junk from the dining room table to make a place for his tray, for Georgia has her machine, and all her literary stuff in the dining room, but we ate his salad and sliced pineapple, and everything, while Georgia showed me the manuscript of her new book. . . . [13]

At this point, she had already completed a second volume entitled *Bronze: A Book of Verse*, which rolled off the presses of the B. J. Brimmer Company, Boston, in 1922. The key to critiquing *Bronze* is a biographical statement that GDJ herself made in 1941 to Arna Bontemps:

> My first book was the Heart of A Woman. It was not at all race conscious. Then some one said—she has no feeling for the race. So I wrote Bronze—it is entirely racial and one section deals entirely with motherhood—that motherhood that has as its basic note—black children born to the world's displeasure.[14]

Consequently, much of *Bronze*—which is her weakest book—reads like obligatory race poetry.

In *Bronze*, GDJ assumes the role of spokesperson for a downtrodden but rising black people. She even prefaces her writing with an "Author's

Note": "This book is the child of a bitter earth-wound. I sit on the earth and sing—sing out, and of, my sorrow. Yet, fully conscious of the potent agencies that silently work in their healing ministries, I know that God's sun shall one day shine upon a perfected and unhampered people."[15] In a manner that this note presages, the ensuing poems tend toward a precious self-consciousness and poetic obliquity. In fact, the dominant image for the entire volume is that of the "mantle," meaning the cloak of "darkness" surrounding the black race: "Sonnet to the Mantled," "The mother soothes her mantled child," and "Cheering the mantled on the thorn-set way"—for example. However, despite its indirectness and conciliatory tone, *Bronze* belongs to the early spate of 1920s black literature that spoke more vociferously of black determination to overturn racial prejudice. Considering GDJ's makeup and the prevailing notion of appropriate womanly behavior, it is difficult to imagine her handling the theme in any other way. Grimké wrote more directly of racial concerns, while Dunbar-Nelson was also reticent in her poetry and short stories but bold in her other work.

GDJ apportions the sixty-five poems of *Bronze* into nine separate sections—"Exhortation," "Supplication," "Shadow," "Motherhood," "Prescience," "Exaltation," "Martial," "Random," and "Appreciations." This establishes a general movement from despair and entreaty to confident determination. The final division consists of poems and sonnets of praise to martyrs in general and to specific individuals such as John Brown, Abraham Lincoln, W. E. B. DuBois, Emilie Bigelow Hapgood (philanthropist), Mary Church Terrell, May Howard Jackson (sculptor), and so on. When not fulsome, they are stately tributes, with some of the concluding couplets being particularly graceful:

> O Alleghanies, fold him to your breast
> Until the judgment! Sentinel his rest!
>
> ("To John Brown," p. 89)

It is also interesting that here GDJ treats motherhood. (Only two of her poems in *Heart* touched on children.) In "The Mother," there occurs what is possibly the most dramatic image in the book: "Her heart is sandaling his feet."

Throughout, GDJ works in a variety of forms (many more than before)—sonnets both Shakespearean and Italian, iambic heptameter lines, her usual quatrains, and even a few free-verse poems. One work, "Hegira," manifests a notable attempt at technical innovation. The initial stanza questions black people about their northern migration; the remainder answer the query in detailed and passionate language:

> I have toiled in your cornfields, and parched in the sun,
>   I have bowed 'neath your load of care,
> I have patiently garnered your bright golden grain, in
>   season of storm and fair,
> . . . .
> My sons, deftly sapped of the brawn-hood of man, self-
>   rejected and impotent stand,
> My daughters, unhaloed, unhonored, undone, feed the
>   lust of a dominant land.

(Pp. 33–34)

Using these techniques, she is able to write a number of effective, sometimes strong, verses—"Calling Dreams," "Prejudice," "Laocoon," "Little Son," "Hope."

Focusing in on other poems also turns up points of interest. There is "Aliens," a neo-treatment of the tragic mulatto, who is called in the poem "the fretted fabric of a dual dynasty." GDJ dedicates it "To You—Everywhere!" in an outburst of emotion that indicates her involvement with this subject. Testifying about this aspect of her importance years later, Cedric Dover writes:

> She has faced and resolved the psychological and social complications of being a near-white, while retaining enough traces of "tragic mulatto" feeling to stress the merit of her conquest. . . . She was the mother who nourished a whole generation of Eurasians and other "Mixed breeds" like myself. We found in her the blood and bone we needed to fight. . . . [16]

A related matter is her, to continue in Dover's words, "philosophy of dawn-men born of the fused strength of tributary sources."[17] She expresses this in "Fusion," a poem that is reminiscent of Jean Toomer's ideas in his long free-verse essay "Blue Meridian."

GDJ even considered this theme sufficiently important that she later wrote or thought of writing a novel about it called "One and One Makes Three," which she synopsized in a catalogue of her writings as follows:

> Story of the life of a child, born of a father with years of intellectual culture in his background, and a mother, with a perfect body, a bit [big?] soul and a warm heart, producing: a child who sums the two parents and adds, comprehension, understanding, tolerance, vigor, energy, beauty and love, such being the resultant of a perfect summation of new world being.[18]

Here, she does not mention racial origins (though how explicit she may have been about this in the novel itself is impossible to say). However, the basic notion is definitely the same.

Her poem "Black Woman" is notable because, like Angelina Grimké's controversial 1920 play *Rachel*, it presents a potential mother who refuses painfully to bring a black child into this world of "cruelty and sin." Also like Grimké, she pushed this protest even further in a one-act play that she mentioned in her catalogue, "Safe." It concerns a young mother who "snuffs out the life of her baby who is being born at the same time" that a black boy is "strung up" by a lynch mob.[19] "Homing Braves," a topical poem, salutes black soldiers returning from the First World War emboldened and proud. Finally, "Credo" is significant because it sets forth the axioms that informed and guided GDJ all of her life—for instance:

> I believe in the ultimate justice of Fate;
> That the races of men front the sun in their turn;
> . . . .
> I believe that the key to the life-mystery
> Lies deeper than reason and further than death.
>
> (P. 53)

DuBois wrote an insulting one-page "Foreword" to *Bronze*. He correctly identifies its theme—"what it means to be a colored woman in 1922"— and speculates about various kinds of readers' response, saying eventually that "none can fail to be caught here and there by a word—a phrase—a period. . . . " He concludes: "Her work is simple, sometimes trite, but it is singularly sincere and true, and as a revelation of the soul struggle of the women of a race it is invaluable." One wonders why GDJ/her friends/the publishers allowed such a bald, condescending statement to be printed. Apparently, the general feeling must have been that even this from DuBois was a boon.

Praise from other commentators was less qualified. The consensus was that GDJ had done a creditable job of writing racial poetry from the unique perspective of the black woman, and that *Bronze* was a valuable book that further enhanced her reputation. The keynotes of this criticism are sounded in this excerpt from the Washington, D.C., *Evening Star:*

> Serious throughout, uplifted at times, rarely bitter, deeply sorrowful, *Bronze* is an unmistakable cry of the human who is still in bondage, not physical bondage, true, but bondage of the spirit in many manifestations. As poetry, the claim of this book cannot be justly denied. It is good poetry, both in the letter of poetic laws and in the spirit of poetic feeling.[20]

One of the most original responses about *Bronze* issued from Alain Locke and Jessie Fauset's *Crisis* column, "Notes on the New Books":

> Mrs. Johnson seems to me to hear a message, a message that gains through being softly but intensely insinuated between the lines of her poems—"Let the traditional instincts of women heal the world that travails under the accumulated woes of the uncompensated instincts of men," or to speak more in her way, "May the saving grace of the motherheart save human-ity."

Though beginning her writing relatively late in adulthood, GDJ rather quickly produced two notable volumes of verse, *The Heart of a Woman* and *Bronze*. Certainly, by the early 1920s, her career as a wife-and-mother turned poet had been auspiciously launched.

ii

On September 10, 1925, Henry Lincoln Johnson, Sr., died of a cerebral hemorrhage caused by a stroke. He had suffered earlier attacks of apoplexy in 1921 and 1923, but this time he succumbed, his large, rotund body having carried all the stress that it could. At an "impressive and imposing" funeral attended by "many high state officials" such as the secretary of labor and postmaster general, he was eulogized as a statesman whose career could be likened to that of Christ. President Calvin Coolidge sent a warmly worded condolence message to Georgia telling her "of my sorrow at his passing and of the sympathy which I feel for you and your sons in your great loss."[21] At this time, she was forty-five years old. Her two children, fifteen and seventeen, were within one and two years of finishing college.

For GDJ, her husband's death was a second turning point. It almost certainly allowed her a freer space in which to write, travel, and the like—as evidenced by her activities of the next few years. But, paradoxically, his loss also complicated her life in ways that rendered writing more difficult.

Chief among these were money and having to bear sole responsibility for the family. It appears that she had not worked extensively outside the home; now she does, in a series of public jobs from sometime around 1924 until she loses the last one in 1934. She is a substitute teacher and librarian for the District of Columbia Public Schools. Then she works as a file clerk for the Civil Service, and Commissioner of Immigration (immigrant inspec-tor) for the Department of Labor. From 1925 to 1934, her title was Com-missioner of Conciliation (labor inspector), Department of Labor, a posi-tion requiring her to investigate "living conditions among laborers."[22]

Having to hold a nine-to-five job sapped her energy—creative and oth-erwise. Time to write, time to write became a constant theme of her existence. A 1928 newspaper article about her begins: "The great fear in Georgia Douglas Johnson's life is that she won't have time to do all the work she has planned to do that she wants to do. Although she works incessantly, her time is too much taken up with making a living to give very much of it to literary work."[23] DuBois hinted at this in a June 21, 1927, letter of recommendation when he wrote: "She has succeeded in writing poetry by the hardest kind of application in the midst of every sort of distraction."[24] GDJ put it even more forthrightly when she said: "If I might ask of some fairy godmother special favors, one would sure be for a clearing space, elbow room in which to think and write and live beyond the reach of the Wolf's fingers."[25] Of course, this has been the dilemma-handicap-cross of practically every black woman who has tried to live and be a conscious artist.

Undoubtedly, the most broadening and spectacular of GDJ's post-1925 activities were the literary evenings at her home, which contributed to her fame and made of Washington, D.C., another mecca for the New Negro Renaissance. According to her, they began in this way:

> Years ago—Jean Toomer said to me "Mrs. J—Why don't you have Weekly Conversations among the writers here in Washington?" It was difficult for me to arrange as home duties had about consumed me before Saturday night, however, I did make an attempt and we began the Saturday evening talks which continued until through about ten years and came to life intermittently now and then to the present.[26]

The first documentation of the group occurs in Gwendolyn Bennett's "Ebony Flute" column, October 1926:

> We who clink our cups over New York fire-places are wont to miss the fact that little knots of literary devotees are in like manner sipping their "cup of warmth" in this or that city of the "provinces." Which reminds me that I have heard Georgia Douglas Johnson say that there is a *Saturday Nighters Club* in Washington, too.[27]

In the years of its flourishing, many black writers, both established and fledgling, partook of the comfort and conversation of GDJ's bay-windowed living room in northwest D.C. They included Jean Toomer, Langston Hughes, Countee Cullen, Marietta Bonner, Bruce Nugent, Angelina Grimké, Lewis Alexander, Jessie Fauset, Wallace Thurman, Arna Bontemps, Effie Lee Newsome, Anne Spencer, James Weldon Johnson, Alain Locke, W. E. B. DuBois, William Stanley Braithwaite, Mae Miller, Willis Richardson, Mary Burrill, Roscoe C. Bruce, E. C. Williams, A. Philip Randolph, Chandler Owens, Kelly Miller, Eric Walrond, Mae Howard Jackson, Charles S. Johnson, Gwendolyn Bennett, Alice Dunbar-Nelson, and Clarissa Scott Delaney.

According to one contemporary reporter, these gatherings were "interesting, lively, many-hued":

> If dull ones come, she [GDJ] weeds them out, gently, effectively. The Negro's predicament is such, Mrs. Johnson believes, that only the white people can afford to have dull leaders. It is a remarkable social phenomenon to see this woman, who works eight hours a day in the Department of Labor, wielding by sheer force of personality an important influence. . . . [28]

The year 1927 was especially brilliant. Two accounts from that summer provide the best picture available of what transpired at these literary evenings. Again, Gwendolyn Bennett tells of the June 4 meeting, where Charles S. Johnson was guest of honor, Angelina Grimké was "particularly pleasing," and the whole company was "a charming medley":

> E. C. Williams with his genial good-humor; Lewis Alexander with jovial tales of this thing and that as well as a new poem or two which he read; Marieta Bonner with her quiet dignity; Willis Richardson with talk of "plays and things" . . . and here and there a new poet or playwright . . . and the whole group held together by the dynamic personality of Mrs. Johnson . . . some poems by Langston Hughes were read.[29]

Dunbar-Nelson's July 23, 1927, journal redaction is even more flavorful. She, GDJ, and another friend are gallivanting and getting lost all over Washington, while the assembled guests are expecting them:

> Georgia looking like the Tragic Muse thinking of the little poets she had invited to meet me and how it was getting on to nine o'clock . . . finally reach Georgia's at 9:45. She and I make explanations. A near-high [?] bunch. Willis Richardson and his wife, the most interesting and little John Davis. Much poetry and discussion and salad and wine and tea and Bobbo [Dunbar-Nelson's husband] rescues me at midnight.[30]

Quite rightly, GDJ wanted to publish a book about her Saturday Nighters. In 1942, she mentions that she has it "sketched out" and that she has kept "letters and original poems" of "our young writers," which "will make a valuable contribution to the early history of these writers."[31] On August 8, 1944, she says that she is "about to begin on Reminiscences of Washington's Young Writers—or something like that."[32] This same project she calls *Literary Salon* in her 1962–63 "Catalogue of Writings," describing it as "the story of literary gatherings . . . where many of the splendid young writers of the present-day received their contactual inspiration."[33] That this work was never completely written or printed and has not survived is almost surely a considerable loss to black American literature.

This latter 1920s period after Link's death was also GDJ's brightest season in the public sun. Sometime in 1926, she made a trip to Chicago, where she was "graciously received" by Harriet Monroe of *Poetry* magazine and spoke with Carl Sandburg "of this and that thing about Negroes and their work."[34] During the fall of 1927 in New York City she met social columnist Geraldyn Dismond, who was impressed not "by the fact that Mrs. Johnson can create a poem or play, but by the charm of her quiet dignity and tender sympathy."[35] Later that same fall, she journeyed to Durham, North Carolina, for a "Black Fact-Finding and Stock-Taking Conference." There she was honored with four other "distinguished ladies"—Mary McLeod Bethune, Charlotte Hawkins Brown, Alice Dunbar-Nelson, and Mrs. Benjamin Brawley.[36] Returning to Washington at 7:25 A.M., she, Dunbar-Nelson, and DuBois taxied to her home, went marketing, then fixed a "breakfast fit for the gods" before going their separate ways.

The spring of 1928 found her in Atlanta, Georgia, delivering the dedicatory talk for a new building being erected by the Neighborhood Union. Generally, at this point, GDJ is doing more speaking/reading in various cities than ever—for example, at the Civic Club in New York City, or the Brooklyn Y.W.C.A. Sometime prior to January 16, 1929, she visited Cleveland, Ohio, and writer Charles Chesnutt and his family, for in a letter of that date to him, she says: "I do not lightly forget the trip I had to Cleveland for standing out most conspicuously is the memory of my talk with you and also my trip to your wonderful home."[37]

Newspaper articles also gave her exposure. Particularly outstanding is a feature written by Floyd J. Calvin that appeared in the Pittsburgh *Courier* July 1928. It is subheaded "Educating Her Splendid Sons, Writing Poems and Plays—Her Days Are Quite Full." Her son Henry is one year away from finishing law at Howard University, and Peter has just completed the first year of medical school, also at Howard—educational expenses that she has borne in addition to keeping their house.

A good portion of the article outlines the five books she has on hand, which "could, on short notice, be prepared for the publishers if she had the time to do it": (1) "'The Torch'—inspirational bits written by famous authors, culled from a lifetime of reading." (2) "The Life and Times of Henry Lincoln Johnson," which "will give a detailed account of her husband's life from the time he entered politics down in Georgia at the age of 9." One of the topics she and Sandburg discussed in Chicago was this material, which he told her "should make a corking story." (3) "Short stories of mixed bloods" called "Rainbow Silhouettes" with plots about a girl passing for white in Salt Lake City, and "a little girl in a colored family, born of a wealthy white woman and her butler." (4) "The Autumn Love Cycle" and (5) "Homely Philosophy" (both discussed below). The remainder of the feature touches upon her as a playwright, her biography, and her current civic and literary interests.

This *Courier* article is a reminder that, whatever else she may have been engaged in, GDJ's celebrity status accrued to her because of her achievements as an author. Sometime during the early to mid-1920s, she took up playwriting, saying in 1927: "Then [after poetry] came drama. I was persuaded to try it and found it a living avenue. . . . "[38] She was successful as a dramatist and, were it not for the peculiarities of the genre and the vagaries of literary fortune, she could just as easily have come down through history known predominantly as a playwright rather than a poet. In fact, noting the emphasis placed upon this form in her self-compiled "Catalogue of Writings," one might conclude that this was her major preoccupation. Nevertheless, that her reputation jelled as a lyric versifier probably has at least as much to do with the reality and image of her as a woman as it does with the objective difficulties of mounting plays.

The first work of hers to win recognition was *Blue Blood*. It was awarded honorable mention in the 1926 *Opportunity* play contest, produced that fall by the Krigwa Players, New York City, and published by Appleton the following year. *Blue Blood* is an interesting creation, in that its essentially comic exterior is built upon a very un-funny substructure—the grim fact of miscegenation via the rape of black women by white men in the South shortly after the Civil War.

As the play opens, May Bush is dressing to marry John Temple, while Randolph Strong, her unsuccessful suitor, is comforted by her mother, Mrs. Bush. John's mother, Mrs. Temple, a pretentious society lady proud of her status, breezes into the kitchen to help with last-minute preparations, whereupon the two mothers proceed to "one-up" each other about their children's worth. Mrs. Bush's revelation that May's father is a rich white banker becomes the dramatic complication for, as Mrs. Temple finally confesses, this man is also John's father.

She tells the story of how she once taught at a country school in Georgia where the banker pursued her, though she was engaged:

I tried to keep away. One night he came to the place where I boarded. The woman where I boarded—she helped him—he bribed her. He came into my room— . . . I cried out. There wasn't any one there that cared enough to help me, and you know yourself, Mrs. Bush, what little chance there is for women like us, in the South, to get justice or redress when these things happen![39]

When the distraught May hears this tale and also finds out her mother's secret, she cries: "Oh God—I've kept out of their clutches myself, but now it's through you, Ma, that they've got me anyway. Oh, what's the use . . . " Thus, GDJ makes a serious statement about this historical problem of black women. Of course, being a comedy, the play ends happily, with Randolph persuading May to elope with him, leaving John and the townspeople none the wiser.

The script is one that would act well. Movement, dialogue, characters are all effective. GDJ's dramaturgical skill is evident throughout—for example, in the way she is able to draw matters out, heightening the suspense and comedy by withholding action until the last possible moment. This works especially well in the scene where the procrastinating Mrs. Temple finally blurts out her story and later when they inform May— probably because GDJ uses the device in a way that enhances her generally deft characterization of the players. The foreshadowing is subtle, and the turns of the plot not totally transparent. Overall, *Blue Blood* is rather sophisticated drama.

The merits of *Blue Blood* notwithstanding, it was her next play, *Plumes,* that won first prize in the 1927 *Opportunity* competition. It is a "folk tragedy" set in the "contemporary" rural South. Black folkways/beliefs/"superstitions"/modes of thought/values saturate the work and are indispensable to it. These elements are pitted against "enlightened" Western thinking, represented by the doctor who wishes to operate on Emmerline, Charity Brown's gravely ill fourteen-year-old daughter. By scrimping and scraping, Charity has saved fifty dollars—the cost of the operation—but also the price of the best funeral (with plumed horses), which she desires for Emmerline if she dies. Charity and her friend Tildy have "no faith a-tall" in doctors, who only think about "cuttin' and killing and taking your money."[40] They drink coffee, about which Charity says, "I love it, but it don't love me—gives me the shortness of breath." Then Tildy reads the grounds left in Charity's cup, which ominously show a funeral procession. While her mother hesitates about which avenue to follow, Emmerline dies.

Charity's conflict is sympathetically portrayed, though it is obvious from the beginning which side will win. No onus attaches to her for her actions—or lack thereof. She does what she does because of who she is, and that identity is sharply limned in the play. She and Tildy together make a good pair who counterpoise each other, as illustrated through these lines of dialogue:

> Charity. I been thinking 'bout Zeke these last few days—how he was put away—
>
> Tildy. I wouldn't worry 'bout him now. He's out of his troubles.
>
> Charity. I know. But it worries me when I think about how he was put away . . . that ugly pine coffin, jest one shabby old hack and nothing else to show—to show—what we thought about him.
>
> Tildy. Hush, sister! Don't you worry over him. He's happy now, anyhow.
>
> Charity. I can't help it! Then little Bessie. We all jest scrooged in one hack and took her little coffin in our lap all the way out to the graveyard. (*Breaks out crying.*)
>
> Tildy. Do hush, sister Charity. You done the best you could. Poor folks got to make the best of it. The Lord understands—(P. 291)

As they talk, they give each other support and understanding, and also concrete womanly aid. Tildy helps sew Emmerline's dress and hangs out a tub of Charity's wash.

This dialogue further reveals GDJ's method of mixing "correct" standard English and traditional black dialect to produce a language that conveys a folk quality while remaining dignified and easily intelligible. Her sense of the dramatic also continues strong. The play's ending is such a stroke, where Charity's final line, "Rip the hem out, sister Tildy," says it all—it having already been established that if Emmerline lives, her dress should be hemmed short, but if she dies, it must be left long to cover her coffined feet.

A New York *Amsterdam News* review stated that *Plumes* met the three conditions for "real Negro literature," namely "a Negro author, a Negro subject, and a Negro audience."[41] This is surely one way of attesting to the genuineness of the work. That GDJ is able to achieve such authenticity is a tribute to her racial feeling and/or her versatile genius as an artist. In *Plumes*, she is as "folk" as she is "academic" in her poetry, striking an authentic roots level that eluded Grimké and Dunbar-Nelson.

GDJ included *Plumes* and *Blue Blood* among her four dramas designated "Primitive Life Plays."[42] The other two (both now lost) were "Red Shoes" and "Well-Diggers." Written for the famous actress Rose McClendon, the first was a domestic play about a mother who bought for her baby's burial red shoes, which are stolen by the drunken father for whiskey. The other concerns two black law partners in the South and the ethical issue of whether they should exploit negative racial stereotypes to secure the acquittal of black clients.

Another category of drama of which GDJ wrote or projected several examples is the "lynching play," recalling Grimké's preoccupation with this theme. However, of the six listed in her "Catalogue," only one is extant. Like almost all black writers and activists of the period, GDJ was intensely concerned about the horrible number of blacks who were being routinely lynched in this country—a figure conservatively set at 1,886 persons for 1900–31.[43] Controversy on the subject was at its height during the early 1920s because of the debate in Congress over the Dyer Anti-Lynching Bill, which, incidentally, was defeated in 1922. Two of her plays explicitly focus on these Congressional "deliberations": "A Bill to be Passed"—"one-act play touching Lynching Bill before Congress, outside of Congressional chamber, four characters"—and "And Still They Paused"—about the continued delay in passing the bill. Her other lost plays in this group are "Safe" (mentioned earlier), a second version of *A Sunday Morning in the South* with a white rather than black church background, and "Blue-Eyed Black Boy": "One-act play, scene kitchen, four characters. Mayor's blue-eyed black son about to be lynched and is saved by mother who appeals to the father and takes the disgrace resulting from her disclosure."[44]

Her one extant lynching play was, apparently, never acted or printed during GDJ's lifetime, and was not readily available until Hatch and Shine published it in their *Black Theatre U.S.A.* collection under the "Black Folk Plays of the 1920's" section. *A Sunday Morning in the South* takes place in "a town in the South" in 1924. Called "a protest play," it explores the theme of the theory versus the reality of justice for black people. Nineteen-year-old Tom Griggs is shabbily identified as the man who allegedly attacked a white woman and, despite his sterling reputation and statements from his good seventy-year-old grandmother and young brother, is taken from the questionable custody of officers and lynched by a mob who "wont gointer be cheated outen they Nigger this time."

The ingredients of the play are staples that GDJ mixes well. This is evident in the predictable action of the plot, and even more so in the characters, who are familiar types, down to their red bandannas, secular Christianity, stomach-rubbing relish for homemade rolls and sausage, and racist disrespect of black "Grannies." A dash of originality comes from her emotional blending in of the spirituals being sung next door at church. This is well done—as is her thorough and efficient exposition, swift but not hasty movement, variegated mix of mood and tone (from comic to pathetic), and tight construction.

Two other one-act plays by GDJ have seen publication—historical works about Frederick Douglass and William and Ellen Craft, respectively. They are black history lessons dramatically packaged, and, as such, accurately present the known facts about their subjects. Clearly, they are meant to inform an audience and would make excellent educational material. Furthermore, as one would expect, if the reader-viewer already knows the history, there is nothing spectacular about the presentations, since the possibility for surprises does not exist. What helps to maintain interest is seeing how GDJ will incorporate the data and what embellishment she will add when there is license—for instance, noting how she works Douglass's telling of the way he learned to read and write into a gingerbread-break conversation with his sweetheart Ann, or watching William's escape plan undergo successive refinements.

William and Ellen Craft is the fresher of the two plays. This is probably because the basic story is more intriguing. Nevertheless, in it, the feelings are stronger, action more desperate, and there is greater diversity of characters. It even becomes relatively exciting when a tattletale slave named Sam sniffs out their plans and has to be permanently silenced:

> Sam.   (*Sneeringly.*) So you is going to try to get away, is ya? (*Moves toward the door.*) Goin' to tell ole Miss goodbye?
> William.   (*Excitedly.*) What you goin' to do?
> Sam.   (*Snarlingly.*) What you reckon, Mr. edicated nigger?
> William.   (*Rushes to him and catches him about the throat.*) So you is goin' to tell! Spyin' on us! I sho ya!
> Mandy.   (*Jumping up overturning her chair in excitement.*) What you goin' to do, William?
> William.   I'm goin' to shut his mouth. . . .
> Mandy.   (*Head on one side listening outside.*) Wonder what William is a doin' to Sam?
> Ellen.   (*Tearfully.*) I dunno. I don't wunt to know.[45]

Both plays share certain repeated motifs (drinking tea/coffee, the passing of locomotives), and end the same way—with a train-whistle getaway and a knee-bent prayer.

In the fall of 1926, *Popoplikahu,* a play written either by GDJ alone or by her and Bruce Nugent (Richard Bruce), was being rehearsed by Barrington Guy for the Washington, D.C., Presidential Theatre.[46] She describes it like this: "Half-cast in Africa falls in love with Claire, daughter of the English Missionary, who is enraged and threatens to kill the half-cast. The lovers become so desperate that he finally stabs her and then, himself. Scene— African Village—with six characters—three scenes."[47] This highly melo-dramatic work seems to shamelessly exploit the Harlem Renaissance taste for *things Africaine*, which characterized the era and was fed in drama by the success of, say, Eugene O'Neill's *The Emperor Jones* (1920). GDJ appar-ently wrote one other play with an African background called "Jungle Love," an even more involved romance with Burmese and African kings, racially illicit lovers, a eunuch, and a python pit.

One final play by GDJ is extant in a sixteen-page manuscript at the Yale University Beinecke Library.[48] Entitled "Starting Point," it is, as the author dubbed it, a story of "average Negro life." Henry and Martha Robinson, conscientious parents getting on in age, think their son Tom, whom they dote on, is "doing so fine up there in the doctor's school in Washington," when in reality, he is writing numbers. He comes home unexpectedly with a surprise wife, their "new daughter Belle—!!" Tom receives a telegram from a friend telling him that his place has been raided and advising him to stay away. Through Belle's prodding, Tom is forced to "come clean" with his parents who are, naturally, broken, traumatized. Scene 2 ends with father and son shouting, father rushing and slapping Tom, and his mother fainting. The play concludes happily, though, with the men reconciled and Tom agreeing to start over from the point of his father's lowly position as porter at the bank. The drama reads rather well. It generally maintains interest, is structured effectively, and utilizes an authenticating vernacular speech.

GDJ placed six other of her now nonexistent plays in this "average Negro life" category. Among these were "Holiday," a Cinderella story about a plain sister who meets love staying at home; "Little Blue Pigeon," which concerns a "young mulatto mother" who passes for white in order to keep her government job, thus enabling her "to take care of her baby— she being a newcomer in Washington, and a stranger;" "One Cross Enough" about a "light colored girl in Germany" who refuses to add her "cross of color" to her Jewish admirer's "Cross of being a Jew"; and "Sue Bailey," a "three-act play based upon the stormy life of an unmarried girl who stabs her paramour, and begins to run away from the consequences of her act."

She also wrote what she termed "Brotherhood" dramas aimed at erad-icating racial "intolerance," and a number of similar plays on interracial themes. The most blatant was "Midnight and Dawn" about a black boy who saves a white boy and loses his eyesight, only to have it restored years later by the white after he becomes rich and important. One or two of her works have war backgrounds and soldiers as characters. And there were a few plays on miscellaneous themes. All together, she listed twenty-eight dramatic works in her "Catalogue."

What is there to say, finally, about GDJ as dramatist? What observations can be made about her themes and subjects, style, significance, and achievements? Definitive assessment is complicated by the unavailability of her total corpus, and by the consideration that one inevitably gives to her "Catalogue" descriptions of the lost works. When both her available and catalogue-described plays are looked at together, the immediate impression is one of variety and scope—in contrast to the plays of, say, Angelina Grimké, who, even in her unpublished dramas, worked and reworked the same themes and situations. It is also very apparent that GDJ was prolific, even though it is impossible to judge that fecund output.

Furthermore, there is a vague impression here of mediocrity, based on one's subjective response to the lack of innovativeness of her subjects and plots—especially as they are synopsized. It is hard to be thrilled by her summaries. However, the summaries of her extant plays are also not gripping, but the plays themselves, when developed (that is, written and then read or seen), range from good to admirable. Clearly, GDJ's genius did not run to thematic originality. She wrote categorizable types of drama—lynching, "primitive" African, passing, miscegenation, interracial "brotherhood," and so on. What she succeeded at was effective dramaturgy: undeniably, she knew how to write one-act plays.

Within her chosen spheres, GDJ made her own mark and displayed creative individuality. As Dover wrote, one of her preoccupations was the situation of visibly mixed-blood blacks. Second, she wrote extensively about women, evidencing great sensitivity about their lives in diverse environments—the young government-worker mother and Ellen Craft as concubine-bound slave woman, for example. Regardless of the topic of her drama, almost without exception, the female characters are center stage. For instance, in *A Sunday Morning in the South*, the principal figure is the grandmother, even though it is the grandson who gets killed.

Thinking about GDJ as playwright, one notes, again, how this aspect of her artistic identity and achievement has been neglected—partly because it is simpler to keep her in her place as lady poet. But her drama must be considered if we are to come to some ultimately accurate conclusions about her as a writer.

During this splendid period following Link's death, GDJ's brilliance was further enhanced by the publication of her third book of poetry in 1928 (truly her red-letter year). It had come into being at least as early as 1921, when it was an intact manuscript called "An Autumn Idyll," which William Stanley Braithwaite was offering to publishers.[49] Finally appearing as *An Autumn Love Cycle* (an apter title, whoever made the change), it tells the story of an autumnal woman's romantic affair, from its heady beginnings to the ultimate resolution. It is almost as hard for us not to read the tale autobiographically as it was for GDJ's friend Alice Dunbar-Nelson, who said of the work: "It makes you blush at times, the baring of the inmost secrets of a soul, as it does. I wonder what Link thinks of it? You might call it poetic inspiration, if you will, but it looks suspiciously to me as if Georgia had had an affair, and it had been a source of inspiration to her."

Whether the product of real life or fancy, *An Autumn Love Cycle* is GDJ's best volume of verse. She continues her mining of "the heart of a woman" with even finer feeling than in that earlier treatment. As Alain Locke avers in the foreword, this is her "special domain" in poetry, if not for her art in general. The poems are, to quote one reviewer, "engagingly candid, sincere, spontaneous, elemental."[50] As such, they have a simple and straightforward power that is not marred by self-conscious poeticizing. Here, GDJ eschews reliance on too-studied conceits and eighteenth-century poetic diction. There also seems to be an increase in the number of free-verse poems, which both indicates and heightens the impression of relative artlessness. The poems ring genuine, authentic—clearly conveying that the narrator *knows* the emotions about which she speaks. And, if the reader has undergone similar joys and sorrows, then they become even more touchingly true.

GDJ adopted the most obvious, but most effective, structure for the book—the organic progress of the romance. The beginning section, "The Cycle," chronicles the initial flaming and disillusion: "Oh Night of Love," "Proving," "Good-Bye," "Parody," and "Sunset." Second comes "Contemplation," a time of reviewing the lived experience and concluding, though without regret, that

> There's nothing certain, nothing sure
> Save sorrow. Fragile happiness
> was never fashioned to endure. . . . [51]

"Intermezzi" is a brief resurgence of springtime passion, a renewal of the "rigors and perfume" of "wildness." It is followed by the utter devastation of "Penseroso," crystallized in the opening poem, "Break, Break My Heart," with its bleak finality: "Darkness / Hide my scars!" Nevertheless,

the poet finds the strength to close in a brief and graceful "Cadence,"
which contains two of her best poems, the stately "Recessional" and
golden "After-glow." "Recessional":

> Consider me a memory—a dream
> That passed away,
> Or yet, a flower that has blown and shattered—
> In a day;
> . . . .
> Consider me a melody
> That served its simple turn,
> Or but the residue of fire
> That settles in the urn, . . .

(P. 67)

Consonant with the cyclical motif of the work, GDJ uses much natural
imagery, as in these metaphors for her lover: "You are the very sun, the
moon, / The starlight of my soul." Some of these images are tied to concepts of fading, sunset, the West. As a woman (especially one who is no
longer young) whose desirability is measured by her youth/beauty, the
speaker is very concerned with time and aging. "Day by day the threads of
white / Multiply," she says, and declares, "I want to die while you love
me, / While yet you hold me fair." Not surprisingly, there is, too, a sense of
(patient or agonized) waiting.

Several of the individual poems in *An Autumn Love Cycle* are interesting,
for diverse reasons. Her "Autumn" is an authentically voiced document of
passionate surprise reminiscent of Gwendolyn Brooks's sonnet "(deep
summer)" from "The Womanhood" section of *Annie Allen:*

> Believe me—when I say
> That love like yours, at this belated hour,
> Overwhelms me,— . . .
> I move as one new-born—
> And strange to swift transitions . . .

(P. 6)

Another provocative poem is "Ivy":

> I am a woman
> Which means
> I am insufficient
> I need—
> Something to hold me
> Or perhaps uphold.
> I am a woman.

(P. 25)

Here, one is reminded of GDJ's contemporary Anne Spencer, who also devised potentially ironic poems. "Ivy" can be read "straight," but there is something unmistakably wry in its chiseled understatement of these two contradictory definitions of "Woman."

Finally, "Welt," one of her most widely known poems, shows that GDJ revised her work and provides some small insight into that process. The version in James Weldon Johnson's Book of *American Negro Poetry* differs in three significant ways from what appears in *Cycle:* (1) "That" for the beginning "Which" of line 2; (2) "And drain this cup so tantalant and fair" instead of "And drain this Cup of Joy so passing fair;" and (3) "parched lips" for "parching lips." The anthology choices are superior in all three cases, with even the seemingly questionable "parched" adding a pleasing Elizabethan flavor to the final lines: "Which meets my parched lips like cooling dew, / Ere time has brushed cold fingers through my hair!" The situation is mixed with her "Lost Illusions" (*Cycle,* "Illusion"), where her revisions improve two of the three recast lines. Thus it appears that GDJ's conscious poetic judgment was erratic.

Though there are many more good lines, even poems, which could be singled out, the impact of *An Autumn Love Cycle* is cumulative. No doubt, this is partly attributable to its narrative mode. The work gives the satisfying completeness that comes from having done well all of the worthwhile task that it set out to do.

GDJ dedicated this volume to the popular white woman writer and critic Zona Gale, "whose appreciation, encouragement and helpful criticism have so heartened me." It is illustrated with a fluid impressionistic line drawing of a cosmically rooted, tragic-visaged woman that is labeled "From a sketch by Effie Lee Newsholme." This name is so close to that of Effie Lee Newsome, also a poet who published during the Renaissance, that what is printed seems to be a mistake. And the fact that the design is *"from* a sketch" makes one wonder if GDJ herself was the artist who adapted it. Physcially, the book was attractive:

> "The Autumn Love Cycle" is delightfully gotten up . . . perfect in all its details. The cover even shows the lovely, softened tints of the fall of the year. Miss Newsholme's frontispiece is thoughtful and beautiful. The titles of the poems are intriguing, the arrangement of them excellent. There are not too many of them and not too few. It is altogether a soul-satisfying book.[52]

Critics reviewed the volume favorably, but although Locke noted her "maturing power and courage of expression,"[53] no known commentator (then or later) pronounced it her best book. Judgments about *Cycle* reflect the fact that love poetry is usually considered a lesser, too-private genre (especially when women write it). Furthermore, for black critics, racial poems that address the material conditions of black people are intrinsically more important and highly valued. These lines of thinking can be traced in the following remarks by Cedric Dover:

> . . . it is unfortunate that *An Autumn Love Cycle* (1928) failed to concentrate her awareness [in *Bronze*]. Instead of enlarging the new vitality, it reverts to the personal notes of her first poems, though it adds the aching maturity of a sensitive woman in her forties. The poet is again overwhelmed by herself.[54]

Dover's negativity, however, is balanced by Anne Spencer's iconoclastic praise. She declares that, "Lovers are the only persons left to us of any elegance at all," and lauds GDJ, a "person of color," for daring "to write of love without hypothecating atavistic jungle tones: the rumble of tom-tom, voodoo ebo, fetish of sagebrush and high spliced palm tree"—thereby effectively denouncing a current fashion in Harlem Renaissance verse.

Actually, as Spencer implies, love poetry is probably the hardest kind to write—simply because the emotions are so universal and commonly treated that it is blissfully easy to pen clichés and much harder to achieve freshness either of feeling or of expression. To a remarkable extent, GDJ is able to do this in a number of the poems and, generally, with the entire book.

During her lifetime, Georgia Douglas Johnson was called "the foremost woman poet of the race," a phrase that was constantly used in reference to her. Considering whether or not she "deserved" that name throws her in juxtaposition to other black women poets and, by extension, to black male and white women poets. Clearly, "foremost" is accurate, for she was better known and more widely published than any of her black sisters. In fact, not one other of them ever collected a volume of her verse, while she produced not just one but three during the ten-year span from 1918 to 1928. Yet, despite her multi-genred prolificness—which approximates that of Langston Hughes—her female life and responsibilities precluded any possibility of Hughes's kind of literary entrepreneurship. Held up with him, Cullen, and McKay, it becomes apparent that the gap between them is not nearly so wide as received critical opinion would have it. And her total achievement eclipses such lesser lights as Arna Bontemps, Fenton Johnson, and Frank Horne.

Throughout, one notes that GDJ held a niche as *woman* poet. Historically, being a lyric writer has necessitated the construction of a strong "I" voice, which has not always been considered compatible with femininity. We are glimmeringly reminded of these attitudes when GDJ's commentators praise her for her "daring" in exposing a woman's secret self. GDJ even hints at the discomfort that heat and candor can cause in "A Paradox":

> I know you love me better cold
> Strange as the pyramids of old . . .
> But I am frail, and spent and weak
> With surging torrents that bespeak
> A living fire.
>
> (P. 13)

That she was stereotyped as a woman poet in other ways is indicated in this excerpt from one of Geraldyn Dismond's Pittsburgh *Courier* columns:

> It so happened that I met Mrs. Johnson before I had read her poems. Consequently, I received a shock. From the place she occupies in the Negro renaissance, I had expected to see a brusque, cold-blooded individual whose efficiency and belief in sex equality would be fairly jumping at one. I imagined she was engrossed in herself and work, sophisticated and self-sufficient. . . . All of which was wrong.
> She is very sensitive, retiring and absolutely feminine.[55]

Embarrassingly operative here is the notion that she can be embraced and liked, despite the "sin" of writing, as long as she remains a nice, soft woman. However, GDJ's race gave her leeway to tackle political subjects (at least in the manner that she did), in contrast to the strictures sometimes laid on her white counterparts. For her, a black woman poet, attacking racial injustice was not only accepted but expected and praised. Interestingly, however, she admitted in a 1941 letter to Arna Bontemps that she does not enjoy "writing racially":

> Whenever I can, I forget my special call to sorrow and live as happily as I may. Perhaps that is why I seldom elect to write racially. It seems to me an art to forget those things that make the heart heavy. If one can soar, he should soar, leaving his chains behind. But, lest we forget, we must now and then come down to earth, accept the yoke and help draw the load.[56]

The mainstream poets with whom she was most frequently compared were Sara Teasdale and Edna St. Vincent Millay. This may have been simply because these two were so popular. GDJ does not write as imagistically as they, or utilize as much personic masking and irony, subsurface meaning and technique. But she was seen, at least by Locke, as belonging to the same school of "modern feminist realism," which had been "rediscovering the Sapphic cult of love as the ecstasy of life, that cult of enthusiasm which leaps over the dilemma of optimism and pessimism, and accepting the paradoxes, pulses in the immediacies of life and rejoices openly in the glory of experience."[57]

Very little criticism has been published about GDJ as poet. James Weldon Johnson points out that "she was the first colored woman after Frances Harper to gain general recognition as a poet," and that her verse may possess "effectiveness precisely because it is at the pole opposite to adroitness, sophistication, and a jejune pretention to metaphysics."[58] Sterling Brown devotes five, mainly factual and descriptive, sentences to her in *Negro Poetry and Drama*.[59] In his more extended treatment, Ronald Primeau seems bent on forcing GDJ into a preset critical mold: her "vision is that of the modern Romantic who stresses man's ability to transform his perception and create new realities through the dynamics of his own mind."[60] Most recently, Erlene Stetson's brief article focuses on "theme and structure" through a New Critical but basically black feminist approach.[61] GDJ's poetry, like her drama, will continue to benefit from new revisionist and radical perspectives.

This second period of GDJ's life was certainly a major one. She moved from her husband's death in 1925 to full participation in the Harlem Renaissance as cultural nexus, prize-winning dramatist, and mature poet. Thus she contributed more than either Dunbar-Nelson or Grimké to the achievement-oriented era of the New Negro.

iii

As was true for almost all Harlem Renaissance artists, the turning of the 1930s meant for GDJ a downswing of fortune and drying up of sustaining resources. There was some slight continuation of 1920s-style activities and recognition, but, in general, she spent the period until the mid-1940s staying close to home and trying to find support and outlets for her writing.

Nowhere is this more evident than in her vain attempts to win fellowships and awards. She was most persistent with the Harmon Foundation, applying for the entire competition period from 1927 to 1930.[62] She was nominated by W. L. Gholston, secretary of Baptist extension work, Atlanta, and by Dunbar-Nelson, who was then executive secretary of the American Inter-Racial Peace Committee, Philadelphia. Dunbar-Nelson stated that she let GDJ fill out "all that she knows about herself," while Gholston wrote a persuasive statement that concluded: "Altogether, Mrs.

Johnson's contributions in literature are more permanent and far-reaching than a slight survey would reveal and I do not believe another woman has accomplished more."

Letters of reference came from Carter G. Woodson, W. E. B. DuBois, James Weldon Johnson, and William Stanley Braithwaite. Their recommendations are characteristic of each of them:

Woodson:	The comments are decidedly favorable. She has a bit of poetic genius. . . . I regard her contributions as unique. She is writing better poetry than any other woman of color.
DuBois:	I think Mrs. Johnson has a real poetic gift and succeeds after work in giving it adequate expression. [And in a second letter], Mrs. Johnson has an unusually sincere, interesting literary message.
Johnson:	She has done some very beautiful lyric poetry.
Braithwaite:	The quality of her achievement in poetic expression: deep feeling, imaginative substance, to which she has given poignant lyric expression. [I endorse her] because I believe no one has worked harder and more faithfully to develop the gifts possessed, and this development has attracted and given her a conspicuous place in contemporary American literature.

Interesting information can be found throughout GDJ's application materials. For instance, one form notes that her poem "Octaroon" from *The Heart of A Woman* was used as "theme, inspiration and frontispiece" for two 1928 (?) novels—Frances Mocatto, *The Forbidden Woman*, and Philip Kenneth Britton, *A Drop of Midnight*. Of more consequence is the fact that GDJ falsified her birthdate, using 1888, which made her two additional years younger than the six years she ordinarily gave herself with the traditional 1886. Only Gholston (from her native Atlanta), who put her down in 1927 as 47, knew the truth. GDJ probably suspected—and rightly—that her age would not be a particular point in her favor.

Throughout this five-year process, there was also correspondence between GDJ and George E. Haynes, a secretary of the Commission on the Church and Race Relations, who administered the Harmon awards. Most of her letters are routine notes accompanying enclosures. However, once or twice, she made more extended, self-revelatory statements, as in this July 26, 1928, letter:

> [I] cannot pay for another volume being published. I have several books formulated that could be gotten out if I had the time.
>
> Is there not a way by which the man who can think can be enabled to have time to think?

Garnering an honorable mention in 1928 was the acme of her success with the foundation. That year, Claude McKay received the gold award, and Nella Larsen, the bronze. In 1929, GDJ received one vote for second place from Alain Locke, one for third from Lewis Mumford, one for fourth from Dorothy Scarborough, and one honorable mention from Joel E. Spingarn. Mumford declared in his October 28, 1929, letter that: "She has sincerity and fine feeling; her verses have steadily improved. Without definite originality, she has still a quiet talent that is capable of further development. She should be put forward in candidacy another year." She was, but with no happier results. A letter that she had written Haynes earlier that year sums up her attitude about her entire endeavor: "I think that those chosen were well worthy and congratulate them and the judges. I am not a bit discouraged, but shall try again sometime when I have done something I think more portent."

Almost ten years later, she asked Spingarn to recommend her for a Knopf fellowship, saying frankly: "Perhaps you know Mr. Knopf personally and might lead him to see the good I might be able to do by being allowed to go forward." She tried a second major foundation, the Julius Rosenwald Fund, in 1942 and 1944.[63] On the first occasion, she sent a flood of published and unpublished material to William C. Haygood, Director for Fellowships, apparently after an exchange with Charles S. Johnson, who was on the board and staff of the fund. Her June 18, 1942, letter to Haygood briefly discussed each of the works she enclosed.

They were (1) "The Torch" and "Homely Philosophy"—"short, pithy, helpful, consoling"; (2) "The Black Cabinet"; (3) *Plumes;* (4) Lynching plays—"pleasing because of the musical background and . . . amenable to strong dramatization without being inflammatory"; (4) "The Story of the African Jungle"; (5) "The Dreams in Me"—"my fourth book of verse and I think, by far my best—of course the people can live without this poetry, yet without a vision the people perish"; (6) a book of about fifteen short stories—"re-written mostly from stories written to me by a strange man whose letters compose another book"; and (7) "Dark Face Literature." Haygood read her material, but, as he informed her in his October 7 reply, it did not suit the purpose: "When Doctor Johnson suggested to me that I ask to see your manuscripts, both he and I were under the impression that the material you were working on was in the field of simplified educational literature which could be used with adult groups of limited reading ability."

For her 1944 attempt, GDJ submitted a two-page application divided into three parts—"Books, Plays And So On Written But Needing Revision and Editing," with five works targeted for the one year of the fellowship and nine others "to follow"; "Already Published"; and "Plan." Her priorities seem to have shifted slightly. "The Black Cabinet" and "Philosophies" still rank in the top five, but that category has been augmented by "Ten Plays of Negro Life," which need "refurbishing"; "White Men's Children," "a novel dealing with the interplay of bloods"; and "Brotherhood," "a book of verse (interracial in character)." For some reason, her two "volumes of universal poetry—The Dreams In Me, I Stand at April" now appear at the bottom of her second list. To her genres, she has added yet another, most modern one—"a moving picture (Love In An African Jungle) (Emperor Jones Style)." Like Dunbar-Nelson, she is trying to remain *au courant*, but she is grafting decaying subject matter to a growing new form.

The most arresting section of the proposal is the plan, which reads more like a statement than a step-by-step outline of work activities:

> With leisure, Freedom from Worry Financially, for time being, with a competent secretary propose to finish the five books in the order named on page 1. And then if there is time available take up the editing of the books named in the second part. (Page 1)
> Believing that each of us has a specific part to play in our individual world, I feel constrained to make this, shall I say last attempt to present these brain children for birth.
>
> > There is such little time
> > And so much to do.

Certainly, GDJ's sixty-four years of age added urgency to her application.

A real need for money also motivated her attempts throughout this period to muster financial support. Early in January 1931 she writes her friend Lugenia Burns Hope (the wife of Atlanta University president John Hope), plaintively asking: "Genie what would I have to do to get some kind of degree (honorary) tacked on to me so that I can get work or something that will not keep me to the grindstone as this job does."[64] After she lost her position with the Department of Labor, she sought library employment. In an October 5, 1934, letter to Arthur Schomburg at the 135th Street branch of the New York Public Library, she candidly lays out her predicament:

> I am trying to get a job in a library and one of the requirements is an A.B. degree, but I have a chance if I can get a statement from those who know me that to their belief, the work I have done is the equivalent of such a degree. . . . I wonder if I could ask you for a letter of recommendation in this behalf.[65]

She states that she "finished library science at Howard University," and that "Dr. Locke and Mr. Charles Houston have generously said that my work is more than the equivalent of an A.B. or Masters degree." Apparently, though, her efforts were not productive. One does not know what library she was applying to, but it is more than ironic that a litterateur of her stature was driven to such lengths to prove bachelor-degree educational ability.

During the early 1940s, she resorted to temporary work. She mentions in passing to Bontemps in July 1941 that she had "worked in the department of the civil service some weeks,"[66] and writes the following to Harold Jackman on June 28, 1942, also as an aside: "This machine makes no C's that is little C's. I am writing in the POOL—this is a big room full of people who are waiting to be called to jobs—I have one and go to my work at three, it is a few minutes before."[67] Of course, there is nothing new about penurious writers—especially black ones—waiting tables and scrubbing floors; but the spectacle of the sixty-two-year-old GDJ—after her many accomplishments—hoping in a clerical pool for a few hours' work is no less disheartening for its dreary familiarity.

In a 1973 oral history interview, poet-novelist Margaret Walker opined that both GDJ's "poetry and her dramatic things sold. . . . She made some *good* money—enough to last her 'til she died in her eighties."[68] However, all of the available data do not seem to corroborate the idea that GDJ lived with ease and comfort on literary royalties. What her precise circumstances were is impossible to decipher. It is no doubt relevant here to recall that, until her death, she, her lawyer son, Lincoln, and his wife, Elizabeth, shared their household. Apparently, Grimké was the only one of these three writers who did not have to worry excessively about money.

Difficulties notwithstanding, this period was not totally devoid of acknowledgment. In 1932, GDJ was listed in *Who's Who of Colored America* as "housewife-writer" and was asked to join the D.C. Women's Party, Poets League of Washington, and Poet Laureate League.[69] The year 1933 finds her being one of an impressive array of associate editors on the letterhead of the Harriet Tubman Publishing Company, Inc. (publishers of "Notable Living Americans of African Descent"; Roscoe Conkling Bruce, editor-in-chief). The next year, she won third prize in a poetry contest sponsored by the D.C. Federation of Women's Clubs with her entry on Frances Perkins, Franklin D. Roosevelt's female Cabinet member. And, throughout, her poems continued to appear in various newspapers, magazines, and anthologies. For instance, "Common Dust" was printed editorially in the New York *Herald Tribune* on January 22, 1940.

GDJ's weekly newspaper column, "Homely Philosophy," also contributed to her ongoing visibility. From 1926 to 1932 it was syndicated by twenty newspapers, including the Pittsburgh *Courier,* Boston *Guardian,* New York *News,* Chicago *Defender,* New York *Amsterdam News,* Philadelphia *Tribune,* and New York *Age.* Writing about this mini-feature, W. L. Gholston said in his Harmon Foundation nomination statement: "At present she is doing an incalculable service through the Negro press with the weekly output of her 'Homely Philosophies.' She is styled The New Frank Crane. These philosophies are used editorially and carry a message of hope, cheer and tonical vigor that is inspirational."[70]

For the modern reader, these "philosophies" are relics of an earlier age, when their "hope, cheer, and tonic" may have expressed what is still called "the American character" and probably did help people over the hump of the Great Depression. The problem with them is that their age-old truths are too often expressed in language that reduces them to clichés. Perhaps the least painful way to convey the nature of these brief secular homilies is to quote some representative titles: "Why Men Fail," "Magnetic Personality," "The Blessings of Work," "What Letters Mean?" "Can You Dream?" "Keeping Friendships in Repair," "A Smile on the Lips," "What Do You Think Of Yourself," "Getting Ahead," "Find Pleasure In Common Things," "Don't Be Envious," "Take Life in Relays," "You Find What You Look For," "Playing A Bad Hand," "Do Not Economize In Love," and so on.[71]

Every so often, one encounters columns that are more palatable than the general run. These usually convey extramundane spiritual awarenesses. "Our Four Eyes" is a good example:

> Four eyes we have with which to look out upon life, observe the course and direct our way—the eyes of the body and the eyes of the mind. The mind's eyes are far keener and more far reaching than the natural eye; they enable us to foresee, to foretell and to foreknow. If you would acquire one of the secrets of the great sages, habit yourself to closing your natural eyes for a while and then look out with the eyes of your mind.[72]

Another in this category is "The Hunch," which begins and concludes with these sentences: "A hunch is a suggestion or whispering from within. . . . Never silence a hunch, but act upon it, for often it is the functioning of your sixth sense—your instruction."[73] One of her Depression-related essays blesses the adversity for forcing individuals back to the simple life, and another predicts its demise: "The sunshine of prosperity and the seasons of plenty will eventually hold sway and life will tear off these grey somber robes and once more assume the rainbow hues of brighter and better days."[74]

In other aspects of her life, too, GDJ seems to have relied heavily on inspirational clichés. For her, however, they were not so much platitudes as simplicities that living had brazened true. Her basic character configuration led her to be genuinely nice, optimistic, trustful, self-abnegating, and nurturing—sometimes to a degree that became inappropriate or discomfiting, especially when she acted impulsively. For instance, in 1929, she wrote Charles Chesnutt a note of appreciation for an award with which he had nothing to do.[75] And, during her second application for a Harmon award, she exuded to Haynes: "You have made my heart feel so much lighter. . . . I feel somehow that I shall be successful this time. I know you are with me and are helping me."[76] The implications of her thanks so alarmed Haynes that he wrote her back immediately, saying "[Your letter] makes me apprehensive, lest you received the wrong impression," and iterating to her that he only secured material and expressed no opinion.

Generally, she was unfailingly gracious and accommodating. When Carl Van Vechten began the founding of the James Weldon Johnson Memorial Collection at Yale University in 1942, she wrote letters to Harold Jackman, giving them suggestions about whom to ask for documents, supplying addresses, and even personally contacting authors.[77] All of these traits exaggerated her tendency to appear a little scattered and dumb. Somehow, she never quite seemed to know who the actual publisher of a book was and how that process worked; and she routinely dashed off material to "important" people in a condition that must have struck them as "unprofessional."

True, GDJ was inherently cheerful and agreeable, yet one wonders how much this may have been augmented by feminine role-playing and/or female socialization. However, it is clear that her relative disregard for formality emanated from her being a psychic, creative person who was not always tuned in to the details of mundane living. Furthermore, as is usually the case, the older she became, the less concerned she was with camouflage.

Half-Way House was her demesne. Although she made occasional jaunts to New York City and sometimes went out socializing, GDJ generally stayed close to home (the same one for over fifty years)—thereby exhibiting the strong attachment to place that characterizes many women's lives and writing. The overwhelming impression is of her reigning at 1461 S Street, Northwest, Washington, D.C., with the world stopping by. Her naming of the space is significant: "I'm half way between everybody and everything and I bring them together."[78] Poet-playwright Owen Dodson recounts an even better explanation that she gave him about her house. She intended to make it a place where anything that even half-way fought to survive could do so:

> She said, "You know why I call this Half-Way House?" She said, "I take not only stray people in, but I try to see if somebody wants to live, and if they want to live, I do . . . my best to help them." She said: "For instance, this morning, I saw a big, fat cockroach who came out of the drain, and so I said, 'Well, I'll just turn on the spigot, and it'll go down.' It did, but then it came up again. I turned on the spigot, and it went down. I knew it was the same one, same size. And, finally, it came up after the third time." She said, "If that cockroach wants to live that much, let it live!"[79]

This cockroach anecdote epitomizes the kind of energy GDJ radiated. A second excerpt from Dodson about her makes this even more explicit:

> She took in anybody—old lame dogs, blind cats . . . any kind of limping animal. I've seen squirrels around there, digging for nuts that she'd hide so they'd play a game. . . . She took in those. Then she took in stray people— mostly artists who were out of money. People like Zora Neale Hurston who stayed there . . . or some artists who were a little berserk. And she was capable of giving them a soothing balm. She knew how to do for people. Of course, the house was a mess! You've never been in any house like it! When you entered the hallway, you knew that you were entering another country.

It was a country where Arthur Schomburg rang her doorbell for a cup of "delicious hot tea," where Glenn Carrington "basked in deep spirituality,"[80] and where scenes like the following occurred (GDJ's description to Charles S. Johnson): "Tomorrow I have two friends in to spend the day. Both have heart trouble. Both travel toward the West, as who doesn't. Both are dear to me. Each shall have her lounge for the day and I shall be the revolving hostess. I am already excited with the prospects of the day."[81] The biographical statement accompanying her retrospective exhibit at the Schomburg Center also noted that she "welcomed casual callers in addition to those she expected, and took delight in the company of all."[82] Another of her lifelong practices was to send poems and cards to friends.

It is enigmatic, but GDJ seems to have been particularly fond of an unusually large number of lesbians and homosexuals—Harold Jackman, Glenn Carrington, Angelina Grimké, Alain Locke, Bruce Nugent, Langston Hughes, Mary Burrill, and Wallace Thurman. She called the younger men her "sons," and they referred to her as "mother." Based on their extant correspondence, her relationships with Jackman and Carrington were closest, and it is through this correspondence that the larger friendship patterns emerge. These letters also indicate that GDJ was aware of their sexual identity.

In December 1932 she writes Carrington that "Nina Grimke is back. . . . Call her up"; and he tells her in 1957 that "Harold and I speak of you often." He also outlines the "several months last year I was occupied with Mr. Locke and his illness," providing an interesting account of how he encouraged Locke, who was weak, to dictate his book to him. Their intimate friendship is evident. Carrington says: "I saw more of him and had more heart to heart talks with him during those last sad weeks than anyone else."[83] Writing to Jackman on October 26, 1942, GDJ imparts: "Langston sent me a letter with some poems from Yaddo or Yazzo— writers colony. Please redirect and forward enclosed to him. He said Mr. V was there—he'll know. Indeed I am rich in sons. Glenn was very lovely to me. . . . "[84]

A later letter of hers, dated December 26, 1944, is a veritable "who's who" of friendly information:

> . . . Bruce Nugent has a book out—*Beyond Where the Stars Stood Still*—it's lovely. Phone him to send you a copy—Watkins 9-7921.
>
> Also Thurman has out a magnificent volume. He's in California. If you wish his address I'll send it. It should be in your collection. Also Bruce's book.
>
> Miss B[urrill] was here last week. Came to bury the lady with whom she used to live. . . . Why is it Nina [Angelina Grimké] does not write to me. Please tell her to. I hope she is not sick.[85]

The next letter she sends him is almost wholly devoted to Mary Burrill. It is long, complicated—and cryptic. It appears that Mary has been asking GDJ for poems, which GDJ suspects her of using as her own. She also seems to think that Mary is "maybe passing." By the time GDJ writes— "Nina knows her but do not speak of these things. She, I mean Mary, may be strictly on the level and Nina may think differently"—the reader is mystified. However, one recalls that Nina and Mary (Mamie) were girl-hood sweethearts, and is intrigued by GDJ's instructions to Jackman: "When you have read this, tear it up that it may never fall into thoughtless hands."[86] Sometime during this period, Grimké herself wrote a flattering little poem "To G.D.J.," which Georgia sent along to Jackman in 1953.[87]

The individuals who made up these interlocking pairs/circles of friendship were writers, artists, critics, and patrons of the arts—from the outset, a very distinct, self-selecting group of kindred spirits. Also, it may well be that were the totality of GDJ's correspondence available, it would reveal that she was similarly involved with pairs and circles of equally undistinguished persons. One tends to doubt this, however, and to see in these particular friendships further evidence of her expansive and individualistic, sensitive and life-giving sympathies. This mixed lesbian-homosexual circle contrasts with the apparently all-female network in which Dunbar-Nelson moved. That there was little contact between the two seems to be suggested by the fact that GDJ does not mention Dunbar-Nelson's name when writing of these friends and otherwise acts as if she is oblivious of her sexuality. Yet, with a subject such as this, one can never be sure of the possible dynamics that may have been operating.

Maintaining Half-Way House and her private relationships was the predominant form that GDJ's social life assumed. However, she belonged to literary-social clubs and organizations such as the American Society of African Culture, the (New York City) Civic Club, the National Song Writers Guild, the Writers' League Against Lynching, the (D.C.) Matrons, the Poet's Council of the National Women's Party, and the League of American Writers. She was also a member of the First Congregational Church. Despite these affiliations, it is obvious that GDJ was not the clubwoman activist that some of her compeers were. Time, temperament, and interest led her in other directions. Unfortunately, this may have isolated her somewhat from other black women.

True to her established pattern, GDJ sustained her commitment to her art. As indicated earlier, however, during this 1930s–mid-1940s era, her efforts consisted mainly of trying to publish some of the voluminous writing she had on hand. She spoke with jaunty seriousness about this subject to Jackman on August 8, 1944:

> Have about eight books here ready to get going—three new books of poetry, thirty plays both one and three act, thirty short stories, a novel, a book of philosophy, a book of exquisite sayings. . . . twenty songs . . . seems I must go to that last peaceful abode without getting them printed . . . but why should I be worrying. Balzac left forty unpublished books. Perhaps you can suggest some avenue that might lead from this present cul-de-sac?[88]

Though her tone here is light, occasionally she betrayed the desperation she began to feel, once going so far as to confess in 1932 after not hearing about a work she had submitted: "I am racked with the tension of waiting with no word."[89]

In her letters, GDJ talked about what she was writing, revising, sending out, and had on hand. Sometimes she gives details about the publishers and their responses and about her own thoughts relative to her prospects. The tone is set in May 1931 when she answers some sort of query from Arthur Schomburg by listing not only her published, but also unpublished, work, and adds: "I tell you this because I do not know the import of your report and am 'always hoping against hope that etc.' And so I tell you of the unfinished things I have on hand with little prospect of getting them done unless something undreamed of befalls."[90]

On August 17 of the next year, she tells him that her biography of her late husband, "The Black Cabinet," is "about ready to go forth to the publishers":

> I had hoped to get the time to refurbish portions of it and perhaps make it less a recital of facts than it seems now to me to be. However, time is always pressing and I have no leisure to follow this up as it should be done, so I may be forced to send it out as it is. . . . I feel that if the book has fallen short of a work of art, it will at least stand as a priceless collection of facts otherwise ungetatable.

GDJ's correspondence to Jackman also contains this kind of information, but it is more extensive and, in addition, chronicles the assistance he gave her efforts by checking on business in New York City for her. Early in 1932, she asks him to phone William Uhl publishers and inquire about her novel "White Men's Children." Five years later, she writes about another (undeterminable) novel: "Finished the last chapter in my novel yesterday and hope to have it in Prof. Braelwy's [*sic*, maybe Brawley's] hands the first of April." It is probably the same work she talks about on July 31, 1938: "Am trying yet to place my novel. I sent seven chapters to Nina Melville . . . but have not heard from her. . . . Could you see if she has a phone and if she received the chapters. . . . Am getting out a new book of poetry if I can find a publisher."[91]

A September 19, 1938, letter to Jackman is especially revealing:

> Because you have such a pleasing personality, I shall impose on you further if you allow me. I feel that you made a very favorable impression on the party on Merlin Street as they spoke well of the book to you. I did as recommended. Sent in the whole book, pages numbered, and asked for the return collect of the first seven chapters. That was in July. I haven't heard from them since and I thought that perhaps it would not be amiss if you would phone Miss Melville again for me. I am so anxious that I am sick. Please do this for me. Also, at the same time . . . I sent a book of verse, The Dreams in Me to The House of Field. . . . They said they had it and thanked me. Please phone them also. . . . Please let me hear from you as the strain is becoming too much.

Finally, in August 1944, she is incorporating "certain suggested additions" into "The Biography," and on the day after Christmas she writes: "Sent away two books yesterday. After[?] A Thousand Years and Brotherhood. Am copying two others and two chapters of the Biography."[92]

Exactly what readers thought of all these works is now a mystery. The one available opinion comes from William Haygood of the Rosenwald Foundation, who volunteered that he had "taken a great deal of pleasure in reading them, especially your short stories and the novel 'White Men's Children.'"[93]

During the Depression thirties, GDJ tried to get into the theater programs of the WPA. Early in 1937, she asked Jackman if he had "any contacts with the WPA Theatre Project." She wished to interest them in her play "Frederick Douglass," which had already been "approved and accepted by the New York Theatre Project board. Only awaits presentation." Sometime a bit later, she tells about having written the director of the Federal Theatre Project, New York City (who guided her to the director of the Negro Theatre, Lafayette). She also apprised a Mr. Farnsworth that she "would like to work with the movement in the special capacity of getting material for use as I have numerous contacts that make it easy for me to get in touch with many new authors of plays." In the summer of 1938, she was apparently still courting an entrée: "Gave Langston [Hughes] five or six plays when he was here. He said they were being read."[94]

Thus GDJ spent this period of her career riding the after-wave of the 1920s, hostessing Half-Way House, and striving for continued literary success and publication. Still, the theme of time is constant—not solely free minutes and hours to write, but the sense of passing years and approaching death. She once admitted: "I am so eager to get to this writing before the taper is snuffed out. Am afraid of dying before I get the things done I hope to do."[95] Contrary to her fears, GDJ's physical self must have been sound. She was hospitalized only once, in September–October 1942, for a kidney operation. At this point, there yet remained ahead of her more than twenty years of living.

iv

It is only by comparison with her earlier years that the last epoch of GDJ's life looks like a decline. In contrast to Dunbar-Nelson and Grimké, GDJ was given almost an extra period at the end of her life (perhaps to compensate for her late beginning). Dunbar-Nelson died relatively early, at the age of sixty, after a lengthy writing career begun when she was young.

Grimké buried herself when she was fifty, although she continued living for another twenty-eight years. Approaching her seventieth birthday in 1950, GDJ rejoiced: "Am finding life most interesting and full of happy surprises—Am utterly refusing to grow old!"[96] Thus, she maintained her vitality and productivity.

During the 1940s, she was, like everyone else, caught up in the war and in the currents of interracialism that accompanied it. Dover phrases her participation in this way:

> The War might easily have extinguished it [her flame], but Mrs. Johnson responded with revived vigor to the changing scene. She added her voice to the Negro struggle for a full share in the democracy that demanded Negro lives and labor. She gave herself unstintingly and, at the same time, poured out a stream of effective poems and fighting songs.[97]

"To Gallant France" appeared in *Opportunity* in March 1941. It compares France's fight to Calvary and concludes: "France, too, though nailed upon the cross / Shall rise in victory!"[98] Other of her war poems exist only in manuscript. In "A Soldier's Letter" (dated November 8, 1943), she speaks out against black soldiers dying for a perpetually racist United States:

> And will you still jim-crow us
> Just as you did before,
> Will you call us "Nigger," order us
> Away from your front door?

Despite the awareness here, her stance is not consistently pacifist, as she can write a poem such as "I Have No Tears to Shed," which feeds the hero mystique of war. Its final stanzas run:

> I cried when you went soldiering
> To distant lands afar
> For you had left the doorway
> Of my empty heart ajar.
>
> But now at length I bend above
> My gallant soldier, dead
> I have no tears to shed upon
> A hero's sacred bed.

GDJ asked Harold Jackman to listen to an April 11, 1945, radio program that would air "Whose Son," a "poem I wrote to accompany a poster showing a black soldier carrying a white comrade."[99] She threw much effort into publicizing her poem "Tomorrow's World," which was set to music by composer Lillian Evanti. In May 1948 she and Evanti sent out a personally signed, mimeographed letter introducing the octavo-form song—taking "pleasure in presenting to you this copy of the song dedicated to world peace" through which "the hearts of fifty-three nations can be crystalized into peaceful thinking." They urge that it be used and circulated, and close: "Your opinion of our song will be valued. Do let us hear from you. Let us together make a happy, free world for the children of Tomorrow."[100]

"Tomorrow's World" is meant to cause reflection upon the needless horror of war:

> Why should we follow brazen drums
>   Into the flames of war
> Since we are brothers of one blood
>   What are we fighting for?
>
> Come before the atom bomb
>   blasts out humanity
> Grinding to ashes all the world
>   In bitter mockery.

It was "read on the floor of the senate by Senator Langer and printed in the Congressional Record."[101]

GDJ was no less enthusiastic about a similar work, the "Brotherhood Marching Song." She wrote in 1945: "Am doing a BROTHERHOOD MARCHING SONG which Norman Corwin of the C. B. Co. thinks well of and has kept for future use. I want this song set to a moving, flaming tune that shall catch fire all over the world. I want contacts in S[outh] A[merica] Europe Africa and all the rest of the musical world."[102] Ending "O come let us know one another, / And march onward in BROTHERHOOD," this typical plea for racial unity was reset "in a very splendid arrangement" by James Dorsey. (GDJ had also written music for it herself.) She mentions in 1946 that she has "about six [additional] interracial songs on TOLERANCE."[103]

In this same vein and intended for the same pageant—radio talk—Brotherhood Day uses, GDJ compiled a book entitled "Bridge to Brotherhood." She described this collection of "80 poems . . . with songs and music" as an "answer to the need for material for schools, colleges and interracial groups to foster and promote good feeling between the races." An interesting September 18, 1948, letter of hers to Jackman presents him with the proposition of finding someone to "sponsor [i.e., publish] this book and write down your commission of the first $1000 dollars accruing therefrom": "I leave it to you. . . . Should be printed AT ONCE. . . . Talk over the matter with friends. . . . Joe Lewis [Louis] is losing $5000 dollars weekly on golf. Perhaps he'd sponsor it."[104] Even if Jackman did respond favorably to this business approach, the book was never published. In February 1950, she was still trying to place it and attributing her difficulty—at least partially—to the fact that it was verse.[105]

Another of her interracial projects that never materialized was a proposed column for the (New York) *Amsterdam News*. Her prospectus reads:

> It will be my privilege to bring to this column the strong and valiant voices of some of the world's mighty personalities. Those whose hearts take in all men of every clime, of every hue. In this column we shall reason together, we shall learn to understand each other, we shall be happier for the widening of our horizons, for the privilege of coming closer together.

She progressed as far as obtaining the editor's consent and contacting appropriate individuals for possible contributions. An October 15, 1941, letter to author Jean Toomer asks him, "among other liberal minded writers, to do your bit toward bringing this [column] about" by sending "something long or short expressing your attitude upon the Brotherhood of Man."[106]

Finally, however, her most successful and enduring work on this theme has proven to be a poem, "Interracial," which Hughes and Bontemps included in their anthology *The Poetry of the Negro*. Midway through, it reads:

> With understanding come to know
> What laughing lips will never show:
> How tears and torturing distress
> May masquerade as happiness:
> Then you will know when my heart's aching
> And I when yours is slowly breaking.[107]

"Interracial," which had first appeared in *The Crisis* and *Phylon* in 1944, captures perfectly the integrationist philosophy of that era.

All of GDJ's songs during this last period were not cause-oriented. Returning to song writing and composing—her first love (as she revealed in 1927)—must have gratified her. From the late 1940s to 1950s, she and composer Lillian Evanti were musical collaborators. Three of their published pieces are "Dedication" (1948), "Beloved Mother" (1952), and "Hail to Fair Washington" (1953). This last is a brisk, patriotic ditty celebrating the District of Columbia and the first president. "Dedication," a "moderately slow secular song in the key of D-major and in 4/4 time," is written for solo voice with difficult piano.[108] GDJ's lyrics, alone melodic, lend themselves easily to instrumental accompaniment:

> Somehow you give me sense of space
> Of shining landscapes in the sun . . .
> You give me sense of altitude
> Of blue skies shining through the trees,
> You take away my solitude
> And mingle dreams with ecstacy.

She claimed twenty-four "written and copyrighted" songs. Only four are dated before 1916; the bulk fall in the 1940s, and three have 1959 designations ("Hoola Hoop Love," "America, I too, Love you," and "Hands Across the Border and a Bridge Across the Sea"). Some of these works are obviously love songs ("Your Eyes are like Violets," "Too Late Sweetheart"), while many are functional or topical ("Georgia State College School Song," "Dedication to Locke," "Little Brown Bomber Lullaby"). She wrote both words and music for all except a handful of them.

Neither was GDJ's poetry relentlessly focused on war and brotherhood. A poem such as "Remember" (from which this middle stanza is taken) echoes her *Heart of a Woman:*

> Know this, the little while of love
> Is fleeting as a cloud,
> As lissom as a zephyr's breath,
> As fickle as a crowd.[109]

"Old Black Men," on the other hand, is in the vein of *Bronze* with its picturing of black men who have learned to live down the bursting of their "sun-minted" hopes. A 1947 work, "Woman," is another of her poems that is either feminine or feminist, depending on whether it is read literally or ironically. The first and third quatrains are:

> Unselfish, silent potently
> Behind each man of history
> A woman stands, upon whose strength
> He leans to cast his shadow's length.
> . . . .
> Aye, some brave woman without crown
> Behind each male-throne huddles down,
> A sentinel to guard his sleep,
> A bosom where he kneels to weep. . . . [110]

GDJ also enclosed little paeans to friendship in occasional letters.

Thus far, GDJ has been viewed as poet, playwright, and journalist. She also wrote short stories—and pursuing this area of her activities leads into yet more surprising facets of her as woman and artist. It also runs one squarely into scholarly frustration. In her "Catalogue of Writings," GDJ lists twenty-one short stories and ten short short stories (although every one of them was probably not published). Furthermore, she revealed to Jackman that she wrote some part of these under a pseudonym, Paul Tremaine.[111] During her lifetime, it appears that a scant one or two stories were printed with her own name—but that her contemporaries remained as uninterested in those as they were unaware of her hidden pseudonymous writings, despite the fact that she sometimes mentioned her prose.[112] Looking for these works today is an exercise that makes finding the proverbial haystacked needle easy.[113] Consequently, discussion of GDJ as fictionist must be based on three items—a short-short story entitled "Free," and two longer ones, "Gesture" and "Tramp Love."

"Free" surfaced in her Library of Congress Harmon Foundation files—a densely printed "short short story complete on this page" "By Georgia Douglas Johnson," but without any other bibliographical clues. It is an engrossing, admirably crafted sketch. Martha Ryan and Rose Delaney have just buried Dr. Ryan, a prosperous Nashville, Tennessee, M.D., who was Martha's husband and Rose's lover. The three have lived together for twenty-five years, Dr. Ryan having brought Rose into their home as his "new nurse" and forced his wife, to her mortification, to accept the arrangement. Now that she is finally "boss in her own house," Martha looks forward to being "free, free from her at last!" Rose, on the other hand, is lost and uncertain. She rises to make Martha a cup of tea, "an easy pleasure" of service that continues the caring she has always given.

As Rose opens the door for the lawyer to read the will, Martha notices for the very first time that Rose, too, is old, that "the years had passed and even Rose had lost her youth." Stunned by this sudden realization, she hears the embarrassed lawyer read a will that leaves the property to "my wife, Martha Ryan, and my adopted daughter, Rose Delaney, equally share and share alike": "The eyes of the two women met, hung together for a moment, and then Rose's glance fell." Saying she'll "cause no trouble," she leaves Martha musing in the hush of the carpeted room and packs her bag to leave. As Rose slowly, sadly walks away, Martha comes to the knowledge of how "still and empty," comfortless, and alone the house will be in days without her: "With a start she awoke to the moment . . . Rose was going, her hand was turning the knob . . . Martha watched with growing panic . . . Rose paused a moment on the threshold, she looked back! And then Mrs. Ryan flung open her arms and cried brokenly, 'Rose!'"

"Free" starkly dramatizes the existences of these two women under capitalist patriarchy—their economic dependence, apparent paucity of alternatives, sexual utilization, and psychological oppression. At the same time, it shows the bonds that their mutual condition has quietly forged between them. This subtle chiaroscuro of sympathy is one of the major strengths of the story. Martha sighs. "Rose Delaney sitting across from Mrs. Ryan, her black hat a little awry, had noted the sigh and seen the shiver. She was keenly aware of her deep agitation. Something called to her from this woman's silence." It is as if, all along, they two have been the ones who mattered, and not Dr. Ryan, at whose funeral Martha had felt "numb and far-away . . . not like it was her own dead she was burying." Under the circumstances, the title "Free" becomes not merely ambiguous but sarcastic.

The story is aracial; no hints are given about the color of the characters. Though one might see them as black because of the author, the Southern setting, or whatever, GDJ clearly intended that issues independent of race focus the work. Autobiographical sources, if they are present, are equally incidental. One thinks, perhaps, of GDJ's tea-making skill, her love of roses, the death of her own prominent husband, and the fact that she and her daughter-in-law Elizabeth lived together in a house externally linked by their son-husband. Throughout, "Free" sustains an ambience of mystery and bare evocativeness. It is a well-executed story—economical, compact, delicate, and true in its psychological depictions.

"Gesture" and "Tramp Love" are the available stories penned by GDJ as Paul Tremaine. What can be pieced together about their history is intriguing. Early in 1936, GDJ sent them to Harold Jackman under the guise of their being beginning efforts by a "protégé." She asked him to give his opinion of them, to write and encourage the protégé, and to consider the stories for publication in *Challenge*, Dorothy West's "literary quarterly" of which Jackman was associate editor. These pieces appeared in the summer 1936 and spring 1937 issues of the magazine. On July 31, 1938, GDJ writes Jackman for second copies of these numbers, and then five weeks later, sends him a new address for Gypsy Drago, the protégé, saying:

> I wrote him [Drago] a week or so ago and heard from him at once. Yes, do write him. . . . He will be tickled about the story's success. Oh, yes, thank you for the copies of the magazines. I intend doing something with them. You see, Paul Tremaine is one of my pseudonyms. I used it on the stories. I rewrote them, you know, and feel a kind of pride in their reception. I only changed the form of expression etc not the content.[114]

This is all rather confusing—and a little circumstantial. As no titles are mentioned, one is not certain what is transpiring. GDJ could be talking about separate stories by her and Drago, or about some one or more joint productions. It is safe to assume, however, that "Gesture" and "Tramp Love" are among the works alluded to, and that she put them into final form.

Whoever Gypsy Drago was, GDJ has a special relationship with him. To her, he narrated fascinating tales drawn from his experiences, which she used as fictional matter. She did not attempt to conceal this process, for not only did she state it to Jackman, she gives even further details in her Rosenwald application and "Catalogue of Writings." To Haygood, she wrote on June 18, 1942, in a listing of her work, that "the book of short stories—there are about fifteen—are re-written mostly from stories written to me by a strange man whose letters compose another book." Her catalogue annotation acknowledges: "Seventeen stories related to this author by one, Gypsy Drago, who was unaware of his Negro blood until thirty. Lived as white until then and reveals his experiences after such knowledge." Her last epistolary reference to him is made on March 31, 1945 to Jackman:

> Think of this surprise. Have a letter from Gypsy Drago. He asked about you and wants to hear from you. . . . Do write to Drago. He's blue and still moving about, but says his wife and he are still in love altho he has not seen her in some time. He'll tell you. He likes you! Get Nina [Grimké] to write him. She should. He has three children now—all boys—all white.[115]

The only other information about Drago occurs in "a letter from Paul Tremaine," from which excerpts were printed in *Challenge* as a biographical note:

> Began life at the age of eleven, when I first learned about myself in an orphan's home, 'way down South. . . . I do not believe in God nor man nor anything much. . . . I have searched everywhere and nearly drove myself insane trying to find an answer that would fit me and my life. . . . I am neither white nor black. The saddest part of it all is that I look too white to be ever taken for a black man. So I am an outcast. From the white race because I am not a hypocrite, and from the black race because they do not want me around with my white manners and white skin.[116]

The problem with this letter is that one does not know if Drago himself or GDJ wrote it, *or* how much of this history is actually true of Drago or represents GDJ creating her "Paul Tremain" persona. It would seem that it is valid Drago data recast, probably, by GDJ.

The fact that "Gesture" is about a hobo indicates its origins as a Gypsy

Drago story. He may not have been a perennial vagrant, but he definitely traveled around. In 1936, he is is Phoenix, Arizona; in 1938, Mackinaw City, Michigan, at the Dixie Rustic Tavern; in 1945, Saginaw, Michigan.[117] Similarly, the narrator of "Gesture" is hitchhiking his way through the Arizona desert. Enroute, he is passed up by a rich white woman in "a large shiny car" chauffeured by a cowboy. Further along, they are halted by a flat tire. After some friendly words with the driver, the hobo fixes it while the woman maintains her haughty demeanor. When it is done, she icily offers him money and a ride, both of which he now refuses—to her chagrin:

> The woman asked, "Don't you want to ride with us? We are going to Prescott."
> The fellow smiled oddly, and shook his head, "No mam, I don't want to ride. I'll walk."
> Her voice was tense with surprise. "It's getting dark already. The sun is going down. You'll be out here all night!"
> "I know it, mam. I like it in the desert at night."
> "Why don't you want a ride now?" she demanded. "You hailed us for one back there."
> "Oh did I? Well, I must have changed my mind."
> He looked into her eyes with a cold smile.

This "gesture" of defiant assertion obviously pleases him, although as he trudges through the chilling night, he "raised a heel of his shoe hard into the seat of his trousers. 'Damn, damn fool,' he muttered."

This little story is a celebration of "the open road" and of the dignity of this particular roamer. He is portrayed as a decent person who joys in the life he meets, be it people, a tiny lizard, an old desert cow and her calf, or the mountain horizon. Showing this is the raison d'être of "Gesture." Its nature descriptions, dialogue, plot, and characterizations all work to support the theme.

"Tramp Love" continues the Gypsy Drago–Paul Tremaine adventures with its treatment of another memorable encounter. This time, the *Challenge* contributor's note reads:

> Paul Tremaine has sent us another story. We last heard that he was in Arizona. By now he is probably in some other far place, still hoboing, still unable to adjust to his discovery that part of his blood is black. We believe that he sends us his stuff first draft, for we do a lot of editing. But we are definitely decided that he has talent and we hope he will send us other things along the way.[118]

Even though it uses the same basic framework as "Gesture," this second story is a great deal richer.

One summer afternoon, the nameless narrator is dozing under a shade tree outside "Columbus" when a girl, also hitchhiking, joins him. She is young (barely twenty), "very blond," trimly dressed, and friendly:

> Her slacks were ordinary white duck. They were men's slacks, worked over. Above them she wore a waist of thin, white silk. I could see the pale green lace brassiere over tiny breasts. Her throat was delicate and the skin was a little red but very smooth. No paint on her face or lips. Just a light coat of powder.

As they smoke, she shares her life story. Having left a Nebraska farm after high school to work, she has proceeded to drift through odd jobs (not finding a steady one) rather than return home as a burden to her already large family. As she says, "I just keep going and going. Doing the best I can, keeping as close to ways I was taught as I can, and still exist." The conversation momentarily deepens when the two of them decide that basically they are alike—philosophical rolling stones who don't have anything, and "don't want anything except security or nothing"—not even a night together. She heads for the next town, leaving the narrator to sleep. He is awakened by a rainstorm and hops a freight to the "weak" and "eerie" sound of the whistle "drifting back along the train."

Despite its allegiance to the hobo-story mode, "Tramp Love" is fundamentally a justification for the existential approach to living. In addition to their rejection of what the world offers, the two characters observe that "no one cares about us" and that they themselves have "nothing to bother about. Nothing to worry about." Beyond this theme, the work is notable for its liberated exploration of the tramp girl, who is an extremely nontraditional woman, especially for her time. She wears (men's) pants, expertly rolls a brown paper cigarette, forwardly joins her companion at her own volition, offers money and her body to him, and generally lives a wayward, "masculine" life. Through her, GDJ is able to touch upon larger "women's questions," as in this passage about work: "She wanted to work, liked to work, but there were so many girls looking for jobs, and so many reasons for jobs suddenly ending. Most times the reasons were men." Men, who expected them to fulfill dual requirements for their positions. As she explodes: "But one thing I refuse to do, and that is work at waiting table or something, and then sleep with the boss to hold the job. I'm willing to do one or the other to get by, but both! Nu-heugh, not this little gal!" Even though the male's race is left unspecified, the woman's whiteness is pronounced. This is crucial realism, since a black woman attempting to pursue this trampish life would quickly have found herself starved, raped, dead—or all three.

Stylistically, "Tramp Love" is not as neat as "Gesture" or as polished as "Free." However, it is competently wrought and proceeds efficiently from beginning to end, its major failing being choppiness of transition in one or two key places. It also seeks verisimilitude by relying heavily on the appropriate jargon—"a dandy smoke," and "You're a good little egg, girlie."

Thinking about "Tramp Love" in relation to where it was published is both illuminating and problematical. *Challenge* was launched in March 1934 as "an organ for the new [black] voice."[119] However, by the appearance of this final issue in spring 1937, Dorothy West was more or less disappointed with the conservative unoriginality of most of the submissions. She wanted good work that dealt with race and class. From the standpoint of class, "Tramp Love" was acceptable. There is a conscious contrast between the hobos and the more affluent society through which they move. For instance, looking at men and women on a golf course, the narrator concedes: "As I watched them I envied them just a little. Their nice white clothes, their parked automobiles, their homes and dinners awaiting them. Cool drinks, cool salads."

A pair of really destitute hitchhikers also make a brief appearance: "They were dirty and tired out. Long, deeply lined faces. Belts with long flapping tongues pulled tightly around thin waists." This Depression world is sharply demarcated into the haves and have nots. Yet, one suspects that at this point of the magazine's demise, the editors may have been a little desperate for fresh material from new names. West's remark about their apparently willing editing of Tremaine's contributions buttresses this theory. It also prompts one to wonder further about GDJ's part in the stories, and, more specifically, about her fictional ability. Interestingly enough, at this same time, she mentions that she is "taking creative writing from the Univ. of Oklahoma."[120] Conceivably, she may have been "practicing" with Drago; but, based on her other story and her general literary output, it is difficult to imagine her writing much below the level of the published "Tramp Love."

One other piece of writing by "Paul Tremaine" has been located—a review of *I'd Do It Again: A Record Of All My Uproarious Years,* the autobiography of James Michael Curley (1874–1958), "once governor of Massachusetts, sometimes Congressman, four times mayor of Boston."[121] It appeared in the *New Republic* on September 9, 1957. Without being told, one would never have suspected GDJ of being the author. Using Curley's own words, Tremaine disrobes him, cooly revealing him as a political rascal whose boundless egomania has blinded him to his own faults. This quote will illustrate both content and style:

> Like the Bedouin chief in *The Seven Pillars of Wisdom*, Curley sees himself as the central figure in a deathless epic, and is so moved by the spectacle that tears come into his eyes, and he speaks of himself in the third person. *I'd Do It Again*, however, is no epic; it is a scenario for a bad film ("The Jim Curley Story") in which the hero (played by himself) indulges in a rather laborious monologue, cataloguing his virtues, reciting his exploits, laughing at his own jokes.

The review is not uncharitable. Tremaine acknowledges Curley's pathos and essential humanity. However, in all good conscience, he must conclude that the book's "only value is that it provides a necessary corrective to a lot of sentimental nonsense about old-fashioned Irish-American politicians; otherwise, it is of dubious value either as a memoir or as a political testament."

This tone of devastating wit is a far cry from the saccharinity of "Homely Philosophy." The fact that this article exists is a reminder that GDJ's life, like Dunbar-Nelson's, constantly touched on politics. From the time of her husband, she was involved with the Republicans and never changed her partisan affiliation even when most black people swung to the Democrats. Her organizational memberships included political groups, such as the Virginia White Speel Republican Club. Furthermore, she wrote songs for the party—e.g., "Hurrah for the G.O.P." (August 26, 1936) and "Dewey and Warren Campaign Song" (1948). This latter she mentions in a September 18, 1948 letter: "Wrote the CAMPAIGN song for the committee and signed a waiver to them. It was played MANY times at opening session here and caused a stir. I was introduced and asked for many autographs. (This for song activity)."[122] She also immortalized Eisenhower's 1953 presidential inauguration in a poem. Thus, it is not as farfetched as it may at first seem for GDJ to write—or to be somehow involved in the writing of—this damning review of Democrat Curley for the *New Republic*.

GDJ's confessing that "Paul Tremaine" was "one of my pseudonyms" makes explicit the fact that she used others. As Dunbar-Nelson wrote in her May 13, 1927, "As in a Looking Glass" column: "Georgia Douglass Johnson has as many aliases as Lon Chaney has faces. One is always stumbling upon another nom de plume of hers." What prompted Dunbar-Nelson's comment was the fact that GDJ had "rather surprised everyone by winning the first prize in the drama department of the *Opportunity* contest [with *Plumes*], under the pseudonym of 'John Temple'" (thus causing Dunbar-Nelson to further credit her with having "as many talents as she has aliases"). Clearly, when other black writers were doing so in the 1920s, GDJ was also employing pseudonyms—as she continued to do until her death.

Not knowing what her pen names were knots her already tangled prose bibliography, especially for her stories. She herself did not help matters by her tendency to refer to her writing and publishing in a maddeningly casual, imprecise (deliberately obscurantist?) fashion. For instance, she tells Jackman on March 27, 1951, that "a magazine in Fort Worth, Texas, is carrying a [her] serial story 'Double Exile.' It is a story of a white girl who chose to be colored—reversing the usual order."[123] Furthermore, there are those thirty-one stories listed in her "Catalogue of Writings"—not to mention other possible pseudonymous work. All of this material has either been lost/destroyed in manuscript or is hopelessly buried in obscure/ defunct magazines.

The GDJ who wrote "Free," "Gesture," "Tramp Love," and the Curley review is visibly related, but not identical, to the GDJ whose image is outlined in the books of poetry, plays, and standard popular commentary. She is less simple and more enigmatic, considerably sharper and more radical. It is clear that writing as a man, disburdened of the weight of her personal, racial, and sexual identity, freed her to express some other selves. Of course, definitive analysis here is complicated by Drago's intermediary role in two of the stories. Nevertheless, her voluntary involvement bespeaks some kind of affinity for the material. One suspects that if additional pseudonymous work of hers were known, the picture would deepen/ darken even further. Considering the fact, say, that one of her poems was published in *Tan Confessions*, it could well be that she, like Wallace Thurman, earned subsistence by writing undisclosed fiction for "trashy," "pulp" publications.[124] What is known for certain about this complex woman does not discourage the taking of rather wide, speculative latitude.

During this final period, GDJ did not try as frantically to locate publishers and subsidy for her work. In the 1950s she gave most of her marketing attention to her novel, "White Men's Children," and the political biography of her late husband, "The Black Cabinet." "A university" and the Black Elks considered "The Black Cabinet."[125] The novel had a much more active history.

GDJ mentions on August 10, 1950, that the New York agent whom Jackman secured for her "has been good enough to keep 'White Men's Children' thus long which makes me feel he may have some faith in it." Seven days later, her faith is wavering, for she becomes agitated and asks Jackman to check on it: "I watch the mailman each day until I am dizzy with hope and fear. I dare not write him [the agent], he might consider me impatient and I don't want to impress him unfavorably. You however know how to be adroit." Later, in November, good news about the novel buoyed her up:

> Had a most encouraging letter from your friend Mr. Schaffner. He is returning the manuscript for 150[?] additional words. I am happy to write them. In fact had already written a third of them some time ago, but hoped they would not be necessary. . . .
>
> He said the book had virility and sincerity. Both are magical words. Also that it depicted life among Negroes in the South very clearly and well. Said it was truly the first half of a very good novel of character study and needed the sequel. I'm doing that according to his suggestions.

By the end of the following January 1951, she had "rounded up the extra pages," but apparently the work was still not placed.[126] This is reminiscent of Dunbar-Nelson's equally unsuccessful counting of words, writing of fiction at the end of her life.

GDJ also repeated her business proposition to Jackman that he or someone else "sponsor" one of her books (this time a collection of one-act plays) and "make his own terms what he will as to royalties etc."[127] In June 1958, she told Glenn Carrington that "the Thurmans at Boston Univ. have my book and I'm invited to go there to talk about it soon." What this book was is unclear. However, speaking about her projects a year later, she is more explicit: "Have a couple of poetry books which I hope will be printed soon: One, Share My World, another: Lovelight."[128] In 1950 and 1964, she made her final attempts at foundation fellowships.[129] On March 2, 1950, she wrote Jackman: "Am trying for the Whitney Opportunity Award, which Robert Weaver is directing. You would be surprised to know how many foundations I have tried, and more surprised to learn that I have still high hopes—am looking with my heart's bright eyes to the bright tomorrow!" This undaunted optimism led her to fill in a 1964 form "from [the] Mary Roberts Rhinehart Foundation in order to have them take an interest in the publication of some book of mine that would be of literary significance ['Literary Salon']."

At this point, GDJ's efforts to publish were both courageous and pathetic. Regardless of how well they may have been written, many of her works had inevitably become dated, passé. And the "old woman" who wrote them must likewise have been regarded as a period piece. It places matters into a startling perspective to think that, while GDJ was attempting to market brotherhood poems and a miscegenation novel, Gwendolyn Brooks was publishing *A Street in Bronzeville* (1945) and Ralph Ellison, *Invisible Man* (1952). Clearly, GDJ was a black writer of another day—and the world had moved on.

Yet, in 1951–52, at over seventy years of age, she asserts that she has "vitality" and is "not dimming out but carrying on with more intensity as the days march!"[130] During the mid-1950s, she found a secretary to take dictation and type, and also inaugurated her habit of working at night (going to bed at 6:30 A.M.) and sleeping during the day. Her later correspondence with Jackman and Carrington suggests that her mind may have been "slipping" a bit since she occasionally repeats more than once a comment or question.[131] However, her always-keen interest in living remains sharp. She visited the West Coast in the summer of 1946 and admonished Carrington to "be sure to see California before the last sun sets for you." In 1954, she asks him: "Tell me this—How does one manage appearances on the show THIS IS YOUR LIFE PROGRAM? Also—What do you know about getting in touch with those who put on T.V. shows." Ten years later, she is talking about responding to an invitation to join the Mensa society for superior intellects.[132]

Descriptions of her during this time illustrate her continuing vigor. Hatch writes:

> Passers-by came to know her as "the old woman with the headband and the tablet around her neck." And indeed she did wear a black headband and, attached to a ribbon around her neck, a pencil and a small, tattered notebook, which she seldom, if ever, removed—"so that when an idea, a word, a line for a poem comes, I can jot it down."[133]

GDJ conceded in 1950 that she was "still vain"—an admission one recalls when Owen Dodson (in a sexist moment) remembers laughingly that she did not hide her "wrinkled bosom" as if to say, "I may be old, but don't you dare try me." Until the end of her life, she attended parties. Again, Dodson recounts an affair (probably during the 1963–64 holiday season) he invited her to:

> Her son Lincoln brought her. She had on her tam o'shanter and her sweatband and one of those big bags. . . . I said "Mrs. Johnson, what is in that big bag?" And she said, "My things." So I said, "Well, let me relieve you of some of this." (She had on a couple of coats.) . . . She said, "No, I'm only going to stay a minute." She stayed until after 4 o'clock and joined in every bit of conversation.[134]

Finally, this anecdote about her highlights her eccentricity and her racial consciousness:

> One day, two young men, their processed hair held by greasy scarves and their backs bent . . . sullenly walked in front of her house cursing. She stopped them with her pointed cane: "Such filth!" she shouted. "Get those

rags off your heads, and walk with your shoulders back! You're black men—you should be proud!" The young men were as startled as Mrs. Johnson's neighbors. They looked at her for a moment; then embarrassed, they removed the scarves and moved on, shoulders back and heads high. "That's more like it!" she shouted, as they crossed the street.[135]

Small items of recognition did continue to cheer her days. In the December 1952 *Crisis,* Cedric Dover published his attention-bestowing article about her, "The Importance of Georgia Douglass Johnson." The authors of *Propaganda and Aesthetics: The Literary Politics of Afro-American Magazines in the Twentieth Century* note that "Johnson's books had been reviewed in *Crisis* and elsewhere, but her career had not previously been discussed in a separate literary essay published in an Afro-American magazine. Dover's article represents a first in the commentary on a poet who had the distinction of extraordinary survival."[136]

GDJ's poems were still seen in outlets such as the *Negro Digest* and the Baltimore *Afro-American.* One of them, a Christmas poem, "received first prize in the [1952] poetry contest in the Professional Writers Club (white)."[137] The Norfolk, Virginia, *Journal and Guide* for November 3, 1962, carries a long letter of appreciation headlined "Tribute to A Poetess, Georgia Douglas Johnson." It begins, "During this week when we pay tribute to American poets, let's not forget our own poetess in Washington, D.C.," and is signed "E. B. Henderson, Falls Church, Va."[138] Her culminating award was an honorary doctor of letters degree from her alma mater, Atlanta University, conferred a year before her death, in June 1965.

Another "moonlighting" activity that kept GDJ busy was running a correspondence club, the "One World" Washington Social Letter Club, Inc. She conducted it under the pseudonym of Mary Strong through a post office box beginning sometime around 1930 until at least 1965. Her first mention of it occurs in a December 8, 1932, letter to Carrington. She informs him: "I run a Letter Writing Club. I haven't told you about it tho. It may be I shall ask you for suggestions about how to get it advertised in New York." He helped her considerably with foreign contacts, giving her, for instance, a membership in the Bahai Fellowship in 1959. She found it invaluable:

> The connections I have made have been worth more than money to me as I am dealing with people all over the world and very specially, Africa. Am sending articles to Africa weekly. The postage is quite a figure, but I consider this part of the offering I am happy to make to the dark Continent. I hope through the Club to bring to those who are eager for touch with the Western world, an avenue.

Carrington also introduced her to an organization called the Caravan of East and West, Inc., whose Pen Friends Guide mailing list she mined for names.[139]

GDJ advertised her club with flyers.[140] One of them is illustrated by a globe encircled with the slogan "One God One World One Hope." Part of the text reads: "Why not meet people at home and abroad? If you can't travel—write! Your life is just what you make it, broad or narrow. Meet lots of people and THEN select those you wish to know better." Further on, the procedure is described:

> Members accepted from 20 to 100 years old. State briefly the sort of people you are interested in and a generous list will be sent to you. Write to THEM FIRST. Others will WRITE TO YOU FIRST. THESE compose YOUR LIST. Joining fee two dollars. You will receive mail from new and various sources for a year. A new list will be sent any time DURING the year for one dollar.

An application blank follows, with spaces for standard demographic data as well as "Complexion," "Musical," and "addresses of lonely friends."

A second flyer touts the club by quoting from "some of the thousands [of letters] received by us from delighted members." They, too, are predictable. From places as diverse as Chicago, Rhode Island, Calcutta, India, and Clarksville, Tennessee, men and women thank "Mrs. Strong" for bringing into their lives "the man of my dreams," the "most loveable little woman that ever lived," "many new friends," and "sunshine." What, one wonders, prompted GDJ to pursue this activity—and for so many years? The two most plausible reasons are money and/or a sincere desire to pull isolated people together.

GDJ's "one world" image is picked up in the title and contents of her final book of poetry, *Share My World* (1962).[141] It is a twilight volume, casting a retrospective glow on the life and work it encompasses. GDJ self-published the thirty-two page collection with the aid of N. Wright Cuney, a typographer and printer whom she refers to as "My Private Printer." (He also enabled her to send her yearly poem to friends and acquaintances.) The soft, blue covers carry the same basic Effie Lee Newsome (now correctly identified) sketch as *An Autumn Love Cycle,* only here the objects floating around the woman are unmistakably planetary bodies.

There is a three-paragraph preface by one Michael Victor Strong, which discusses the poet as "Sappho and Miriam combined," a writer who unites the "passion, storm and sweep of Sappho" with the "tranquility" and "calm" of the "nun-like" biblical Miriam. It also points out that "this modern Southern poet" utilizes a Heine-like "concise and condensed

quatrain style." Something about this preface within the contextual circumstances of the book's publication suggests that Michael Victor Strong
(otherwise unidentifiable) is next-of-kin to Mary Strong—is, in all proba-
bility, another of GDJ's pseudonymous faces. Except for its physical production, everything about this volume—from the adapted illustration, to
the decorative roses on the title page, through the "Preface" and "Author's
Word," on to the dedication to Dorsey K. Offutt (also unknown)—feels
like GDJ.

A few poems from her earlier books are reprinted in *Share My World,* as
are later works from newspapers and periodicals—for instance, "I Want to
Die While You Love Me," "Common Dust," and "Credo." Many of the
verses resound her familiar themes. There are those which treat the
ephemerality of joy and deathlessness of love—"My Happiness" and
"Love Is So Small a Thing." And, of course, racial and brotherhood poems
are included—"The Return," "The Man to Be," and "Inevitably." By far,
the largest category is that which presents the author's personal summa-
tion and general philosophy of life.

Reviewing the years gone by, GDJ reminisces about "old love letters"
that remind her, "I was loved once—long ago," and enjoys "savoring" the
"bitter-sweet" past. She reveals that she has steadily pursued a "dream
life":

> Always the world has ever been
> A fairy-land to me.
> No road was just a common road
> No tree a common tree.
>
> . . . .
> About each tree-trunk hung a spell
> Whose pebbles, bits of glass
> In hidden nests were images
> To bring my dreams to pass. . . .

(P. 15)

Perhaps the most poignant inclusions are "The Gift of Years" and "One
Lives Too Long." The "mellow years" have brought "the infinite peace of
forgetting, / the joy of remembering":

> A key to earth-born melodies,
> A deaf ear to its din
> Eyes that see only the beautiful,
> And a heart that is young again.

(P. 12)

A truly somber poem, "One Lives Too Long," laments that "days grow pale / And endless creep the nights" and admits that "the gift of death / Is merciful—when understood."

Yet, despite this funereal tone, the overall message is for one to live audaciously, gazing into the sun. For the writer, this is essential:

> How much living have you done?
> From it the patterns that you weave
> Are imaged.
>
> (P. 18)

In "Lovelight," the title poem for one of her projected books, life and death are "darkened doors / And love the light between."

Themes rather than technique distinguish these final poems. Most of them are brief, many being no more than a quatrain long. There is no egregious lapsing of GDJ's lyric instinct and, occasionally, she still manages to seize the reader with an unexpectedly perfect word. All in all, the poet's sharing of her waning world is a queenly gesture.

Writing a foreword for another 1962 poetry collection brought GDJ to her second foray into formal literary criticism. The first had occurred more than thirty years previously in the "Book Chat" column of the Norfolk, Virginia, *Journal and Guide,* October 4 (?), 1930. In the wake of her splendid successes as a dramatist, GDJ assesses the contemporary black theater scene and gives advice to the younger playwrights. She begins:

> Drama in the past has portrayed the Negro farthest down. That was good as a starter, in fact, it was the only kind of play that would have been welcomed or even received by the great universal public. Now, however, the time is about ripe for plays of a different nature. Stories that tell of the hopes, dreams, yearnings, heartbreaks and yes, even the joys and fulfillments of today—the history of our great middle class should be written.

Then she avers that youth wants present life depicted, and that their mothers and fathers would welcome some modern, perhaps even escapist, drama. There is much bygone and present truth in her statement, "Most of the plays in the past have had a kitchen setting." While GDJ recognizes the market conditions that foster the outmoded dialect work, she judges that "the good old ignorant Negro, the poor old ignorant Negro, the bad old ignorant Negro" need to be largely replaced with fresher images, which she exhorts the young writers to provide. Here GDJ is calling for the same kind of development in drama that Grimké declared was necessary for the short story.

GDJ's second critical essay prefaced *Second Movement,* a volume of poems by Robert E. Fennell.[142] In its first paragraph, she gives some information about the fledgling author and then veers to a discourse about poets and poetry. Except for her brief comment—"Poetry is the art of the passionate few. A poem is like ice on a stove. Zip, and then it's gone"[143]—these remarks are her only published words on the subject. However, being romanticist, they are not particularly novel. She outlines the stages of a poet's progress from nascent sensibility and then concludes that "few poets, however, preserve this rich ecstasy into age, yet, some few have done so and thus mightily enriched the literature of the world." Here, GDJ might have had herself in mind. Whether or not poets are really "God's envoys," she asserts that "they are indeed set apart."

These two pieces finally exhaust GDJ's genres and repertoire as a writer. However voluminous it may appear, this available work represents only a fraction of her total corpus. When she died, her papers included much more of her own writing as well as a wealth of correspondence and other irreplaceable literary material. Owen Dodson provides the sole, deplorable account of what happened to these documents:

> I do know that she had a great deal of unpublished material—novels, poems, essays, memoirs, remembrances, all kinds of things. But as the car stopped in front of her house [returning from her funeral], the men were cleaning out the cellar, and I clearly saw manuscripts thrown into the garbage. I said, "A lifetime to the sanitation department!"[144]

The sadness/horror/rage one feels contemplating this scene is inexpressible. All too obviously, GDJ's black female creativity was not valued by those close to her, who saw her pages of writing as so much junk and clutter. Fortunately, enough of her output survived to prove that she was, unquestionably, a rare woman and a dedicated writer. For fifty-five years, she had produced literature ranging from aphorisms to plays to novels. Simply focusing on her published work reveals her to be, first of all, a gifted lyric poet, and second, a fine dramatist. Overall, her writings—and her life—expand to the point of astonishment one's consciousness about authorship for an individual of her race, her gender, and her era.

A wonderful, late glimpse of GDJ comes from black woman poet Julia Fields, who wrote her elegy in the October 1966 *Negro Digest.*[145] Fields evokes her "marvelous, scandalous living room . . . sown with treasures," with GDJ "holding seance" "like a brilliant old / Genius of an Empress on a throne of chintz-bound chair." They attended the National Poetry Festival together, where GDJ sat, "silent, vibrant again as the phoenix / Young it seemed as I, and with a better, purer grace."

Her youthfulness was the growing backwards into second beginnings. In May 1966 she suffered a stroke and was taken to Freedman's Hospital, where she died quietly on Saturday, May 14, almost eighty-six years old. Her Episcopal rites were conducted by the Rev. W. A. Van Croft, and her body interred in Lincoln Cemetery.[146] At her funeral, Dodson argued with the minister, who reluctantly agreed to let him read two of her poems, "I Want to Die While You Love Me" and "Your World," prior to the regulation service. Dodson ends the story:

> So I said, "Alright. I'm not going to fight you and God at the same time." So I read the poems and I just touched her casket while I was reading them. They had dressed this old lady in surprise pink and put a fresh sweat-band around her head, one of those 20's things. It was a nice, beautiful, fitting touch.

The image is roses. Sometime soon after her husband's 1925 death, GDJ planted rosebushes in the yard of Half-Way House.[147] She loved and tended them—grew them with such pride and success that they curtained the walkway to her door and neighbors called her front "The Riviera."[148] When Owen Dodson saw her a month before she died, she was stirring about her roses—it was the spring—and crying out that she did not want "to be buried in that ground."[149] Her son Lincoln, who people said did not understand his mother, brought to her burial an old bag filled with roses from the forty-year-old plants—and sprinkled them on her coffin. The bushes at 1461 S Street, Northwest Washington, continue to bloom with pink, red, red-pink roses.

Julia Fields wrote further of her 1960s visit with GDJ:

> We discussed reincarnation. You said to me, "And you, what would You choose to come back as?" "A butterfly," I said. "Ah," we heard You sigh. "And what other thing?" "A rose, I think and very red." Smiling into quiet delight, you said, "That's beautiful. And I think that I would too return here as a rose. . . . "[150]

CHAPTER V • AFTERWORD

Color, Sex, and Poetry: The Renaissance Legacy

After the Harlem Renaissance, black women writers continued to explore what Gloria Wade-Gayles describes as "the narrow space of race, the dark enclosure of sex."[1] Paralleling Afro-American social, political, and literary history, they have advanced to sharper, more sophisticated racial-sexual self-definitions and a more integrated and provocative handling of these ubiquitous themes. How they treat this material is still an amalgam of personal, racial, sexual, and societal factors impinging upon them as individual creative artists. It proves that, in matters such as this, things change even as they remain the same. Later writers both echo and extend the issues—personal, thematic, stylistic—of their earlier sisters in an ever-increasing variety of ways. Even a brief look at the poets and writers is revealing.

In the generally depleted 1930s, Zora Neale Hurston's culturally based exploration of black female selfhood in her 1937 novel, *Their Eyes Were Watching God*, was revolutionary. It opened the way for Ann Petry to depict Lutie Johnson entangled in a destructive web of race-sex-class (*The Street*, 1944), and for Dorothy West to evoke the neuroses of Cleo Judson wrought by the same deadly skein (*The Living is Easy*, 1947). Poets, too, were breaking free of limiting notions of poetic femininity and speaking with stronger, surer voices. In her prize-winning 1942 volume, *For My People*, Margaret Walker assumed the griot voice of "her people" to chronicle their defeats and triumphs, celebrate their heroes and heroines, and consider her own specific place in this complex lineage.

Gwendolyn Brooks began presenting the characters from *A Street in Bronzeville* in 1945, often using them as the narrative personae of her poems and ballads. When she wrote *Annie Allen* in 1949, she made explicit her earlier attention to black women by elevating a plain young woman named Annie to the status of an epic hero in "The Anniad." She also embodied a racial-stylistic dilemma reminiscent of the Harlem Renaissance writers when she wrote of Annie in the learned, allusive, and dense academic language of the mainstream poetic elite in order to prove that she, a black woman poet, could also "write well." Brooks's preoccupation with the browns, blacks, tans, chocolates, and yellows of Afro-American color—especially as this schema victimizes her darker-skinned female characters—brings out openly in black women's literature what had been previously submerged or subverted.

Like their earlier counterparts, both Brooks and Walker also wrote novels, the lyrical *Maud Martha* (1953) and the historical *Jubilee* (1966), respectively. Theirs, however, are very successful ones that creatively utilize the autobiographies of their authors. *Jubilee* is based on the life of Walker's great-grandmother during slavery and Reconstruction, while the title character of *Maud Martha* is a fictionalized Gwendolyn Brooks, an ordinary black woman with her own kind of dandelion beauty. It also bears mentioning that Walker spent twenty-seven years writing *Jubilee* because of interruptions resulting from marriage, childbirth, childrearing, scarce money, teaching jobs, and lack of time.

When Afro-American poetry exploded in the 1960s–70s, women were well represented. Mari Evans announced *I Am a Black Woman* (1970) and wrote movingly from that core. Lucille Clifton celebrated husband and children, and her own vaselined legs and nappy hair. Nikki Giovanni catalogued a long list of black martyrs, then asked her brethren and sistren if they, too, knew how to kill.

Sonia Sanchez suggests the amazing new range of the black female poet. Writing with a harsh, "unfeminine" militancy, she can flatly declare:

> blues ain't culture
>   they sounds of
> oppression
>   against the white man's
> shit/[2]

In a beautiful, cadenced standard English that contrasts with her rhythmic black street dialect, she eulogizes Malcolm X. However, she also writes of relationships between black men and women, of the problems and possibilities that lie in black children, and, most poignantly, of personal/black female selfhood and pain:

> but i am what i
> am. woman. alone
> amid all this noise.[3]

Throughout, she autobiographically, culturally, and artistically centers herself as

> this honeycoatedalabamianwoman
> raining rhythms of blue/black smiles[4]

Clearly, the Black Power and Black Arts movements provided inspiration and outlet for these new Afro-American women poets as the Harlem Renaissance had for the writers of that era. Interestingly, they, too, found themselves discriminated against because of their sex and gender, so much so that Audre Lorde could protest acidly that "Black is / not beautiful baby,"

> not
> being screwed twice
> at the same time
> from on top
> as well as
> from my side.[5]

Though these contemporary women poets could not be dismissed for the araciality of their subjects or the delicacy of their tones or the anachronism of their style, they could still be relegated to second place in a movement that was designed, in more than rhetorical terms, for "the black man."

However, the late 1970s–80s added a new ingredient: the women's/ feminist movement. Black women, who by right of blood belonged to both the women's and the black movements, found themselves decrying racism in the one and sexism in the other. They were also confronted with the falsely dichotomized but still vexing question of which was paramount— their race or their sex. Though earlier women sometimes wrote as if they could not make up their internal minds about this issue (one recalls, for example, Dunbar-Nelson's many fragmentations and evasions), no one so directly posed the challenge (sometimes accusation) of choice. Again, Lorde crystallizes the dilemma in her "Who Said It Was Simple." This poem features a black woman at a feminist demonstration realizing that she is "bound by my mirror / as well as my bed" and wondering "which me will survive / all these liberations."[6] Despite apparent contradictions, the women's/feminist movement—in its critique of patriarchy and raising of female consciousness—contributed significantly to the bold, self-assured honesty of Afro-American women's work. At the same time, it provided them with another (sometimes alternative) audience and means of support. Notably, the acceptance of lesbianism and other heretofore too-personal, too-female themes saved the literary lives of many women poets, both black and white. Angelina Grimké's tragedy did not have to be replayed.

The ascendancy of poetry and drama in the 1960s–70s was challenged by the fiction writers of the late 1970s–80s. Unlike the earlier decades when the post–Harlem Renaissance period of fiction was dominated by the names of men such as Richard Wright, Ralph Ellison, and James Baldwin, this new age did not witness the disappearance of women. In fact, the primary writers are female—for example, Toni Morrison, Gayle Jones, Alice Walker, Toni Cade Bambara, Gloria Naylor, and Paule Marshall. Critic Barbara Christian makes a statement about these women writers that links them to their pioneering cohorts and simultaneously points out the distance traveled. She posits: "The extent to which Afro-American women writers in the seventies and eighties have been able to make a commitment to an exploration of self, as central rather than marginal, is a tribute to the insights they have culled in a century or so of literary activity."[7] This ability to maintain "an overtly self-centered point of view" distinguishes modern Afro-American women writers; but it is a stance made possible by the wobbly steps in that direction of forebears like Alice Dunbar-Nelson, Angelina Grimké, and Georgia Douglas Johnson.

From this surety of self, black women writers are consciously exploring their ancient wisdoms and spiritual selves, their relationships with other women (as mothers, sisters, friends, lovers), their ties to their black communities and culture, their place in the African diaspora, their multivalent eroticism, their personal relationships to the politics and history of their age, and so on. More than this, out of their sense of a black female "writerly" self, they are, like their white contemporaries, devising new, more appropriate forms in which to package their experiences. Walker's *The Color Purple* (1982) utilizes the crude but eloquent letters of uneducated black women. Billie Holiday could sing the lines that Alexis DeVeaux writes about her in *Don't Explain: A Song of Billie Holiday* (1980). Paule Marshall chants an African praise poem in her *Praisesong for the Widow* (1983) and uses the non-naturalistic techniques of dream and hallucination. Audre Lorde invents a form, biomythography, in which to tell her story in *Zami: A New Spelling of My Name* (1982). ntozake shange unifies poetry, drama, and women's nonliterary expressionistic forms in her "choreopoem," *for colored girls who have considered suicide/when the rainbow is enuf* (1977), while in her more recent *sassafras, cypress, and indigo* (1982), she incorporates recipes and voodoo charms. Michelle Parkerson combines poetry, fiction, science fiction, and film in her experimentally effective *Waiting Rooms* (1983). And this already long list could be indefinitely extended.

There is some fear that the current black female literary renaissance may prove to be as much of a "fad" as the New Negro one of the 1920s. However, whether white people and the literary establishment remain thrilled with what black women write should not be the measure of these writers' achievement. Though Afro-American women in general are fighting some of the same old gorgons with fresh-sprung heads, the scribes are depicting this as well as myriad new realities in works that will endure. Some dawns are, in truth, the beginning of a brand-new day.

NOTES

As with all the women writers of the Harlem Renaissance except Zora Neale Hurston, extensive biographical and literary criticism does not exist for Alice Dunbar-Nelson, Angelina Weld Grimké, and Georgia Douglas Johnson. Furthermore, their work is mostly out of print and not easily available (a fact for which I have tried to compensate by ample quotations, when necessary). This situation will change for Dunbar-Nelson when Oxford University Press publishes a two-volume collection of her work as part of the "Oxford Library of Black Women's Writings" in September 1987. Fortunately, however, for these three writers, original, archival material has been preserved. Dunbar-Nelson's papers were kept after her death by her niece, Pauline A. Young, and have been recently acquired by the Morris Library, University of Delaware, Newark, Delaware. Grimké's documents are an important part of the Grimké family papers at the Moorland-Spingarn Research Center, Howard University, Washington, D.C. Primary sources for Johnson are more widely scattered in the major Afro-American repositories, with the holdings at the Trevor-Arnett Library, Atlanta University, Atlanta, Georgia, being particularly valuable.

Chapter 1: Introduction

1. Alice Dunbar-Nelson, "As in a Looking Glass," the Washington *Eagle,* February 25–September [?], 1927. "April Is on the Way," *Ebony and Topaz,* ed. Charles S. Johnson (*Opportunity,* 1927).

2. Letter from Langston Hughes to Angelina Weld Grimké, May 8, 1927. The AWG Collection, Moorland-Spingarn Research Center, Howard University, Washington, D.C. *Caroling Dusk: An Anthology of Verse by Negro Poets,* ed. Countee Cullen (New York: Harper & Brothers, 1927).

3. Gwendolyn Bennett, "The Ebony Flute," *Opportunity* (July 1927): 212. *Give Us Each Day: The Diary of Alice Dunbar-Nelson,* ed. Gloria T. Hull (New York: W. W. Norton, 1984), p. 185.

4. Nathan I. Huggins, Introduction to his anthology *Voices from the Harlem Renaissance* (New York: Oxford University Press, 1976), p. 9. The following general information about the period draws from this source as well as from two others: *Black Writers of America,* ed. Richard Barksdale and Keneth Kinnamon (New York: The Macmillan Company, 1972); Darwin T. Turner's Introduction to Jean Toomer, *Cane* (New York: Liveright, 1975).

5. Alice Dunbar-Nelson, "As in a Looking Glass" column, the Washington *Eagle,* June 14, 1929. Unprocessed Dunbar-Nelson materials, Morris Library, University of Delaware, Newark, Delaware.

6. Huggins, *Voices From the Harlem Renaissance,* p. 5.

7. Elise Johnson McDougald, "The Task of Negro Womanhood," in *The New Negro,* ed. Alain Locke (1925; New York: Atheneum, 1974), p. 369.

8. Langston Hughes, "Madam's Past History," in his *Selected Poems* (New York: Alfred A. Knopf, 1959), p. 201.

9. Blanche Taylor Dickinson, "Revelation," in *Caroling Dusk,* p. 108.

10. This information comes from an interview of Ethel Ray Nance conducted by Ann Allen Shockley in 1970. Fisk University Library Oral History, Nashville, Tennessee.

11. David Levering Lewis, *When Harlem Was in Vogue* (New York: Alfred A. Knopf, 1981), p. 123. Lewis's extensively researched, eminently readable work is an invaluable reference for the social-literary history of the period, and functioned as an important sourcebook for this introductory chapter.

12. Ibid., p. 127.

13. Biographical sketch of Anne Spencer taken from the program of the landmark dedication of her home, February 26, 1977. Biography file, Fisk University, Nashville, Tennessee.

14. Langston Hughes, *The Big Sea* (New York: Hill & Wang, 1932), p. 218.

15. Lewis, p. 96.

16. Owen Dodson interviewed by James V. Hatch, December 3, 1971. Tape collection, Atlanta University Library, Atlanta, Georgia. My transcription.

17. Hurston's comments about Locke are contained in a letter to James Weldon Johnson. Quoted from Jervis Anderson, *This Was Harlem: A Cultural Portrait, 1900–1950* (New York: Farrar, Straus & Giroux, 1982), p. 201.

18. Lewis, pp. 81, 85, 87, 88, 153.

19. Ibid., p. 196.

20. Ibid., p. 209.

21. A description of Van Vechten's parties given by Allen Churchill in *The Literary Decade*. Quoted from Jervis Anderson, *This Was Harlem*, p. 214. The succeeding quotation also comes from Anderson, p. 214.

22. Letter from James Weldon Johnson to Charles W. Chesnutt, January 31, 1928. Chesnutt Collection, Fisk University Library, Nashville, Tennessee.

23. Letter from James Weldon Johnson to Edwin R. Embree, August 22, 1931. Rosenwald Papers, Fisk University Library, Nashville, Tennessee.

24. Lewis, p. 293.

25. This information about McKay comes from Lewis, pp. 140–42, 225–26.

26. *Give Us Each Day: The Diary of Alice Dunbar-Nelson*, p. 313.

27. The Pittsburgh *Courier*, July [5, 16 ?], 1928.

28. Lewis, p. 167.

29. Statement prepared for the Harold Jackman Memorial Committee by Regina M. Andrews, the Schomburg Center Vertical File; Lewis, p. 213.

30. Lewis, p. 266.

31. Ibid., p. 140.

32. Ethel Ray Nance interview with Ann Allen Shockley.

33. Cited in the Introduction to Robert Hemenway's edition of Hurston's autobiography, *Dust Tracks On a Road* (1942; Urbana: University of Illinois Press, 1984), pp. x–xi. Professor Cheryl Wall has discovered that Hurston was born on January 7, 1891, rather than January 1, 1901.

34. Georgia Douglas Johnson, "Welt." Quoted from *The Book of American Negro Poetry*, ed. J. W. Johnson (New York: Harcourt, Brace, 1931), p. 183.

35. Johnson, *The Book of American Negro Poetry*, p. 279. The poets discussed here are best represented in Johnson's anthology, Cullen's *Caroling Dusk*, and *The Poetry of the Negro*, ed. Langston Hughes and Arna Bontemps. The Hayford poem quoted below is taken from *Caroling Dusk*, p. 200.

36. Lewis, p. 140.

37. Greene's work resulted in *Time's Unfading Garden: Anne Spencer's Life and Poetry* (Baton Rouge: Louisiana State University Press, 1977).

38. McKay in *Home to Harlem*. Quoted from Arthur P. Davis, *From the Dark Tower: Afro-American Writers 1900–1960* (Washington, D.C.: Howard University Press, 1974), p. 40.

39. Letter from Charles S. Johnson to Angelina W. Grimké, January 6, 1925. AWG Collection, Moorland-Spingarn Research Center, Howard University, Washington, D.C.

40. Cedric Dover, "The Importance of Georgia Douglass Johnson," *The Crisis* 59 (December 1952): 635.

41. This poem is included in her *Bronze: A Book of Verse* (Boston: B. J. Brimmer Co., 1922).

42. Review of *Plumes*, New York *Amsterdam News*, November 23 (?), 1927.

43. Letter from Georgia Douglas Johnson to Arna Bontemps, July 6, 1941. The Cullen-Jackman Collection, Trevor Arnett Library, Atlanta University, Atlanta, Georgia.

44. *Caroling Dusk*, p. 47.

45. Letter from Georgia Douglas Johnson to Arna Bontemps, July 19, 1941. GDJ Papers, the Cullen-Jackman Collection.

46. The New York *Ecclesiastical Review*, February 1900.

47. Letter from Bliss Perry to Alice Dunbar-Nelson, August 22, 1900. AD–N Papers, the University of Delaware Library, Newark, Delaware.

48. Lewis, p. 94.

49. Alain Locke, Foreword to Georgia Douglas Johnson's *An Autumn Love Cycle* (New York: Harold Vinal, Ltd., 1928), p. xviii.

50. Johnson's third-person headnote in *Caroling Dusk*, p. 74.

51. This statement exists in an incomplete holograph draft. Grimké wrote it in response to a November 28, 1925, request for information from a student studying her work.

52. Reprinted in *The World Split Open: Four Centuries of Women Poets in England and America, 1552–1950*, ed. Louise Bernikow (New York: Vintage Books, 1974), p. 262.

53. Barbara Christian, "Afro-American Women Poets: A Historical Introduction," in *Black Feminist Criticism: Perspectives on Black Women Writers* (New York: Pergamon Press, 1985), p. 122.

54. Cheryl A. Wall, "Poets and Versifiers, Singers and Signifiers: Women of the Harlem Renaissance," in *Women, the Arts and the 1920's in Paris and New York*, ed. Kenneth W. Wheeler and Virginia Lee Lussier (New Brunswick, N.J.: Transaction Books, 1982), p. 75.

55. Helene Johnson, "Poem," in *Caroling Dusk*, p. 219. Bessie Smith, "Young Woman's Blues," quoted from Cheryl A. Wall, pp. 90–91.

56. Letter from William Haygood to GDJ, October 7, 1942. Rosenwald Collection, Fisk University, Nashville, Tennessee.

57. Lewis, p. 238.

58. Letter from GDJ to Harold Jackman, August 8, 1944. Cullen-Jackman Collection.

59. Erlene Stetson, "Rediscovering the Harlem Renaissance: Georgia Douglas Johnson, 'The New Negro Poet,'" *Obsidian* 5 (Spring/Summer, 1979): 33.

60. Letter from Charles S. Johnson to Angelina W. Grimké, May 28, 1925. AWG Collection.

61. Letter from Georgia Douglas Johnson to George E. Haynes, July 26, 1928. The Harmon Foundation Records, Manuscript Division, Library of Congress, Washington, D.C.

62. *Caroling Dusk*, p. 105.
63. Lewis, pp. 120–21.

Chapter 2: Alice Dunbar-Nelson

1. Letter from Alice Dunbar-Nelson to Paul Laurence Dunbar, March 7, 1899. Unprocessed Alice Dunbar-Nelson materials, Special Collections, Morris Library, University of Delaware, Newark, Delaware. Unless otherwise noted, all letters, documents, and unpublished materials cited come from this source.
2. Undated letter from Alice Dunbar-Nelson to Paul L. Dunbar, probably ca. December 1898.
3. *Give Us Each Day: The Diary of Alice Dunbar-Nelson*, ed. Gloria T. Hull (New York: W. W. Norton, 1984), p. 107.
4. *Journal of the Lodge*, August 18, 1894.
5. Alice Ruth Moore, *Violets and Other Tales* (The Monthly Review, 1895). Page numbers are hereafter given parenthetically in the text.
6. Letter from Dunbar-Nelson to Arthur Schomburg, July 23, 1913. The Schomburg Center, New York Public Library.
7. *Give Us Each Day*, p. 276.
8. Ibid., p. 394. In her October 5, 1928, diary entry, Dunbar-Nelson also mentions this date as the beginning for one of her youthful romances with a sweetheart, Nelson Mitchell.
9. Letter from Dunbar-Nelson to Arthur Schomburg, July 23, 1913. The Schomburg Center, New York Public Library.
10. A phrase in quotes that Sylvanie F. Williams used to describe the author, Dunbar-Nelson, in the Preface to *Violets*, p. 10.
11. Letters from Alice Dunbar-Nelson to Paul L. Dunbar, March 29, 1898, and June 8, 1897.
12. Letter from Alice Dunbar-Nelson to Paul L. Dunbar, February 8, 1898.
13. Letter from Alice Dunbar-Nelson to Paul L. Dunbar, January 29, 1898.
14. Letter from Alice Dunbar-Nelson to Paul L. Dunbar, January 12, 1898.
15. *Give Us Each Day*, p. 333.
16. "Women in Clubdom," no date (ca. 1899), no place (probably Denver, Colorado).
17. The Philadelphia *Afro-American*, September 28, 1935.
18. Letter from Alice Dunbar-Nelson to Paul L. Dunbar, March 27, 1898.
19. Virginia Cunningham, *Paul Laurence Dunbar and His Song* (1947; New York: Biblo and Tannen, 1969), p. 172.
20. The New York *Mail and Express*, January 31, 1899.
21. Lincoln, Nebraska, newspaper, October 1899.
22. Letter from Alice Dunbar-Nelson to Paul L. Dunbar, February 8, 1898.
23. Letter from Alice Dunbar-Nelson to Paul L. Dunbar, February 27, 1899.
24. Letter from Alice Dunbar-Nelson to Paul L. Dunbar, October 6, 1897.
25. Letter from Alice Dunbar-Nelson to Paul L. Dunbar, January 26, 1898.
26. Letter from Alice Dunbar-Nelson to Paul L. Dunbar, October 10, 1897.
27. Letters from Alice Dunbar-Nelson to Paul L. Dunbar, January 1 and February 21, 1898.
28. Letter from Alice Dunbar-Nelson to Paul L. Dunbar, February 27, 1900.
29. Letter from Alice Dunbar-Nelson to Paul L. Dunbar, April 24, 1901.
30. Letter from Alice Dunbar-Nelson to Paul L. Dunbar, September 13, 1898.

31. Letter from Alice Dunbar-Nelson to Paul L. Dunbar, undated, probably ca. December, 1898.

32. This information and the succeeding quotes are taken from Andrew Alexander, "The Dunbar Letters: The Tragic Love Affair of One of America's Greatest Poets," the *Washington Post* Magazine, June 28, 1981.

33. Letter from Alice Dunbar-Nelson to Paul L. Dunbar, January 15, 1898.

34. "Paul L. Dunbar in Denver," *Literary Life,* Saturday, October 7, 1899.

35. "Mrs. Paul Laurence Dunbar, Wife of the Colored Poet and Novelist," Chicago *Recorder,* August 4, 1902.

36. "The Dunbar Letters."

37. Cunningham, p. 176.

38. Letter from Alice Dunbar-Nelson to Paul L. Dunbar, February 27, 1900.

39. Letter from Alice Dunbar-Nelson to Paul L. Dunbar, January 29, 1898.

40. Letter from Alice Dunbar-Nelson to Paul L. Dunbar, February 25, 1899.

41. The Glasgow *Evening News,* September 30, 1899; the [?] *Mail and Express,* December 16, 1899.

42. New York *Mail and Express,* August 31, 1899.

43. New York *Evening Sun,* October 11, 1900.

44. Alice Dunbar, *The Goodness of St. Rocque and Other Stories* (New York: Dodd, Mead and Company, 1899). Page references are given parenthetically in the text.

45. "Paul Dunbar's Gifted Wife," Philadelphia *Post,* April 21, 1900.

46. Pittsburgh *Christian Advocate,* December 21, 1899.

47. Alice Dunbar-Nelson, "Hope Deferred," *The Crisis* (September 1914): 238–42.

48. The New York *Eccelesiastical Review,* February 1900.

49. The New York *Evening Post,* August 28, 1900; the Houston *Post,* December 1899; the New York *Tribune,* December 17, 1899.

50. Washington, D.C., *Times,* September 3, 1899.

51. *Mail and Express,* December 16, 1899.

52. Dallas *Christian Advocate,* August 9, 1900.

53. Pittsburgh *Post,* December 25, 1899; New York *Tribune,* December 17, 1899.

54. The New York City *Chute* (?), May 1900.

55. Newspaper clipping, no name, July 4, 1928. From the Schomburg Center vertical file.

56. The stories being discussed here are all to be found in the Alice Dunbar-Nelson materials, University of Delaware library. Publication information is given in the text.

57. Dunbar-Nelson made a list of the volume's contents—titles of eleven stories and their lengths in words (combined wordage 58,300).

58. "Mrs. Paul Laurence Dunbar, Wife of the Colored Poet and Novelist," Chicago *Recorder,* August 4, 1902.

59. Alice Dunbar-Nelson to Paul R. Reynolds, April 9, 1902. Paul Laurence Dunbar Collection, the Schomburg Center.

60. Paul R. Reynolds to Mrs. Paul Laurence Dunbar, November 22, 1902. There are allusions to published stories other than the ones here mentioned—for example, a March 18, 1902, reference by her to "selling that story to the Herald that time."

61. Alice Dunbar-Nelson to Paul L. Dunbar, March 23 and March 27, 1901.

62. J. N. M. [?] to Alice Dunbar-Nelson, July 16, 1903. For this "expert opinion" Dunbar-Nelson paid five dollars.

63. Alice Dunbar-Nelson to Paul R. Reynolds, August 27, 1901. Paul Laurence Dunbar Collection, the Schomburg Center. She wrote the other letter to Reynolds on April 19, 1901.

64. Letter from Dr. Francis R. Lane, Director of High Schools, to Alice Dunbar-Nelson, February 24, 1902.

65. Letter from Booker T. Washington, Principal, to Alice Dunbar-Nelson, May 20, 1905. He informed her that Tuskegee was not at present keeping a summer session.

66. Alice Dunbar-Nelson, "Training of Teachers of English," *Education* 29 (October 1908): 97–103.

67. Alice Dunbar-Nelson, "Negro Literature for Negro Pupils," *The Southern Workman*, February 1922, pp. 59–63. Quoted from *An Alice Dunbar-Nelson Reader*, ed. R. Ora Williams (Washington, D.C.: University Press of America, 1979), p. 134.

68. Correspondence with a friend "Lu" at the World Book Company, Publishers, 1918.

69. Letter from Edgar D. Hellweg of the Doubleday Page Educational Department to Alice Dunbar-Nelson, February 20, 1918.

70. Alice Dunbar-Nelson, "Why I Like Jane Austen." Paper for Professor Schelling, December 12, 1903.

71. Ora Williams gives the details of Dunbar-Nelson's scholarly activities in the Preface to her *An Alice Dunbar-Nelson Reader*, pp. v–viii.

72. *Modern Language Notes* 24 (April 1909): 124–25.

73. *Give Us Each Day*, pp. 419–20.

74. Carroll Smith-Rosenberg, "The Female World of Love and Ritual: Relations Between Women in Nineteenth Century America," *Signs: Journal of Women in Culture and Society* I, 1 (Autumn 1975): 1–29.

75. *Give Us Each Day*, pp. 374–75.

76. Letter from Major C. A. Fleetwood to Alice Dunbar-Nelson, July 18, 1909.

77. *Give Us Each Day*, pp. 397, 398. The following entry occurs on p. 432.

78. Ibid., p. 163.

79. Charles H. Wesley, *Henry Arthur Callis: Life and Legacy* (Chicago: The Foundation Publishers, 1977), p. 44.

80. "Colored Citizens of Wilmington Hold Monster Patriotic Parade," the Philadelphia *Tribune*, June 22, 1918; "Prominent Woman Responsible for Flag Day Celebration," unnamed newspaper clipping, June 28–29, 1918.

81. *Give Us Each Day*, p. 88.

82. "Mrs. Nelson, Teacher, is 'Locked Out,'" unnamed Wilmington, Delaware, newspaper, October 5, 1920.

83. Alice Dunbar-Nelson, "Politics in Delaware," *Opportunity* (November 1924): 339–40. Quoted from *An Alice Dunbar-Nelson Reader*, pp. 177–79.

84. These selections can be found in *An Alice Dunbar-Nelson Reader*. Where necessary, page numbers are given in parentheses in the text. Original publication data are as follows: "Hysteria: The Old Time Mass Meeting Is Dead," *The Competitor* (February 1920): 32–34. "Is It Time for the Negro Colleges in the South to Be Put into the Hands of Negro Teachers?" *Twentieth Century Negro Literature*, ed. D. W. Culp (Toronto: J. L. Nichols, 1902). "People of Color in Louisiana," Parts I and II, *Journal of Negro History* (October 1916): 361–76, and (January 1917): 51–78. "These 'Colored' United States; No. 16—Delaware: A Jewel of Inconsistencies," Parts I and II, *The Messenger* (August 1924): 244–46, and (September 1924): 276–79. "Lincoln and Douglass," *The Dunbar Speaker and Entertainer*, ed. Alice Dunbar Nelson (Naperville, Illinois: J. L. Nichols, 1920). "A Life of Social Service as Exemplified in David Livingstone," *Masterpieces of Negro Eloquence*, ed. Alice Dunbar

(Harrisburg, Pennsylvania: Douglas Publishing Co., 1914), originally delivered at Lincoln University, Pennsylvania, on March 7, 1913, the centenary of the birth of David Livingstone.

85. The Paul L. Dunbar Collection, the Schomburg Center.

86. Letter from Alice Dunbar-Nelson to Arthur Schomburg, October 19, 1913. Paul L. Dunbar Collection, the Schomburg Center.

87. Letter from Alice Dunbar-Nelson to Arthur Schomburg, May 29, 1918. Paul L. Dunbar Collection, the Schomburg Center.

88. Alice M. Dunbar-Nelson, *Mine Eyes Have Seen, The Crisis* 15 (1918): 271–75. Page numbers are given parenthetically in the text. This play has been reprinted in *Black Theatre, U.S.A.: Forty-Five Plays By Black Americans, 1847–1974*, ed. James V. Hatch and Ted Shine (New York: The Free Press, 1974).

89. Letter from Caroline Bond to Alice Dunbar-Nelson, March 28, 1918.

90. Alice Dunbar, *The Author's Evening at Home, The Smart Set* (September 1900): 195–96. Quoted in *An Alice Dunbar-Nelson Reader*.

91. Unidentified July 4, 1928, clipping from the Schomburg Center vertical file.

92. *Give Us Each Day*, pp. 74–75.

93. Ibid., p. 97. The following quotations appear on pp. 118, 101.

94. Alice Dunbar-Nelson, "A Song of Love," *Munsey's Magazine* (July 1902): 603. Quoted from *An Alice Dunbar-Nelson Reader*, p. 2. "Summit and Vale" was published in *Lippincott's Magazine* (December 1902): 715, and on p. 17 of the *Reader*. Unless otherwise noted, the poems discussed can be found in this source.

95. Alice Dunbar-Nelson, "A Little Bird Sings." This poem and other unpublished poems can be found in Dunbar-Nelson's papers at the University of Delaware library.

96. *Give Us Each Day*, p. 421.

97. "The Lights at Carney's Point," "To the Negro Farmers of the United States," and "I Sit and Sew" were originally published in *The Dunbar Speaker and Entertainer*, 1920.

98. As a contest entry, "To Madame Curie" was published in the August 21, 1921, Philadelphia *Public Ledger*.

99. "Forest Fire" was published in the journal *Harlem* in 1928; "Snow in October" in Countee Cullen's 1927 anthology, *Caroling Dusk*.

100. "The Proletariat Speaks" can be found in *The Crisis* 36 (1929): 378; "Harlem John Henry Views the Airmada" in *The Crisis* 39 (January 1932): 458, 473.

101. June 18, 1931. *Give Us Each Day*, p. 435.

102. Robert T. Kerlin, *Negro Poets and Their Poems* (Washington, D.C.: Associated Publishers, 1935), p. 144. Sterling Brown, *Negro Poetry and Drama* and *The Negro in American Fiction* (1937; New York, 1969), p. 63.

103. *Give Us Each Day*, p. 313.

104. "Mrs. Paul Laurence Dunbar, Wife of the Colored Poet and Novelist," Chicago *Recorder*, August 4, 1902. "Alice Dunbar-Nelson, Eagle Columnist, Executive Secretary to Direct Interracial Peace Work," Washington *Eagle*, July 6, 1928.

105. Letter of Alice Dunbar-Nelson to Hannah Clothier Hull, April 2, 1931.

106. *Give Us Each Day*, p. 429.

107. Quoted as an epigraph to Dunbar-Nelson's February 25, 1927, *Eagle* column.

108. The Pittsburgh *Courier*, undated clipping, about 1930.

109. Cover of the December 9, 1927, *Inter-State Tattler*, reproduced in David Levering Lewis, *When Harlem Was in Vogue* (New York: Alfred A. Knopf, 1981).

110. These are her April 17, May 8, May 22, July 17, and September 4, 1926, columns. These and the rest of the columns drawn on here can be found in the

Alice Dunbar-Nelson materials, the University of Delaware library. Some of them carry no date.

111. AIPC National Negro Music Festival, May 25, 1929, program cover statement.

112. "Alice Dunbar Nelson Thrills Great Los Angeles Audience on World Peace and the Negro," California *Eagle*, March 14, 1930.

113. Tuesday, June 17, 1930, *Give Us Each Day*, p. 374.

114. *Give Us Each Day: The Diary of Alice Dunbar-Nelson*, ed. with a Critical Introduction and Notes by Gloria T. Hull (New York: W. W. Norton, 1984).

115. Letter from Arthur B. Spingarn to Alice Dunbar-Nelson, April 11, 1931.

116. Patricia Beer, *Reader, I Married Him* (New York: Barnes and Noble, 1974), p. 1.

117. Letter from August Lenniger to Alice Dunbar-Nelson, February 12, 1931.

118. *Give Us Each Day*, p. 177.

119. "Attends Premiere," July 10, 1934, and "A New Photograph of Mrs. Nelson," 1933. Newspaper clippings, no source, but probably the Philadelphia *Tribune* or *Afro-American*. The Harrisburg, Pennsylvania, *Morning Telegraph*, October 12, 1934.

120. Letter from "Melvin" (probably Chisum) to Alice Dunbar-Nelson, April 21, 1933.

121. Letter from Alice Dunbar-Nelson to Arthur Schomburg, January 22, 1934. The Schomburg Center, New York Public Library.

122. "Alice Dunbar Nelson, Noted Teacher, Author Crosses Bar," the Philadelphia *Tribune*, n.d. Her "burial" wish was reported in the Philadelphia *Afro-American*, September 28, 1935.

Chapter 3: Angelina Weld Grimké

1. Angelina W. Grimké, "A Biographical Sketch of Archibald H. Grimké," *Opportunity* III (February 1925).

2. The *Boston Sunday Globe*, July 22, 1894, in a headnote to one of Angelina's juvenile poems, "Street Echoes."

3. Grimké was being interviewed in January 1955 by Katharine DuPre Lampkin for her *The Emancipation of Angelina Grimké* [Weld] (Chapel Hill: The University of North Carolina Press, 1974). The quote appears in the Acknowledgments, p. xv.

4. Letter of Archibald H. Grimké to Angelina Weld Grimké, September 7, 1897. The Angelina W. Grimké Collection, Manuscript Division, Moorland-Spingarn Research Center, Howard University Library, Washington, D.C. Unless otherwise noted, all quotes and information from letters, manuscripts, and other unpublished sources come from this collection.

5. Letter of Emma A. Tolles to Angelina Weld Grimké, May 7, 1900.

6. Letter of Angelina Weld Grimké to Archibald H. Grimké, August 25, 1914. The Archibald H. Grimké Collection, Moorland-Spingarn Research Center, Howard University.

7. Gerda Lerner, *The Grimké Sisters from South Carolina* (Boston: Houghton Mifflin, 1967), p. 365. The poem to Weld was published in the *Norfolk County Gazette*, November 25, 1893.

8. This photograph can be found in the Archibald H. Grimké Collection.

9. Letters from Archibald H. Grimké to Angelina W. Grimké.

10. *The Colored American Magazine* I (1900): 160–63.

11. Her nickname also echoes that of her great-aunt Angelina Grimké, who was called "Nina" by her family and close friends.

12. Guiney's letter, n.d., is pasted in one of Grimké's early scrapbooks/notebooks. It was obviously written around the time of the poem's publication in the *Gazette* on May 27, 1893.

13. *The Boston Transcript:* "May" (May 7, 1901), "Where Phyllis Sleeps" (July 31, 1901), and "Longing" (April 16, 1901).

14. Quoted from Anna J. Cooper, *Life and Writings of the Grimké Family* (Copyright Anna J. Cooper, 1951), p. 28.

15. This story can be found in Alice Dunbar-Nelson's papers at the Morris Library, University of Delaware, Newark, Delaware.

16. Robert T. Kerlin includes this poem in his *Negro Poets and Their Poems* (Washington, D.C.: Associated Publishers, Inc., 1935), p. 154.

17. Archibald H. Grimké Collection.

18. Lerner, *The Grimké Sisters from South Carolina*, p. 365.

19. Archibald H. Grimké Collection.

20. Letter of Emma A. Tolles to Angelina Weld Grimké, May 22, 1900.

21. Letter of Archibald H. Grimké to Angelina Weld Grimké, October 2, 1907.

22. Play program. The Washington, D.C., premier production sponsored by the Drama Committee of the District of Columbia Branch of the N.A.A.C.P., March 3 and 4, 1916.

23. Angelina W. Grimké, *Rachel: A Play in Three Acts* (College Park, MD.: McGrath Publishing Co., 1969). Reprint of the 1920 edition published by the Cornhill Co., Boston. All excerpts of the play are taken from this edition.

24. Angelina W. Grimké, "'Rachel' The Play of the Month: The Reason and Synopsis by the Author."

25. Ibid.

26. Letter of Meta W. Fuller to Angelina Weld Grimké, May 31, 1917.

27. "'Rachel' . . . The Reason and Synopsis," p. 82.

28. Arthur P. Davis, *From the Dark Tower: Afro-American Writers 1900 to 1960* (Washington, D.C.: Howard University Press, 1974), p. 58.

29. Letter of Angelina Weld Grimké to Archibald H. Grimké, August 16, 1916. Archibald H. Grimke Collection.

30. Letter of John G. Underhill to Angelina Weld Grimké, May 17, 1915.

31. Letter to Angelina Weld Grimké, December 3, 1924.

32. Letter of Angelina Weld Grimké to Archibald H. Grimké, August 25, 1919. Archibald H. Grimké Collection.

33. Letter of Meta W. Fuller to Angelina Weld Grimké, May 25, 1917.

34. Letter of Montgomery Gregory to Angelina Weld Grimké, March 5, 1916.

35. Excerpted from the *Washington Post,* March 19, 1917. Play program for *Rachel.* The Neighborhood Playhouse, New York City, April 26, 1917.

36. Ibid.

37. Review of *Rachel* in *The Freeman,* March 2, 1921.

38. Letter of Maud Cuney Hare to Angelina Weld Grimké, May 24, 1917.

39. Letter of Meta W. Fuller to Angelina Weld Grimké, May 25, 1917.

40. Whether Grimké profited from the book is not clear. The Cornhill Company went bankrupt and was bought by the Cornhill Publishing Company. On January 4, 1925, Grimké wrote them an angry letter charging violation of contract in regard to royalties. They replied on January 8, 1925, informing her of the bankruptcy and the fact that her contract was thereby rendered void. They also offered to sell her the remaining copies of *Rachel,* including the copyright, below cost. After they twice lowered the price from $200, Grimké agreed on April 7, 1926 and paid $50

for 400 bound and 300 unbound copies of the play, which were shipped to the Associated Publishers, Incorporated, of Washington, D.C.

41. "'Rachel' . . . The Reason and Synopsis," p. 51.

42. The *Grinnell Review*, Grinnell, Iowa, January 1921.

43. The Washington, D.C., *Star.* December 5, 1920.

44. The Rochester, New York, *Post-Express*, September 14, 1920.

45. The Utica, New York, *Daily Press*, October 8, 1920.

46. The Wilmington, Delaware, *Every Evening*, September 4, 1920.

47. The Washington, D.C., *Star*, December 5, 1920.

48. *Grinnell Review*, January 1921.

49. *The Catholic World*, New York, New York, December 1920.

50. The Buffalo, New York, *Courier*, October 3, 1920.

51. The Columbus, Ohio, *Dispatch*, September 26, 1920.

52. The Buffalo, New York, *Courier*, October 3, 1920.

53. *The Catholic World*, December 1920.

54. Letter of H. G. Wells to Angelina Weld Grimké, envelope postmarked December 6, 1921.

55. Sterling Brown, *Negro Poetry and Drama* and *The Negro in American Fiction* (1937; New York: Atheneum, 1969), p. 129.

56. Letter of John G. Underhill to Angelina Weld Grimké, February 9, 1915.

57. Angelina Weld Grimké, Diary, 1903.

58. *The Birth Control Review* (September 1919): 10.

59. Quoted from the typescript of "The Closing Door," p. 14.

60. Announcement on the magazine cover.

61. Judging from a letter written on October 28, 1920, by Gertrude Nafe, the editor, to Grimké, the story appeared in two consecutive issues of the magazine, printed right after the date of her letter.

62. This letter exists in Grimké's papers as an undated draft.

63. Quoted from the typescript of "Goldie," p. 1.

64. Trudier Harris, *Exorcising Blackness: Historical and Literary Lynching and Burning Rituals* (Bloomington: Indiana University Press, 1984), p. ix. Her succeeding remark occurs on pp. xii–xiii.

65. Letter of Archibald H. Grimké to Angelina Weld Grimké, November 16, 1899.

66. Letter of Montgomery Gregory to Angelina Weld Grimké, March 5, 1916.

67. Archibald H. Grimké Collection.

68. This letter exists in an undated draft. It was obviously written sometime shortly after World War I.

69. Letter of Charles S. Johnson to Angelina Weld Grimké, May 7, 1925.

70. Underwood is described in Charles S. Johnson's *Ebony and Topaz* as "a poet, novelist and translator of international reputation, author of *The Passion Flower, The Pageant Maker* and other volumes" (New York: *Opportunity* Magazine, 1927), p. 161. Johnson sent Underwood's handwritten notes about "Jettisoned" to Grimké probably in his May 7, 1925, letter.

71. Zona Gale, "The Negro Sees Himself," *The Survey* (Graphic Number) LIV, no. 5 (June 1, 1925): 300.

72. Letter of Charles S. Johnson to Angelina Weld Grimké, January 6, 1925.

73. This speech exists in a two-page holograph text.

74. In 1905, DuBois asked if his wife and daughter Yolande could stop with them, the Grimkés, in Washington. Archibald questioned his motives, wondering if the request should be interpreted as an olive branch or a move toward the Howard

presidency (Letter to Angelina Weld Grimké, June 24,1905). It seems also that the Grimkés were loyal to Roscoe Bruce, whom DuBois did not particularly like. As Grimké phrased it in a November 13, 1910, letter to her father: " . . . there is so little good blood between the two men" (Archibald H. Grimké Collection).

75. Letter of Dr. Anna Nussbaum from Vienna to Angelina Weld Grimké, January 25, 1928.

76. Harper & Bros. returned her "Grief and Despair" (Letter of Archibald H. Grimké to Angelina Weld Grimké, June 24, 1905, in which he mentions this). *The Smart Set* rejected one of her manuscripts in a note postmarked February 28, 1913.

77. Letter of Charles S. Johnson to Angelina Weld Grimké, February 6, 1924.

78. For example, poems by her appear in the following: Cromwell, Turner, and Dykes, *Readings from Negro Authors for Schools and Colleges* (ca. 1931—letter of thanks to her March 5, 1931); Woolbert and Smith, *Fundamentals of Speech* (letter from Harper & Bros. asking her permission April 12, 1934); Walter Loban, *Adventures in Appreciation* (ca. 1947—she received a letter prior to her complimentary copy March 14, 1947); and, of course, standard anthologies such as Hughes and Bontemps, *The Poetry of the Negro* (1949, 1970).

79. Letter of Henry B. Jones to Angelina Weld Grimké, May 1, 1932.

80. *The Boston Evening Transcript*, November 11, 1908, in prefacing her poem "Joseph Lee."

81. Letter of Julia Parks to Angelina Weld Grimké, postmarked May 4, 1928.

82. In an October 24, 1909, diary entry, Grimké grumbles about the trouble she is having with Lottie while Frank (Francis Grimké) is away, mentioning such things as their spatting over who will fix the fires: "Things she never dreams of doing while he is here she does when he is not. She gets real sprightly." (At this point in her life, Lottie is semi-invalid.) And on November 11, 1910, Grimké's father writes: "I am particularly pleased that your Aunt Lottie no longer disputes your position in the home. That I know makes your management much easier."

83. Quoted from *Negro Poets and Their Poems*, p. 155.

84. Letter of Mamie Burrill to Angelina Weld Grimké, February 25, 1896.

85. This letter exists in a draft written on the back of some physics notes dated October 27, 1896.

86. This play is included in *Black Theater, U.S.A.: Forty-five Plays by Black Americans, 1847–1974*, ed. James V. Hatch with Ted Shine (New York: The Free Press, 1974).

87. Quoted from *Caroling Dusk: An Anthology of Verse by Negro Poets*, ed. Countee Cullen (New York: Harper and Row, 1927), p. 42.

88. Quoted from *Caroling Dusk*, p. 46.

89. Ibid., p. 41.

90. "The Puppet Player," *Caroling Dusk*, p. 46.

91. "Paradox," *Caroling Dusk*, pp. 43–44.

92. Quoted from *Caroling Dusk*, p. 37.

93. These remarks exist in an incomplete holograph draft.

94. Quoted from *American Negro Poetry*, ed. Arna Bontemps (New York: Hill and Wang, 1963), p. 17. This version of the poem has been slightly revised from its form in Locke's *The New Negro* (1925).

95. Quoted from *American Negro Poetry*, p. 16.

96. "The Want of You," *Negro Poets and Their Poems*, p. 154.

97. Brown, *Negro Poetry and Drama*, p. 62.

98. This poem is reprinted in *The World Split Open*, p. 262.

99. Alice Walker, "In Search of Our Mothers' Gardens," *MS* Magazine (May 1974), p. 67.

100. Julia Bumry Jones, "Talk O' Town," the Pittsburgh *Courier*, September 28, 1935.

101. *The Negro Caravan*, ed. Brown, Davis, and Lee (1941; New York: Arno Press and The New York *Times*, 1969), p. 804.

102. In *Opportunity* magazine, December 1924.

103. Ellen B. (Nelly) Stebbins wrote Grimké a long, very interesting letter dated January 21, 1936, in which she recalls her relationship with her and her father. In it, she gives accounts of such events as the Grimké-Stanley wedding and of seeing Angelina as a baby "in short clothes." She also confesses to once kissing Mr. Grimké, a fact "*Not* for incorporation in your biography." This last statement suggests that Grimké was thinking about writing the life of her father at the time.

104. Letter of Georgia Douglas Johnson to Angelina Weld Grimké, December 2, 1955.

105. Letter of Angelina Weld Grimké to her father, December 6–11, 1899 (Archibald H. Grimké Collection); letter of Archibald H. Grimké to Angelina Weld Grimké, August 28, 1912.

106. Charles S. Johnson in a letter to her on June 1, 1927, after receiving her photograph: "I should not alter the haughty sadness of your face even if it were possible to do it."

107. Letter of Archibald Grimké to Angelina Weld Grimké, September 7, 1897. Angelina Weld Grimké to her father, November 13, 1910 (Archibald H. Grimké Collection); letter of Angelina Weld Grimké to her father, April 3, 1921 (AHG Collection); letters of Nelly Stebbins to Angelina Weld Grimké, January 17, 1928, and May 6, 1931.

108. Cooper, *Life and Writings of the Grimké Family*, p. 27.

109. Letter to her father, August 22, 1913. Also see Angelina Weld Grimké to Archibald H. Grimké, August 26, 1913, August 9 and August 11, 1914. All in the Archibald H. Grimké Collection.

110. Her arguments with her uncle and the doctor exist in rough drafts of letters and a long list of charges.

111. Letter of Solomon C. Fuller to Angelina Weld Grimké, March 24, 1929; letter of Anna J. Cooper to Angelina Weld Grimké, "Easter Day 1930."

112. In a January 30, 1934, letter to her, Joseph Robinson states: "I hope you will now be able to find interest in your work, for which you originally came to New York."

113. This conclusion results from perusal of the Harmon Foundation Records, Manuscript Division, The Library of Congress, Washington, D.C.

114. Cooper, p. 27.

115. "Biographical Notes," *American Negro Poetry*, p. 190.

116. This letter is the sole item in the Angelina Grimké–Harold Jackman correspondence file, Small Collections, James Weldon Johnson Memorial Collection, Yale University Library, New Haven, Connecticut.

117. Letter from Georgia Douglas Johnson to Harold Jackman, December 26, 1944. The Cullen-Jackman Collection, Trevor Arnett Library, Atlanta University, Atlanta, Georgia.

118. "Angelina W. Grimké, Poet, Ex-Teacher, 78," the *New York Times*, June 11, 1958. Vertical File, the Schomburg Center, New York Public Library.

Chapter 4: Georgia Douglas Johnson

The following abbreviated references are used to designate the four major archival sources that are repeatedly cited in these notes:

C-J   The Cullen-Jackman Collection. Trevor Arnett Library, Atlanta
             University, Atlanta, Georgia.
Fisk   Manuscript holdings. Fisk University, Nashville, Tennessee.
JWJ   The James Weldon Johnson Memorial Collection. Collection of
             American Literature, The Beinecke Rare Book and Manuscript Li-
             brary, Yale University, New Haven, Connecticut.
Schomburg   The Schomburg Center for Research in Black Culture. New York
             Public Library, New York City.

1. For instance, it is most unlikely that she would have entered Atlanta University's normal course when she was seven years old. The *Washington Post*'s obituary also gives her age at death in 1966 as eighty-six.

2. Her autobiographical headnote in *Caroling Dusk: An Anthology of Verse by Negro Poets*, ed. Countee Cullen (New York: Harper & Row, 1927), p. 74. Her parents' names are given in the *Who's Who in Colored America*, here quoted from the "Through the Lorgnette" column, Pittsburgh *Courier*, October 29, 1927.

3. GDJ letter to Harold Jackman, March 31, 1945. C-J. GDJ's handwriting, typing, and spelling were notoriously atrocious. Here, and subsequently, I have corrected and sometimes regularized her spelling without altering her meaning or intent.

4. Information that she provided on her 1930 application for a Harmon Foundation fellowship. Harmon Foundation Records, Manuscript Division, the Library of Congress, Washington, D.C.

5. "The Contest Spotlight," *Opportunity* (July 1927): 204.

6. Biographical statement written by Glenn Carrington to accompany a GDJ retrospective exhibit at the Schomburg Library, New York City, August 1966. Carrington Collection, Schomburg.

7. GDJ letter to Arthur Schomburg, May 15, 1931. Schomburg.

8. *Caroling Dusk*, p. 74.

9. "Gossamer," *The Crisis* 12 (May 1916): 42; "Fame," *The Crisis* 12 (September 1916): 229; "My Little One," *The Crisis* 12 (October 1916): 273.

10. Introduction, *The Heart of A Woman and Other Poems* (Boston: The Cornhill Co., 1918), p. vii. This edition is the source for subsequent references to these poems, with the page numbers given in parentheses.

11. Cornhill Company brochure for *The Heart of A Woman*. Carrington Collection, Schomburg.

12. "Georgia Douglas Johnson Fears She Won't Have Time To Complete All Of The Work She Has Planned," Pittsburgh *Courier*, July [5, 16?], 1928.

13. *Give Us Each Day: The Diary of Alice Dunbar-Nelson*, ed. Gloria T. Hull (New York: W. W. Norton, 1984), pp. 87–88.

14. GDJ letter to Arna Bontemps, July 19, 1941. GDJ Papers, C-J.

15. GDJ, *Bronze: A Book of Verse* (Boston: B. J. Brimmer Company, 1922), p. 3. This edition is used in the subsequent discussion, with page numbers given in parentheses.

16. Cedric Dover, "The Importance of Georgia Douglass Johnson," *The Crisis*, 59 (December 1952): 635.

17. Ibid.

18. "Catalogue of Writings by Georgia Douglas Johnson," p. 4. This is an unpublished 19-page document that she compiled some time after 1962–63. C-J.

19. Ibid., p. 10. Grimké's story with a very similar plot is "The Closing Door." It was published in the April 1919 issue of the *Birth Control Review*. Clearly, black women—as mothers and potential mothers—felt a unique horror about lynching.

20. Quoted from her "Catalogue," p. 18. The quote from Locke and Fauset comes from *The Crisis* 25 (February 1923): 161.

21. The Washington *Daily American*, September 15, 1925.

22. Clipping from the Moorland-Spingarn Research Center, Howard University, Washington, D.C., vertical file. No date or source is given for this "Current Comment" translation and reprinting of an article by Dr. Anna Nussbaum, Vienna, Austria, which appeared in the German newspaper *Der Tag*.

23. The Pittsburgh *Courier*, July [5, 16?], 1928.

24. W. E. B. DuBois letter of recommendation to the Harmon Foundation, June 21, 1927. Harmon Foundation Records, the Library of Congress.

25. *Opportunity* (July 1927): 204.

26. Synopsis of a proposed work called "Dark Face Literature," which GDJ sent to William Haygood of the Rosenwald Foundation in June of 1942 exploring funding possibilities.

27. "The Ebony Flute," *Opportunity* (October 1926): 322.

28. Biographical headnote, *Black and White: An Anthology of Washington Verse*, comp. and ed. J. C. Byars, Jr. (Washington, D.C.: Crane Press, 1927), p. 42.

29. "The Ebony Flute," *Opportunity* (July 1927): 212.

30. *Give Us Each Day*, p. 185.

31. GDJ letter to William Haygood of the Rosenwald Foundation, June 18, 1942. Fisk.

32. GDJ letter to Harold Jackman, August 8, 1944. C-J.

33. "Catalogue of Writings by Georgia Douglas Johnson," p. 4. C-J.

34. "The Ebony Flute," *Opportunity* (November 1926): 357.

35. "Through the Lorgnette" column, Pittsburgh *Courier*, October 29, 1927.

36. Entries for December 9 and 10, 1927, *Give Us Each Day*, p. 207.

37. Letter of GDJ to Charles Chesnutt, January 16, 1929. Charles Chesnutt Collection, Fisk.

38. "The Contest Spotlight," *Opportunity* (July 1927): 204.

39. *Blue Blood*, in *Fifty More Contemporary One Act Plays*, ed. Frank Shay (New York: Appleton-Century Co., 1938), p. 302. This is the edition used for all quotations from the play.

40. *Plumes* was published by Samuel French, New York, in 1927. The edition used here is *Plays of Negro Life: A Source Book of Native American Drama*, ed. Alain Locke and Montgomery Gregory (New York: Harper & Brothers, 1927).

41. "Book Review," New York *Amsterdam News*, November 23(?), 1927.

42. "Catalogue of Writings by GDJ," pp. 7–8. C-J.

43. C. Eric Lincoln's statistics in *The Negro Pilgrimage in America*, 1967. Quoted from headnote to GDJ's play *A Sunday Morning in the South*, in *Black Theatre U.S.A.: 45 Plays by Black Americans 1847–1974*, ed. James V. Hatch and Ted Shine (New York: Free Press, 1974), p. 211.

44. "Catalogue of Writings by GDJ," p. 10. C-J.

45. *William and Ellen Craft*, in *Negro History in Thirteen Plays*, ed. Willis Richardson and May Miller (Washington, D.C.: Associated Publishers, 1935), pp. 183–85.

46. As reported by Gwendolyn Bennett, "Ebony Flute," *Opportunity* (November 1926): 357.

47. "Catalogue of Writings," p. 9. C-J.

48. "Starting Point." JWJ.

49. Entry for October 1, 1921, *Give Us Each Day*, p. 88. The succeeding quote also appears here.

50. "The Bookshelf," *The Chicago Defender*, March 16, 1929. This review, the most perceptive one I have encountered, was written by Blanche Watson.

51. *An Autumn Love Cycle* (New York: Harold Vinal, Ltd., 1928), p. 26. This is the source for all of these poems, with page numbers provided in parentheses.

52. *The Chicago Defender,* March 16, 1929.

53. Foreword to *An Autumn Love Cycle.*

54. Dover, "The Importance of Georgia Douglass Johnson," p. 634. The Anne Spencer review appeared in *The Crisis,* 36 (March 1929): 87.

55. "Through the Lorgnette," Pittsburgh *Courier,* October 29, 1927.

56. GDJ to Arna Bontemps, July 6, 1941. C-J.

57. Foreword to *An Autumn Love Cycle,* p. xviii.

58. GDJ headnote, *The Book of American Negro Poetry* (New York: Harcourt, Brace & World, Inc., 1931), p. 181.

59. Sterling Brown, *Negro Poetry and Drama* (1937; rpt. New York: Atheneum, 1969).

60. Ronald Primeau, "Frank Horne and the Second Echelon Poets of the Harlem Renaissance," in *The Harlem Renaissance Remembered,* ed. Arna Bontemps (New York: Dodd, Mead & Company, 1972), p. 265.

61. Erlene Stetson, "Rediscovering the Harlem Renaissance: Georgia Douglas Johnson, 'The New Negro Poet,'" *Obsidian: Black Literature in Review* 5 (Spring/Summer 1979): 26–34.

62. Unless otherwise noted, the information about the Harmon awards comes from the Harmon Foundation Records at the Manuscript Division, Library of Congress, Washington, D.C.

63. Unless otherwise noted, the material pertaining to the Rosenwald Fund is taken from the Julius Rosenwald Papers, Fisk University, Nashville, Tennessee.

64. GDJ to Lugenia Burns Hope. C-J.

65. GDJ to Arthur Schomburg, October 5, 1934. Schomburg.

66. GDJ to Arna Bontemps, July 6, 1941. C-J.

67. GDJ to Harold Jackman, June 28, 1942. JWJ.

68. Oral History Tapes, Fisk University. July 18, 1973, interview of Margaret Walker Alexander by Ann Allen Shockley. My transcription. In a November 1986 conversation with me, Walker explained that what she meant to emphasize was the *popularity* of GDJ's work.

69. GDJ letter to Schomburg, September 20, 1932. Schomburg.

70. Harmon Foundation Records, Library of Congress, Washington, D.C.

71. The "Homely Philosophy" columns used here were taken from the GDJ vertical file of the Schomburg Center.

72. The Boston *Guardian,* January 16, 1932.

73. The *Guardian,* December 5, 1931.

74. Pittsburgh *Courier,* September 17, 1932.

75. GDJ to Charles Chestnutt, January 16, 1929; Chesnutt to GDJ February 2, 1929. Chesnutt Collection, Fisk.

76. GDJ to George E. Haynes, August 21, 1928. His reply is dated August 24, 1928. Harmon Foundation Records, Library of Congress.

77. For example, GDJ to Jackman, May 15, 1942. JWJ.

78. "Georgia Douglas Johnson, noted poet, author dies," The Baltimore *Afro-American,* May 28, 1966.

79. Owen Dodson made these and the following comments in an interview with James V. Hatch. Tape Collection, C-J. Transcription mine.

80. Schomburg to GDJ, June 26, 1936; Carrington to GDJ, May 7, 1955. Schomburg.

81. GDJ to Charles S. Johnson, [December] 1946. Charles S. Johnson Collection, Fisk.

82. Glenn Carrington composed this statement, which comes from the Carrington Collection, Schomburg.

83. GDJ to Carrington, December 8, 1932. Carrington to GDJ, February 28, 1957 and May 7, 1955. Carrington Collection, Schomburg.

84. GDJ to Jackman, October 26, 1942. C-J.

85. GDJ to Jackman, December 26, 1944. C-J.

86. GDJ to Jackman, January 10, 1945. C-J.

87. GDJ enclosed the poem in a letter dated January 29, 1953. C-J.

88. GDJ to Harold Jackman, August 8, 1944. C-J.

89. GDJ postcard to Jackman, January 21, 1932. C-J.

90. GDJ to Arthur Schomburg, May 15, 1932. Schomburg. The next letter quoted (August 17, 1932) is also from the Schomburg Collection.

91. GDJ to Jackman: January 21, 1932 (C-J); March 22, 1937 (JWJ); July 31, 1938 (C-J).

92. GDJ to Jackman, September 19, 1938, August 8, 1944, and December 26, 1944. C-J.

93. William Haygood to GDJ, October 7, 1942. Rosenwald Collection, Fisk.

94. GDJ to Jackman: March 17, 1937, and n.d. (JWJ), and August 4, 1938 (C-J).

95. GDJ to Jackman, June 28, 1942. JWJ.

96. GDJ to Jackman, March 2, 1950. C-J.

97. Cedric Dover, "The Importance of Georgia Douglass Johnson," *The Crisis* 59 (December 1952): 634.

98. *Opportunity* 19 (March 1941): 104. The manuscript poems discussed in this section come from C-J.

99. GDJ to Jackman, March 31, 1945. C-J.

100. Unless otherwise noted, the material on "Tomorrow's World" is taken from JWJ.

101. GDJ to Jackman, February 15, 1950. C-J.

102. GDJ to Jackman, March 31, 1945. C-J.

103. JWJ Collection; GDJ to Jackman, June 17, 1946.

104. GDJ to Jackman, September 18, 1948. C-J.

105. GDJ to Jackman, February 15, 1950. C-J.

106. GDJ to Jean Toomer, October 15, 1941. Her column prospectus accompanied this letter. Jean Toomer Collection, Fisk.

107. *The Poetry of the Negro 1746–1970,* ed. Langston Hughes and Arna Bontemps (1949; New York: Doubleday, 1970), p. 78.

108. From an unpublished paper by Ora Williams et al., "American Black Women Composers: An Annotated Bibliography." Ora Williams kindly supplied me with copies of these three scores. "Dedication" was published by Handy Brothers Music Co., Inc., New York City.

109. Both "Remember" and "Old Black Men" are from *The Poetry of the Negro,* pp. 75 and 77.

110. *Opportunity* 25 (Winter 1947): 15.

111. GDJ to Jackman, August 4, 1938. C-J.

112. As in the previously mentioned July 16, 1928, Pittsburgh *Courier* article about her.

113. Checking her name, "Paul Tremaine," and the story titles in *Readers' Guide to Periodical Literature* and the more than half-dozen short-story indexes yields nothing. Neither do black publications such as *The Crisis, Opportunity, Negro Digest,*

and short-story anthologies. Other, less-standard, methods have thus far proven to be just as fruitless.

114. GDJ to Jackman: February 4, 1936, and undated (JWJ); July 31, 1938, and August 4, 1938 (C-J).

115. GDJ to William Haygood, June 18, 1942. The Rosenwald Papers, Fisk. "Catalogue of Writings by Georgia Douglas Johnson," p. 4. C-J. GDJ to Harold Jackman, March 31, 1945. C-J.

116. *Challenge: A Literary Quarterly* (June 1936): 47. "Gesture" appeared in this issue, too, pp. 13–17.

117. GDJ to Jackman: undated, probably 1936 (JWJ); August 4, 1938, and March 31, 1945 (C-J).

118. *Challenge: A Literary Quarterly* (April 1937): 42. "Tramp Love" appeared in this issue, pp. 3–8.

119. This information about *Challenge* is taken from Abby Arthur Johnson and Ronald Maberry Johnson, *Propaganda and Aesthetics: The Literary Politics of Afro-American Magazines in the Twentieth Century* (Amherst: The University of Massachusetts Press, 1979), pp. 112–16.

120. GDJ to Harold Jackman, August 4, 1938. C-J.

121. Paul Tremaine, "His Excellency's Looking-Glass," *New Republic* 137 (September 9, 1957): 17–19.

122. "Catalogue of Writings" and GDJ to Harold Jackman, September 18, 1948. C-J.

123. GDJ to Jackman, March 27, 1951. C-J.

124. Ibid. The poem was "I Want to Die While You Love Me."

125. GDJ to Jackman, March 27, 1951, and November 26, 1952. C-J.

126. GDJ to Jackman, postcard August 10, 1950; August 17, 1950; November 13, 1950; and January 30, 1951. C-J.

127. GDJ to Jackman, December 2, 1952. C-J.

128. GDJ to Glenn Carrington, June 1, 1958, and July 28, 1959. Carrington Collection, Schomburg.

129. GDJ to Jackman, March 2, 1950. C-J Collection. GDJ to Carrington, January 4, 1964. Carrington Collection.

130. GDJ to Jackman, March 27, 1951, and December 31, 1952. C-J.

131. For example, GDJ to Mozelle C. Hill, editor of *Phylon* magazine, October 15, 1956, and GDJ to Langston Hughes, January 8, 1955. C-J.

132. GDJ to Carrington: postcard August 2, 1946, May 15, 1954, and January 4, 1964. Carrington Collection.

133. *Black Theatre U.S.A.: 45 Plays by Black Americans 1847–1974*, ed. James V. Hatch and Ted Shine (New York: Free Press, 1974), p. 211.

134. GDJ to Carrington, May 18, 1950. Carrington Collection. Taped interview of Owen Dodson by James V. Hatch, Atlanta University. My transcription.

135. *Black Theatre U.S.A.*, p. 211.

136. Abby Arthur Johnson and Ronald Maberry Johnson, p. 143.

137. GDJ to Jackman, December 26, 1952. C-J.

138. The Norfolk, Virginia, *Journal and Guide*, November 3, 1962. Home Edition, p. 15.

139. GDJ to Carrington, December 8, 1932, July 28, 1959, and March 27, 1965. Carrington Collection, Schomburg.

140. The two flyers described were found in the Carrington Collection, Schomburg.

141. GDJ, *Share My World* (Washington, D.C.: The Author, 1962). Page numbers for the poems quoted are given in parentheses.

142. Robert E. Fennell, *Second Movement* (Copyright: The Author, 1962).

143. This quote concludes the obituary article about her in the *Afro-American*, May 28, 1966.

144. Both this quote and the final one about her funeral are taken from James V. Hatch's taped interview with Dodson, Atlanta University. My transcription.

145. Julia Fields, poem, "Georgia Douglas Johnson," *Negro Digest* 15 (October 1966): 48.

146. "Georgia Douglas Johnson, noted poet, author dies," the Baltimore *Afro-American*, May 28, 1966.

147. Ibid. This article also tells about Henry Lincoln Johnson, Jr., placing the roses on her grave.

148. One of GDJ's S Street neighbors gave me this information.

149. Dodson tape, C-J.

150. Fields poem, "Georgia Douglas Johnson."

Chapter 5: Afterword

1. Gloria Wade-Gayles, *No Crystal Stair: Visions of Race and Sex in Black Women's Fiction* (New York: The Pilgrim Press, 1984).

2. Sonia Sanchez, from "liberation/poem," in *We a BaddDDD People* (Detroit: Broadside Press, 1970), p. 54.

3. Sonia Sanchez, from "personal letter no. 2," in *Home Coming* (Detroit: Broadside Press, 1969), p. 32.

4. Sonia Sanchez, from *A Blues Book for Blue Black Magical Women* (Detroit: Broadside Press, 1974), p. 41.

5. Audre Lorde, from "Hard Love Rock #II," in *The New York Head Shop and Museum* (Detroit: Broadside Press, 1974), p. 24.

6. Audre Lorde, from "Who Said It Was Simple," in *From a Land Where Other People Live* (Detroit: Broadside Press, 1973), p. 39.

7. Barbara Christian, "Trajectories of Self-Definition: Placing Contemporary Afro-American Women's Fiction," in her *Black Feminist Criticism: Perspectives on Black Women Writers* (New York: Pergamon Press, 1985), p. 172.

INDEX

Africa: Dunbar-Nelson on white
exploitation of, 88; use of as background
by Johnson, 172–73
Akerson, George: Dunbar-Nelson on racist
comments of, 89–90
Anderson, Regina: contribution to Harlem
Renaissance, 5
Austen, Jane: Dunbar-Nelson on, 61–62
The Author's Evening at Home: place in
works of Dunbar-Nelson, 72–73
An Autumn Love Cycle: as collection of love
poetry, 175–77; natural imagery, 176;
dedicated to Zona Gale, 177; critical
response, 177–78

Bennett, Gwendolyn: contribution to
Harlem Renaissance, 6; poetry related to
art, 13; on Johnson's literary evenings,
165, 166
Black Power: influence on new Afro-
American women poets, 214
Blue Blood: as comedic treatment of racial
theme, 168–69
Blues: lyrics as poetry, 24–25
Bontemps, Arna: corresponded with
Johnson, 179
The Book of American Negro Poetry: inclusion
of Dunbar-Nelson, 82; exclusion of
Grimké, 136; included version of
Johnson's "Welt," 177
Boston: as intellectual background of
Grimké, 109–10
Braithwaite, William Stanley: encouraged
early poetry of Johnson, 156; wrote
introduction for *The Heart of a Woman*,
157
Britton, Kenneth: novel inspired by
Johnson's "Octaroon," 181
Bronze: A Book of Verse: as racial poetry,
160–63; motherhood as theme, 161;
critical response, 163–64
Brooks, Gwendolyn: portrayal of black
women in novels, 212–13
Brown, Sterling: on poetry of Dunbar-
Nelson, 82; commented on Johnson as
poet, 180
Bruce, Richard: relationships with Langston
Hughes, Johnson, and Carl Van Vechten,
8
Bryant, Louise: assisted Claude McKay, 10

Burrill, Mary: relationship with Grimké,
139; commented on by Johnson, 188

Callis, Arthur: marriage to Dunbar-Nelson,
65–66
Calvin, Floyd J.: wrote feature article on
Johnson, 167
*Caroling Dusk: An Anthology of Verse by
Negro Poets*: inclusion of poems by
Grimké, 1
Carrington, Glenn: relationship with
Johnson, 187–88, 204
Chesnutt, Charles: racial concerns as
themes, 19–20; visited by Johnson, 167
Class: Dunbar-Nelson and A'lelia Walker,
11; maintenance of position by Dunbar-
Nelson, 98
Clement, E. H.: praised Grimké's poetry,
114
Clifton, Lucille: poetry on theme of black
woman, 213
Color: as preoccupation of Harlem
Renaissance, 17; influence on Dunbar-
Nelson, Grimké, and Johnson, 17, 18; in
Dunbar-Nelson's *The Goodness of St.
Rocque*, 52; as theme in short stories of
Dunbar-Nelson, 55–56; and life of
Dunbar-Nelson, 101–102. *See also* Race;
individual authors
Coolidge, Calvin: sent condolences to
Johnson on death of husband, 164
Cooper, Anna: on personality of Grimké,
148, 149
Cooper, Lane: consulted Dunbar-Nelson on
Wordsworth and Milton, 62
Craft, William and Ellen: subject of play by
Johnson, 172
The Crisis: published *Mine Eyes Have Seen*,
71; featured Dunbar-Nelson's "Harlem
John Henry Views the Airmada," 81;
published early poetry of Johnson, 156;
article on Johnson, 206
Curley, James Michael: subject of short
story by Johnson, 201–202

Davis, Arthur P.: on *Rachel*, 118
Delaney, Clarissa Scott: eulogized in poem
by Grimké, 137

Dialect: attempts at poetry in by Dunbar-Nelson and Grimké, 112–13; Grimké's use of in "Jettisoned," 135; Johnson's use of in *Plumes*, 170

Dickinson, Blanche Taylor: representation of women during Harlem Renaissance, 5

Dismond, Geraldyn: reported on literary parties during Harlem Renaissance, 7; compared to Dunbar-Nelson as a columnist, 84; impression of Johnson, 167, 179

Dodson, Owen: on Johnson at home, 187; on Johnson in later years, 205–206; on destruction of Johnson's papers, 210; read poems at Johnson's funeral, 211

Dorsey, James: set poem by Johnson to music, 193

Douglass, Frederick: subject of play by Johnson, 172

Dover, Cedric: on racial poetry of Johnson, 162; criticized *An Autumn Love Cycle*, 178; on Johnson's activities during World War II, 192; article on career of Johnson, 206

Drago, Gypsy: as source of material for short stories by Johnson, 197–99

DuBois, W. E. B.: wrote foreword to *Bronze*, 163; on working conditions of Johnson, 165

Dunbar, Paul Laurence: marriage to Dunbar-Nelson, 42–47; and Dunbar-Nelson as professional writing couple, 47–50

Dunbar-Nelson, Alice: topics of newspaper columns, 1, 86–89; on genteel and bohemian schools of literature during Harlem Renaissance, 3; class and A'lelia Walker, 11; narrowly defined as poet, 14–15; life and literature compared and contrasted with Grimké and Johnson, 15–31; relationship with Johnson, 15; contemporary reputation, 16; skin tone and racial attitude, 17; separated black concerns from literary work, 19–20; sexual role, 20–21; and lesbianism, 21; portrayal of gender, 21–22; concept of literature, 23–24; genres other than poetry, 25, 26; works summarized, 27–28; family history, 33–34; education, 35, 61–62; early development as a writer, 35–36; preface of first book, 36–37; ambivalence toward women's roles in early works, 39–40; teaching career, 41–42, 60–61, 68, 91; participation in black women's club movement, 42, 90–91; marriage to Paul Laurence Dunbar, 42–47, 100; and Dunbar as professional writing couple, 47–50; short stories, 53, 54–57; autobiographical elements in short stories, 54–55; interest in psychology, 56; publication of short stories in periodicals, 57; attempted two novels, 57–58; method of writing, 58–59; professional publications, 61; on Jane Austen, 61–62; relationship with Edwina B. Kruse, 62–63; biographical novel based on Kruse's life, 64; relationship with Major C. A. Fleetwood, 65; marriage to Arthur Callis, 65–66; marriage to Robert J. Nelson, 66–67, 94–95; activities during World War I, 67–68; relationship with Emmett J. Scott, 68; political activities, 68–69; educational and political stance reflected in writing, 69–70; edited volumes on oral tradition, 70–71; as speaker, 71, 92; plays, 71–73; attempts at screenplays, 73–75; as poet, 75–82; "I Sit and Sew" as feminist poem, 79–80; separated race from imaginative literature, 80–81; as a journalist, 83–90; literary reviews, 87–88; as executive secretary of American Inter-Racial Peace Committee, 91–93; lesbian relationships, 95–97; diary, 97–99; attempted autobiographical novel, 100–101; use of pseudonyms, 101, 102; attempted poetry in dialect, 112–13; on domestic life of Johnson, 160; on Johnson's literary evenings, 166; on Johnson's *An Autumn Love Cycle*, 175; nominated Johnson for Harmon Foundation award, 180; on Johnson's pseudonyms, 202. See also *The Author's Evening at Home*; *The Goodness of St. Rocque and Other Stories*; *Mine Eyes Have Seen*; *Violets and Other Tales*

Dyer Anti-Lynching Bill: lobbied for by Dunbar-Nelson, 69; controversy as influence on Grimké, 131; defeated in 1922, 171. *See also* Lynching

Eaton, G. D.: on use of pseudonym by Dunbar-Nelson, 102

Evans, Mari: poetry on theme of black woman, 213

Evans, W. B.: on Grimké as teacher, 116

Evanti, Lillian: musical collaboration with Johnson, 156, 193, 194–95

Farmers Cookery School: Dunbar-Nelson on racist policies of, 89

Fauset, Jessie: contribution to Harlem Renaissance, 5; love poetry, 13; aided

Johnson, 23; criticized for realistic
fiction, 26; reviewed *Bronze*, 163–64
Feminism: and Dunbar-Nelson's "I Sit and
Sew," 79–80; interpretation of Johnson's
The Heart of a Woman, 157; poetry of
Johnson, 195; influence on work of
Afro-American women writers, 214–15.
See also Women
Fields, Julia: wrote elegy for Johnson,
210–11
Fleetwood, C. A.: relationship with
Dunbar-Nelson, 65
Forten, Charlotte: eulogized in poem by
Grimké, 137–38
Fuller, Meta Warrick: reaction to *Rachel*,
119; on audience response to *Rachel*, 120

Gale, Zona: on "Jettisoned," 134–35; *An
Autumn Love Cycle* dedicated to, 177
Gholston, W. L.: nominated Johnson for
Harmon Foundation award, 180
Giovanni, Nikki: poetry on racial themes,
213
"Goldie": basis and motivation of story,
129–31
The Goodness of St. Rocque and Other Stories:
and development of Dunbar-Nelson as a
writer, 50–52, 53–54; compared to
Grimké's "The Closing Door," 51–52;
critical response, 52–53
Gordon, Eugene: on Dunbar-Nelson as a
journalist, 84
Graves, Ralph: on *Rachel*, 120
Gregory, Montgomery: reaction to *Rachel*,
119–20; on racial mission of Grimké,
132
Grimké, Angelina Weld: poems included in
*Caroling Dusk: An Anthology of Verse by
Negro Poets*, 1; narrowly defined as poet,
14–15; life and literature compared and
contrasted with Dunbar-Nelson and
Johnson, 15–31; relationship with
Johnson, 15, 147; contemporary
reputation, 15–16; skin tone and racial
attitude, 17, 18; race themes of period as
motifs, 18; sexual role, 20, 21;
lesbianism, 21, 140–41, 145; portrayal of
gender, 22; cessation of writing, 23, 137,
149–50; romantic concept of poetry, 24;
genres other than poetry, 25; works
summarized, 26, 150–51; "The Closing
Door" compared to Dunbar-Nelson's *The
Goodness of St. Rocque*, 51–52; family
background, 107–109, 147; early short
stories, 110; early poetry, 110–11;
attempted poetry in dialect, 112–13;
relationship with father, 114–15, 149;

education, 115–16; teaching career, 116;
decision not to marry, 124; racial themes
compared with Johnson's, 128, 163;
lynching as theme, 128–32; racial
consciousness, 132; as author of short
stories, 135–36; publication of poetry,
136; attempted collection of poetry, 137;
elegies, 137–38; love lyrics, 138–41; on
creative process, 142–43; compared with
imagists, 143; nature poetry, 144;
assessment of poetry, 145; miscellaneous
writings, 145–47; personality, 148–49;
obituary and epitaph, 151–52; wrote
poem to Johnson, 188. *See also* "Goldie";
"Jettisoned"; "Mara"; *Rachel*
Grimké, Archibald: early life of, 108;
encouraged Grimké's poetry, 113; on
Grimké's critics, 114; expressed
disapproval of Grimké, 115; on Grimké's
teaching career, 116
Grimké, Nancy Weston: sketch of by
Grimké, 107
Guiney, Louise I.: on early poetry of
Grimké, 111

Harding, Warren G.: presented with racial
concerns by delegation including
Dunbar-Nelson, 69; described by
Dunbar-Nelson, 97
Hare, Maud Cuney: on audience for *Rachel*,
120
Harlem Renaissance: contributions of
Dunbar-Nelson, Grimké, and Johnson, 2;
historical context, 2–3; critical debate
over genteel and bohemian schools of
literature, 3; overall place of women, 4–
7; male attitudes toward women, 7; as
racial movement, 17; preoccupation with
skin tones, 17; emergence of women as
writers, 25; sexual-literary politics, 29–
30; role of women writers, 30–31; role
of Dunbar-Nelson, 75–76, 82–83;
fashion for use of pseudonyms, 101
Harmon Foundation: Grimké did not apply
for award, 149; Johnson's applications
for awards, 180–82
Hayford, Gladys Mae: poetry and African
origins, 14
Haygood, William C.: received unpublished
material from Johnson, 182; on works of
Johnson, 191
Haynes, George E.: corresponded with
Johnson, 181
The Heart of a Woman: as feminist work,
156–59; autobiographical elements, 157,
158

Hill, Leslie Pinckney: relationship with Dunbar-Nelson, 93

Hope, Lugenia Burns: corresponded with Johnson concerning honorary degree, 183

Hughes, Langston: representation of women during Harlem Renaissance, 4–5; relationship with Alain Leroy Locke, 8; financial support by patrons, 9

Hunt, Charles S.: refused to publish racial poem by Grimké, 111–12

Hurston, Zora Neale: and Alain Leroy Locke, 8; misrepresented birthdate, 12–13; treatment of black female selfhood, 212

Jackman, Harold: corresponded with Grimké, 151; correspondence with Johnson, 155, 184, 186, 188, 190–91, 197, 203–204

"Jettisoned": nonviolent, racial theme, 133–35

Johnson, Charles: contribution to Harlem Renaissance, 6; male circles of power, 9; as mentor, 30; on "Jettisoned," 134; helped Grimké publish poetry, 137

Johnson, Georgia Douglas: won 1927 *Opportunity* competition for *Plumes*, 1, 169, 202; literary evenings, 6, 165–66; lack of time to write, 10–11, 164–65; misrepresented birthdate, 12–13, 181; narrowly defined as poet, 14–15; life and literature compared and contrasted with Dunbar-Nelson and Grimké, 15–31; relationship with Grimké, 15, 147, 151; contemporary reputation, 15, 16; skin tone and racial attitude, 17; racial themes in works of, 18–19; sexual role, 20; handling of gender in works of, 21; all books prefaced by men, 23; genres other than poetry, 25–26; works summarized, 26–27; racial themes compared with Grimké's, 128, 163; early life, 155; education, 155; interest in music, 156, 194–95; teaching career, 156; marriage to Henry Lincoln Johnson, 156, 159–60; poetry as song lyrics, 159; Dunbar-Nelson on domestic life of, 160; poetry on racial themes, 160–64; death of husband, 164; attempted book about literary evenings, 166–67; uncompleted works, 167–68; as dramatist, 168, 174; collection of "Primitive Life Plays," 170–71; lynching as theme in plays, 171–72; black history as theme of plays, 172; subjects of lost plays, 173; plays on interracial themes, 173–74; position as

woman poet, 178; on "writing racially," 179; compared with contemporary poets, 179–80; attempts to win fellowships and awards, 180–83; search for employment in 1930s, 183–84; newspaper columns, 185–86, 194; personality, 186; entertaining in home, 186–87; fondness for lesbians and homosexuals, 187–88; on Mary Burrill, 188; personal relationships as evidenced by correspondence, 188–89; on attempts to publish works, 189–91, 203–204; later years compared with Dunbar-Nelson and Grimké, 191–92; activities during World War II, 192–93; compiled book of poems on racial unity, 193–94; returned to song writing and composing, 194–95; theme of poetry in later years, 195; short stories, 196–203; use of pseudonyms, 196, 197, 198, 199, 201, 202–203, 206, 207–208; relationship with Gypsy Drago, 197–99; political writings, 202; eccentricity in later years, 205–206; ran "one world" correspondence club, 206–207; literary criticism, 209–10; destruction of papers, 210; death and funeral, 210–11. See also *An Autumn Love Cycle; Blue Blood; Bronze: A Book of Verse; The Heart of a Woman; Plumes; Share My World; A Sunday Morning in the South*

Johnson, Helene: poetry characteristic of Harlem Renaissance, 13–14

Johnson, Henry Lincoln: marriage to Georgia Douglas, 156; political career, 159; patriarchal attitudes, 159–60; death and funeral, 164

Johnson, James Weldon: discovered Anne Spencer, 6; anthologized most sex-stereotyped of female poetry, 23; novel reviewed by Dunbar-Nelson, 87; on Johnson as poet, 180. See also *The Book of American Negro Poetry*

Kerlin, Robert: on poetry of Dunbar-Nelson, 82

Knoblauch, Mary: solicited story by Grimké for *The Birth Control Review*, 129

Kruse, Edwina B.: relationship with Dunbar-Nelson, 62–63

Larsen, Nella: novel reviewed by Dunbar-Nelson, 87

Lee, Joseph: eulogized in poem by Grimké, 137

Lesbianism: hidden nature of women's sexual lives, 21; in poetry of Grimké, 22,

26, 140–41, 145, 215; Dunbar-Nelson's
    relationships, 95–97; acceptance of
    during 1960s–70s, 215
Lewis, Ira F.: correspondence with Dunbar-
    Nelson concerning payment for columns,
    85–86
Lewis, Lillian: on personality of Grimké,
    148
Lewis, Sinclair: aided Claude McKay, 11–
    12
Locke, Alain Leroy: misogynistic attitude,
    7–8, 30; reviewed *Bronze*, 163–64;
    wrote forword to *An Autumn Love Cycle*,
    175
London, Helene Ricks: relationship with
    Dunbar-Nelson and Fay Jackson
    Robinson, 95
Lorde, Audre: poetry on oppression of
    black women, 214
Lynching: political activities of Dunbar-
    Nelson, 69; as theme in works of
    Grimké, 128, 131–32; as theme in
    Johnson's plays, 171–72. *See also* Dyer
    Anti-Lynching Bill

McDougald, Elise Johnson: on place of
    women in Harlem Renaissance, 4
McKay, Claude: financial support by
    patrons, 9–10; aided by Sinclair Lewis,
    11–12
"Mara": compared and contrasted to
    Rachel, 124–28; autobiographical
    elements, 127
Micheaux, Oscar: collaboration proposed
    by Dunbar-Nelson, 74
Miller, Dean Kelly: encouraged early poetry
    of Johnson, 156
Mine Eyes Have Seen: intended to persuade
    blacks to support World War I, 71–72;
    interracialism, 72; compared with *The
    Author's Evening at Home*, 72–73
Mocatto, Frances: novel inspired by
    Johnson's "Octaroon," 181
Mumford, Lewis: on Johnson as poet, 182

Nance, Ethel Ray: contribution to Harlem
    Renaissance, 5; on women and smoking,
    12
Nelson, Robert J.: marriage to Alice
    Dunbar, 66–67, 94–95; on Dunbar-
    Nelson's retention of Dunbar's name,
    93–94
Nerney, May Childs: reaction to *Rachel*, 120
New Orleans: description of in early works
    of Dunbar-Nelson, 37, 50
Newsome, Effie Lee: children's verse, 13;
    frontispiece of *An Autumn Love Cycle*, 177

Nussbaum, Anna: requested permission to
    translate poetry by Grimké, 136

Petry, Ann: depiction of race-sex-class, 212
Pickett, Clarence E.: farewell
    commendation to Dunbar-Nelson, 93
Plumes: 1927 *Opportunity* competition, 1,
    169, 202; as folk tragedy, 169–70; use of
    dialect, 170
Poetry: preeminent literary form during
    Harlem Renaissance, 13; lyric as proper
    genre for women, 14, 23; avoidance of
    modern styles by Dunbar-Nelson,
    Grimké, and Johnson, 24; of Dunbar-
    Nelson, 75–82; of Grimké, 137–45;
    Afro-American in the 1960s–70s, 213–
    14. *See also* individual authors and titles
Primeau, Ronald: on Johnson as poet, 180

Race: as theme in works of Grimké, 18,
    111–12, 128–32, 133–35, 163; as theme
    in works of Johnson, 18–19, 128, 160–
    64, 171–72; as theme in works of
    Dunbar-Nelson, 80–81, 88–89. *See also*
    Color; individual authors and titles
Rachel: as race propaganda, 117–24; stage
    presentations, 119; publication
    subsidized by Grimké, 121; critical
    response, 121–22; possible
    autobiographical elements, 124;
    compared and contrasted with "Mara,"
    124–28
Realart Picture Corp.: considered
    screenplay by Dunbar-Nelson, 74–75
Republican Party: participation of Dunbar-
    Nelson, 68–69; participation of Johnson,
    202
Reynolds, Paul R.: as agent for Dunbar-
    Nelson, 57–58, 59
Robinson, Fay Jackson: relationship with
    Dunbar-Nelson, 95–96

Sanchez, Sonia: poetry on racial themes,
    213–14
Sandburg, Carl: meeting with Johnson, 167
Schomburg, Arthur: assisted Dunbar-
    Nelson, 71; correspondence with
    Johnson, 190
Schuyler, George S.: corresponded with
    Dunbar-Nelson, 99
Scott, Emmett J.: relationship with
    Dunbar-Nelson, 68
Share My World: retrospective collection of
    poetry, 207–209
Smith, Bessie: blues lyrics as poetry, 24–25

Society of Friends: Dunbar-Nelson as
executive secretary of American Inter-
Racial Peace Committee, 91–93; racism
and sexism noted by Dunbar-Nelson, 93
Spencer, Anne: as hostess in Harlem
Renaissance, 6; poetry of, 13; on racial
topics, 19; poetry compared to
Johnson's, 177; on *An Autumn Love
Cycle*, 178
Stanley, Sarah E.: relationship with Grimké
as mother, 108–109
Stetson, Erlene: on Johnson as poet, 180
Strong, Michael Victor: preface to *Share My
World*, 207–208
A Sunday Morning in the South: lynching as
theme, 171–72

Tolles, Emma Austin: on relationship of
Grimké with mother, 108–109
Tremaine, Paul: as pseudonym of Johnson,
196, 197, 198, 199, 201

Underhill, John G.: advised Grimké on
Rachel, 119, 123
Underwood, Edna Worthley: on
"Jettisoned," 134

Van Vechten, Carl: literary parties during
Harlem Renaissance, 7; lifestyle, 9
Violets and Other Tales: and development of
Dunbar-Nelson as a writer, 36–40

Walker, A'lelia: literary parties during
Harlem Renaissance, 6–7; lack of
support to writers, 11; class and Dunbar-
Nelson, 11
Walker, Margaret: poetry on black
tradition, 212; novel based on life of
great-grandmother, 213
Wallace, Thurman: skin tone as theme of
novel, 17

Walton, Lester A.: on Dunbar-Nelson, 99–
100
Weld, Angelina Grimké: relationship to
Grimké, 108
Weld, Theodore D.: relationship with
Grimké, 109–10; provided for education
of Grimké, 115
Wells, H. G.: on *Rachel*, 122
West, Dorothy: on Johnson's "Tramp
Love," 201; depiction of race-sex-class,
212
Women: overall place in Harlem
Renaissance, 4–7; male prejudice, 7–8;
greater support provided to male authors,
10; female support networks, 11;
socialization interfered with search for
support, 11–12; opportunity limited by
geographic immobility, 12; lyric poetry
as proper genre, 14; lives determined as
much by gender as race, 20; emergence
as writers during Harlem Renaissance,
25; experiences of in Dunbar-Nelson's
The Goodness of St. Rocque, 51–52; black
women writers after the Harlem
Renaissance, 212–16; continuing
oppression of black women poets, 214.
See also Feminism; Lesbianism; individual
authors and titles
Women's club movement: described by
Dunbar-Nelson, 42; offices held by
Dunbar-Nelson, 69, 90–91
Wooten, Ray: locked Dunbar-Nelson out of
classroom, 68
Wyman, Lillie Buffum Chace: advised
Grimké to attempt work with less violent
racial theme, 132–33; novel reviewed by
Grimké, 146

Young, Leila: relationship with Dunbar-
Nelson, 60

GLORIA T. HULL

is Professor of English at the University of Delaware. She is co-editor of the anthology *All the Women Are White, All the Blacks Are Men, But Some of Us Are Brave: Black Women's Studies* and editor of *Give Us Each Day: The Diary of Alice Dunbar-Nelson.*

Book designer

Sharon L. Sklar

Jacket designer

Sharon L. Sklar

Production coordinator

Harriet Curry

Typeface

Meridien

Compositor

Keystone Typesetting

Printer

Braun Brumfield